SPECIAL PLACES TO STAY

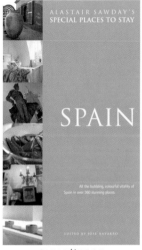

£14.99/$23.95

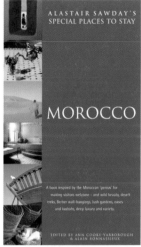

£10.99/$17.95

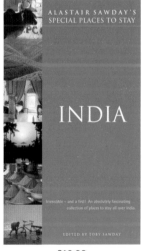

£10.99

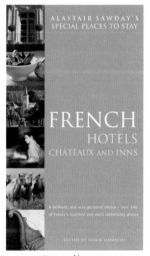

£13.99/$19.95

Credit card orders (free p&tp) 01275 464891
www.specialplacestostay.com

In US: credit card orders (800) 243-0495, 9am-5pm EST,
24-hour fax (800) 820-2329 www.globepequot.com

Third edition
Copyright © March 2005
Alastair Sawday Publishing Co. Ltd
Published in March 2005
Alastair Sawday Publishing Co. Ltd
The Home Farm Stables,
Barrow Gurney, Bristol BS48 3RW
Tel: +44 (0)1275 464891
Fax: +44 (0)1275 464887
Email: info@specialplacestostay.com
Web: www.specialplacestostay.com

The Globe Pequot Press
P.O. Box 480, Guilford,
Connecticut 06437, USA
Tel: +1 203 458 4500
Fax: +1 203 458 4601
E-mail: info@globepequot.com
Web: www.globepequot.com

Design:
Caroline King

Maps & Mapping:
Bartholomew Mapping, a division of
HarperCollins, Glasgow

Printing:
Pims, UK

UK Distribution:
Penguin UK, 80 Strand, London

US Distribution:
The Globe Pequot Press, Guilford,
Connecticut

A catalogue record for this book is
available from the British Library.

**Alastair Sawday has asserted his right
to be identified as the author of this
work.**

ISBN 1-901970-57-4

Printed in UK on Revive Silk: 75% de-inked
post-consumer waste, 25% mill broke and
virgin fibres.

The publishers have made every effort to
ensure the accuracy of the information
in this book at the time of going to
press. However, they cannot accept
any responsibility for any loss, injury
or inconvenience resulting from the
use of information contained therein.

ALASTAIR SAWDAY'S
SPECIAL PLACES TO STAY

PORTUGAL

Contents

Back

Photo Rio Arade, entry 189

Alastair Sawday Publishing

We began by chance, in 1993, seeking a job for a friend. On my desk was a file: a miscellany of handsome old houses in France, some that could provide a bed, and some a meal, to strangers.

I ran a small travel company at the time, taking people off the beaten track; these places were our 'finds'. No chain hotels for us, no tourist restaurants if we could possibly visit old manor houses, farms and châteaux whose owners would breathe new life into our enthusiasm for France.

So Jane set off with a file under her arm and began to turn it into a book. We were then innocent enough to ignore advice and print 'far too many' – 10,000. We sold them all, in six months – and a publishing company was born.

We exhorted readers to enjoy a 'warm welcome, wooden beams, stone walls, good coffee' and nailed our colours firmly to the mast: 'We are not impressed by TVs, mini-bars and trouser-presses'. We urged people to enjoy simplicity and authenticity and railed against the iniquities of corporate travel. Little has changed.

Although there are now more than 25 of us working out here in our rural idyll, publishing about 20

books, we are holding tightly to our original ethos and gradually developing it. Our first priority is to publish the best books in our field and to nourish a reputation for integrity. It is critically important that readers trust our judgement.

Our next priority is to sell them – fortunately they sell themselves, too, such is their reputation for reliability and for providing travellers with memorable experiences and friendships.

However, publishing and selling books is not enough. It raises other questions: what is our impact on the world around us? How do we treat ourselves and other people? Is not a company just people working together with a shared focus? So we have begun to consider our responses to those questions and thus have generated our Ethical Policy.

There is little intrinsically ethical about publishing travel guides, but there are ways in which we can improve. Firstly, we use recycled paper and seek the most eco-friendly printing methods. Secondly, we are promoting local economies and encouraging good work. We seek beauty and are providing an alternative to the corporate culture that has done so much damage. Thirdly, we celebrate the use of locally sourced and organic food

Who are we?

among our owners and have launched a Fine Breakfast scheme in our British bed & breakfast guides.

But the way we function as a company matters too. We treat each other with respect and affection. An easy-going but demanding office atmosphere seems to work for us. But for these things to survive we need to engage all the staff, so we are split into three teams: the Green team, the Better Business team and the Charitable Trust team.

Each team meets monthly to advise the company. The Green team uses our annual Environmental Audit as a text and monitors progress. The Better Business team ponders ethical issues such as flexible working, time off in lieu/overtime, and other matters that need a deep airing before decisions are made. The Trust team allocates the small sum that the company gives each year to charities, and raises extra money.

A few examples of our approach to company life: we compost our waste, recycle the recyclable, run a shared car to work, run a car on LPG and another on a mix of recycled cooking oil and diesel, operate a communal organic food ordering system, use organic or local food for our own events, take part in Bike to Work day, use a 'green' electricity supplier, partially bank with Triodos

Photo Paul Groom

(the ethical bank in Bristol), have a health insurance scheme that encourages alternative therapies, and sequester our carbon emissions.

Especially exciting for us is an imminent move to our own eco offices; they will conserve energy and use little of it. But I have left to the end any mention of our most tangible effort in the ethical field: our Fragile Earth series of books. There are *The Little Food Book*, *The Little Earth Book* and T*he Little Money Book* - hugely respected and selling solidly. Look out for new titles in the Fragile Earth series.

Perhaps the most vital element in our growing Ethical Policy is the sense of engagement that we all have. It is not only stimulating to be trying to do the right thing, but it is an important perspective for us all at work. And that can only help us to continue to produce beautiful books.

Alastair Sawday

Acknowledgments

Laura Kinch, who worked on the last edition of this guide with Marie Hodges, has now taken the project thoroughly under her wing. She cut her editorial teeth on one of our biggest books, *British Bed and Breakfast*, and richly deserved the exotica of Portugal.

The fact that the book has grown dramatically and has taken on new energy owes all to Laura. She has thrown herself into the task with prodigious commitment and energy, criss-crossing the country with zeal and sympathy, and taking to Portugal and its deep culture like a cod to a waiting net. She has tackled the task largely on her own but with the help of a sterling band of inspectors, the most experienced of whom is our good friend Carol Dymond, and has done so with massive success. If the owners in this book, and the readers of it, get as much out of it as Laura has put into it, they will be happy indeed.

Alastair Sawday

Series Editor
Alastair Sawday

Editor
Laura Kinch

Editorial Director
Annie Shillito

Managing Editor
Jackie King

Production Manager
Julia Richardson

Web & IT
Russell Wilkinson, Matt Kenefick

Production
Rachel Coe, Paul Groom,
Allys Williams, Ezra Chambers

Copy Editor Jo Boissevain

Editorial
Roanne Finch, Maria Serrano,
Danielle Williams

Sales & Marketing & PR
Siobhán Flynn, Paula Brown,
Sarah Bolton

Accounts Sheila Clifton, Bridget
Bishop, Christine Buxton, Jenny
Purdy, Sandra Hasell

Writing Jo Boissevain, Viv Cripps,
John Dalton, Marie Golding, Laura
Kinch, Helen Pickles, Hamish Wills

Inspections Laura Kinch, Carol
Dymond, Marie Golding, Amy Herrick,
Carlos Jardim, Alethea Tonner

Special Thanks
Vasco Guerreiro, Solomon Wright,
João Grama

Previous Editors John Dalton,
Guy Hunter-Watts

A word from Alastair Sawday

Portugal – the First Global Village? That is a reference to the title of an illuminating book by Martin Page that I bought out there but is, sadly, not available here. The book puts Portugal, tiny and often peripheral, into its historical perspective – with some panache. For most of us it is hard to grasp what Portugal is about. We wrestle with the elusive significance of facts, such as Portugal's colonization of Brazil and vast chunks of Africa, or her brief dominance of maritime trade, or her once-glitteringly lovely capital, or her sheer wealth. She has punched way beyond her weight for centuries, and for several of those centuries she was a heavyweight. So travelling about in Portugal is as rich an experience as you might expect, especially if you have learned quite how grand she once was and quite how modest she now affects to be.

This revealing and stimulating book about Special Places – apparently about nothing other than where to lay your head – reflects all of Portugal's history. You will find castles that terrified towns and fought off invaders. There are great houses that nurtured the impossibly wealthy, farms that nourished thousands and estates that impress us still. You may want to be less exposed to the great forces of history and just stay in a little cottage by the sea, or in a townhouse in a university town – but you won't get away from the sheer exhilaration of being so close to the story of Europe.

Wherever you go you will be greeted by lovely people, whose gentleness and modesty is unexpected in a Latin country. You will be folded into family life if you wish, or left to wallow in the magnificence of some of Portugal's finest buildings. For we have absorbed most of her Pousadas – state-run until recently – into this book, acknowledging that they are exceptional places and that to stay in them is a privilege. Do give yourselves a treat and try a Pousada for a night, at least.

But give yourselves a big treat anyway – and use this book. Your holiday in Portugal deserves no less.

Alastair Sawday

Photo Paul Groom

Introduction

THESE SPECIAL PEOPLE IN THEIR SPECIAL PLACES WILL LOOK AFTER YOU LIKE THEIR OWN...

Portugal has got firmly under my skin and it will touch you too. Its deeply traditional society resists change, so the images, the sounds and the smells are still a delight.

For this edition I visited over 60 places, and was treated everywhere with warmth and generosity. I travelled across the sun-burnt plains where people shelter under olive trees surrounded by sheep, saw whitewashed churches with golden carved interiors, soaked up soft views of corn and grapes and bathed in deep green pools. In the mountains, I've seen the sun set down a deep gorge, the rays reflecting on the water below, goats jostling importantly past cars, donkeys working the land and hill-forts rising from the earth. And down by the sea: icy water and crashing waves, wild winds, colourful boats and deep-lined faces.

I've tasted bittersweet orange juice, homemade peach jam, freshly-picked nuts, lemons and figs. I've become addicted to the soft sweetness of a *pastel de nata*, a flaky custard pastry. I've gorged on fresh crabs and lobster in the *cataplana* stew, and feasted on olive oil-drenched flaky fish and clam and pork stew.

The people have stirred my soul: an old lady singing Fado inside Castelo de São Jorge in Lisbon, the melodies sad and beautiful, grape pickers touching their caps to me, old ladies in black stockings carrying mountains of lettuce on their heads, people almost singing *Bom dia* and children shyly kissing my cheeks. In one manor house, the family elder showed me the precious traditional dresses saved for religious festivals. I saw people washing clothes in mountain water troughs with smiles that reach the eyes and the heart.

These special people in their special places – including some on Madeira – will look after you like their own. You will surely enjoy Portugal as much as I do.

Photo left Quinta do Arco, entry 215
Photo opposite Pousada de Arraiolos, entry 156

Introduction

How we choose our Special Places

We choose places where we, our friends and family, would like to stay. My sister loves funky hotels where she can be anonymous, luxuriate in the bath and sleep on the best quality sheets; my father likes history: old houses filled with antiques and conversations with the family over dinner; I like both. We all enjoy different things at different times, with peace and plenty of space.

The places in this book are richly diverse – there is something for everyone. There are cottages, palaces, pousadas, windmills & castles – simple, modern, traditional, quirky, peaceful... flick through the pages and take your pick. The write-ups can be subtle – do read them carefully, and take the hard work out of choosing the right place to stay.

We like people who are 'human' and flexible, kind when you call to say you're late and who may look after the kids while you go out for a meal. Most hotels & pousadas we have are smallish yet you may not have much personal contact with the owners (which you may prefer). But whatever you choose, even self-catering, the personality and flair of those running it will be evident.

We like the fact that each place is different. The atmosphere, people, setting, architecture and character all play a part. It's a balance – not everywhere will be right for everyone, or perfect in every detail, but the positives will far outweigh the negatives. We absolutely do not like mass-market tourism, unwelcoming hosts, dreary bedrooms or grotty bathrooms.

Readers write to us with their recommendations, which is great. Others tell owners they should contact us. We visit all new places and regularly revisit those that have been in the book for some time. We like to have a friendly and informal relationship with both our owners and our readers.

What to expect

This guide to mainland Portugal and Madeira contains B&Bs, self-catering houses, small properties and pousadas. Many B&Bs and hotels

also have self-catering options –
we've mentioned this on their entry
and flagged them accordingly on the
map pages.

Pensão: a guesthouse, the
Portuguese equivalent of a bed and
breakfast, though breakfast is not
always included in the price
Quinta: a country estate or villa; in
the Douro wine-growing area it
often refers to a wine lodge
Fortaleza: a fort
Residencial: a guesthouse; slightly
more expensive than a pensão and
normally serving breakfast
Solar: a manor house

Tourist Definitions – these are
marked on blue road signs to help
you find a place.

Turismo de habitacão: B&B in stately
home
Turismo rural: rustic house
Agroturismo: B&B on a farm
Casa de campo: simple rural private
house
Hotel rural: rural hotel

Types of property
This list serves as a rough guide to
what you might expect to find
behind each name.

Albergaria: an upmarket inn
Casa: a house, old or new
Castelo: a castle
Estalagem: an inn, more expensive
than an albergaria
Herdade: a large farm or estate
Monte: a long, low Alentejo
farmhouse, usually on top of a hill
Paço: a palace or country house
Palacio: a palace or country house,
but grander than a Paço

B&Bs and self-catering
In B&Bs you stay as a guest in
someone's home which may be
a grand, old manor house or
somewhere much simpler. You may
eat at the polished wooden dining
table, perhaps with your hosts, your
bedroom may have antique furniture
and the feel will be personal.
The Portuguese tourist board would
describe this type of place as a
'turismo de habitacão'. It is often the
largest house in the village and may
have its own chapel.

Photo Convento de São Saturnino, entry 89

Introduction

A Turismo rural is also a B&B but in a more rustic house in the countryside. These places often also have self-catering apartments on their land.

An Agroturismo is a B&B on a working farm. Owners of these places too have often converted outbuildings on their land and created wonderful self-catering places. (A 'residencial' is an urban B&B that may have some hotel-like facilities.) Short breaks are often available at self-catering places. Check with the owners for details (mentioned in the entry where possible).

Hotels

Those we choose normally have under 50 rooms. They are family-run with friendly staff and many are in old buildings. An albergaria is a small, upmarket inn that is good value for money and generally not as smart as a hotel.

Pousadas

Their hotels are in historic buildings such as monasteries, convents and castles and they use local food in their restaurants. We have visited them all and have included those that we find special. They stand in some of the most beautiful places in Portugal, many with the most spectacular views. If you like hotels and enjoy staying in majestic buildings with breathtaking views, then pousadas may well be for you.

The pousadas in this guide belong to a group of just over 40 hotels that was set up in the 1940s by the government. Recently the Pestana Group (a successful worldwide hotel group) has become an important shareholder and deals with marketing and promotions.

Depending on the season, current room prices in pousadas range from €90–€220 which is on the high side, but they are regenerating some of the oldest buildings in the country. However, for better value, make the most of the numerous special deals

Photo above Pousada de Guimarães – Santa Marinha, entry 19
Photo right Pousada da Murtosa-Torreira/Ria, entry 52

Introduction

that you may find on the pousada web site or when booking. A few examples (subject to change) are:

A 40% discount for the over 60s at all pousadas, from Sundays to Thursdays. If you are aged between 18 and 30, you also receive a discount. Every month, you can stay in three places on offer, but only pay the price for two. You can buy a 'passport' which gives you four nights in your choice of pousadas for a set rate. They also do deals on car hire and staying in the Pestana Palace, in Lisbon.

Pousadas de Portugal
Avenida Santa Joana Princesa nº 10
1749-090 Lisboa
Tel: +351 218 442 001
Fax: +351 218 442 085
e-mail: guest@pousadas.pt
www.pousadas.pt

Casas Brancas & Montes Alentejanos
We have also formed associations with Casas Brancas (in south-western Portugal) and Montes Alentejanos (in central Portugal). Each is a group of B&Bs and self-catering places which markets itself collectively. Their contact details can be found at the back of the book in the quick reference section.

How to use this book
Map
Go to the maps at the front of the book. The properties are labelled with the entry page number. Blue labels show overnight accommodation, pink self-catering, blue/pink a mixture of the two. We have also included one place just across the Spanish border.

Rooms
We give the range in single, double, twin or triple rooms or in apartments, suites, cottages or houses. Extra beds can often be added for children. Many twin beds can be zipped together to make doubles. Ask your host for more details.

Bathrooms
Bathrooms are not always ensuite, so check when booking.

Prices
Prices for B&B and hotels are per night for two people and give a range from low season to high

Photo: Rua Relógio, entry 118

season. Self-catering prices are given per night and per week. Owners have given us prices for 2005, which may rise in 2006. Always check prices when booking. Many owners do special deals for off-season or longer stays. If there is a single room, the 'singles' price is for a single room. Alternatively, the price is for single occupancy of a double or twin room.

Symbols
There is an explanation of these on the inside back cover of the book. Use them as a guide, not as a statement of fact. If an owner does not have the symbol that you're looking for, it's worth discussing your needs; the Portuguese generally love to please. Most owners speak some English – and there is an 'English spoken' symbol (Hello).

Quick Reference Indices
At the back of the book is a quick reference section to direct you to places that produce their own wine or olives, are close to walking and cycling routes, have local festivals, or are within 10km of a good river beach.

Practical Matters
Bookings
It is best to make your booking in writing. Often you will need to pay a deposit, the equivalent of one night's stay or 30% of a week's holiday. You can do this by credit card (if the

owner has the symbol), personal cheque or bank transfer. If you make your booking by telephone, many hotels will ask you for a credit card. Do make sure that you have written confirmation, ask for detailed directions and let smaller places know if you want dinner. Book well ahead if you plan to be in Portugal during the holidays. August is very busy in tourist and beach areas so you might choose to head for the remoter places in this book.

Portugal is on the same time zone as the UK but if you pop across the border to Spain, it is one hour ahead of Portugal.

Arrivals
Many city hotels will only hold a

Introduction

reservation until the early evening, even if you booked months in advance. So warn them if you are planning to arrive late. It remains law that you should register on arrival but hotels have no right to keep your passport.

Tipping
Tipping is not as widespread in Portugal as in the UK and US. However, the more expensive restaurants do expect a 10% service charge, if it is not already included.

Public Holidays & Festivals
In Portugal everything closes down at Easter, Christmas and New Year, and on the following public holidays:

Feb/March: Carnival Tuesday (day

before Ash Wednesday)
March/April: Good Friday
April 25: Liberty Day: commemorating the 1974 Revolution
1 May: Labour Day
May/June: Corpus Christi (ninth Tuesday after Easter)
10 June: Portugal Day; Camões & the Communities Day
15 August: The Feast of the Assumption
5 October: Republic Day: commemorating 1910 declaration of Portuguese Republic
1 November: All Saint's Day
1 December: Independence Day – commemorating 1640 restoration of independence from Spain
8 December: Feast of the Immaculate Conception

See our quick reference section for more Festival information.

Telephones
Calling Portugal from another country:
From the UK: 00 351 then the number.
From the USA: 011 351 then the number.
Landline numbers begin with 2, mobile phone numbers with 9.

As well as public phone boxes (for which you can buy phone cards in most newsagents) and phone boxes inside post offices (look for *Correios*), virtually every café has a phone for which customers pay the *impulsos* used, counted on a meter. Many owners answer the phone with '*estou*' which literally means 'I'm ready'.

Electricity
Virtually all sockets now have 220/240 AC voltage (usually 2-pin). Pack an adaptor if you travel with electrical appliances.

Driving
The maps in this guide give an approximate idea of where places are; use with an up-to-date detailed road map for navigation. Avoid driving on public holidays and, preferably, August when there is a mass exodus to the countryside and the coast. It is compulsory to have a spare set of bulbs, a warning triangle, a fire extinguisher and a basic first aid kit in the car.

It is an offence to drive without having your driving licence on you. Remember that foreign number plates attract attention in the big cities so never leave your car with valuables inside. Use a public car park; they are cheap and safe.

The following are general guidelines:

Auto-estradas – toll motorways (*portagems*), usually with two to three lanes. Indicated with blue

Photo Herdade da Matinha, entry 161

signs and numbers preceded by 'A'. Generally shown on maps with a bold double red line. Make sure you take the toll ticket. *Itinário-principal* (IP) & *Itiniário complementar* (IC) are the main non-toll roads. Beware as sometimes the road names change mid-route. *Estradas Nacionais* (national two-lane roads) are usually prefixed with an N.

Petrol is more expensive in Portugal than in the UK (and much more expensive than in the USA). Don't wait until you hit red on the gauge before filling up as you can often go for many miles (even on the biggest roads) without coming across a station. You have been warned!

Public transport
You can get almost everywhere by train or bus. Trains are inexpensive and some lines very scenic, but it's usually quicker to go by bus, especially for shorter journeys. Buses marked *carreiras* (or CR) are the slow local buses. *Expressos* are direct

Introduction

buses between large towns and *rápidas* fast regional buses. We give details at the back of the book about getting to Portugal by plane, train or ferry and travel within Portugal. One of the the quick reference indices at the back of the book tells you the entry numbers for those places which you can easily reach by public transport. Sometimes the owners are willing to pick you up from the train or bus station – ask for details.

Food

It can be inexpensive to eat out in Portugal. The set meal, *ementa turistica*, may offer a small choice, while à la carte, *á lista*, is a full choice. The dish of the day, *prato do dia*, is usually a local speciality and helpings can be enormous. It is perfectly normal to ask for a *meia dose*, half portion, or for two adults to ask for *uma dose*, a portion, to share between two.

At virtually any restaurant in Portugal you will be given things to nibble before your meal arrives – olives, *chouriço*, sardine spread. But you will be charged for whatever you eat. If you don't want it, just say so. *Bacalhão*, salted cod, is the national dish: there are said to be 365 different ways of preparing it! Pork, as in Spain, is also popular; the homemade vegetable soups are delicious and so is fresh fish near the coast.

Many 'Special Places' have restaurants or make authentic local dishes. The 🍏 symbol shows those places which can provide vegetarian dinners, which may be welcome in a mainly carnivorous country.

Environment

Portugal is becoming more 'green' and most places have a recycling centre. Do try to recycle your waste. For information about the environment in Portugal check out www.naturlink.pt

Portuguese Tourist Offices
UK: 11 Belgrave Square, London
SW1X 8PP Tel: 0845 3551212
tourism@portugaloffice.org.uk

Photo above Rio Arade, entry 189
Photo right Cabana dos Rouxinois, entry 173

www.visitportugal.com
USA: 4th Floor, 590 Fifth Avenue,
New York, NY 10036-4785
Tel: 212 354 4403
tourism@portugal.org
www.portugalinsite.com

Subscription

Owners pay to appear in this guide.
Their fee goes towards the high
costs of inspecting and producing an
all-colour book. We only include
places that we like and find special
for one reason or another, so it is
not possible to buy – or bribe! –
your way in.

Internet

www.specialplacestostay.com has
online pages for all the places
featured here and from all our
other books – around 4,500 places
to stay in total. There's a searchable
database, a snippet from the write-
up and colour photos. New kid
on the block is our dedicated
UK holiday home web site,
www.special-escapes.co.uk

Disclaimer

We make no claims to pure
objectivity in choosing these places.
They are here simply because we
like them. We try our utmost to
get our facts right but we apologise
unreservedly if any errors have
sneaked in.

We do not check such things as fire

alarms, swimming pool security or
any other regulations with which
owners of properties receiving
paying guests should comply. This
is the responsibility of the owners.

And finally

Thank you to all those who have
taken the time to share your
opinions with us. You have helped
make this edition of the book even
better than the last! Please let us
have your comments; there is a
report form at the back of this book.
Or email us at
portugal@sawdays.co.uk
We'd particularly love your
recommendations for Madeira
and hope to go further afield for
the next edition (to the Azores).
Please tell us your favourite haunts
there too. Happy travels.

Laura Kinch

Photo left Pousada de Manteigas, entry 63
Photo right Monte da Fornalha, entry 136

General Map

On the following map pages:
places with self-catering accommodation are marked in pink **86**
places with overnight accommodation are marked in blue **84**
places with a mixture are marked with both **85**

Map 1

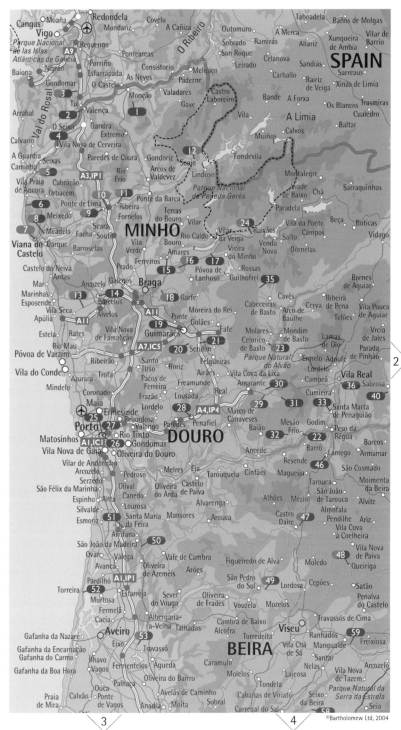

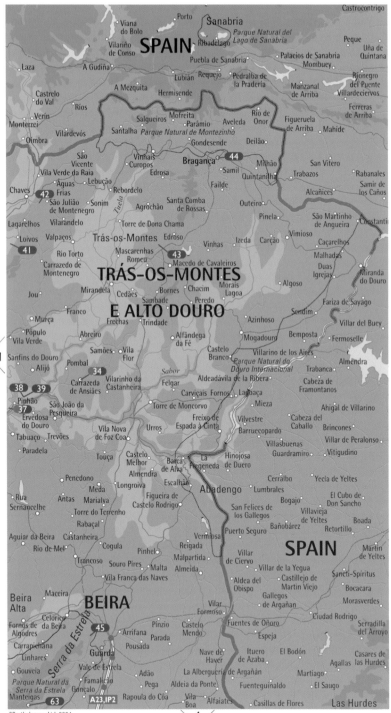

Map 3

©Bartholomew Ltd, 2004

1   2

57   60 Lagares da Beira   São Romão   Belmonte   64   Sortelha   Sabugal   Quadrazais   Aldeia Velha   Lajeosa

Tábua   Oliveira do Hospital   62   Loriga   Teixoso   Caria   Casteleiro   Vale de Espinho   Navasfrías

61   Parque Natural da Serra da Estrela   Covilhã   Escarigo   Meimoa   Valverde del Fresno   Eljas   Villamiel

Coja   Unhais da Serra   Dominguiso   Tortozendo   Capinha   Benquerença

Secarias   Paul   Silvares   Fundão   Fatela   Penamacor   Cilleros

Arganil   Unhais-o-Velho   Souto   65   Vale de Prazeres   Aranhas

Colmeal   Fajão   Barroca da Casa   Aldeia do Bispo   Salvador   Penha Garcia

Cabril   Orvalho   São Vicente da Beira   Soalheira   Orca   Medelim   Monfortinho

Pampilhosa da Serra   Lardosa   Proença-a-Velha   Monsanto

Álvares   Foz Giraldo   Sobral do Campo   **BEIRA**   Idanha-a-Velha

Álvaro   Estreito   Tinalhas   Escalos de Cima   **Beira Baixa**   Alcafozes   Zarza la Mayor

Madeirã   Oleiros   Salgueiro   Alcains   Escalos de Baixo   Idanha-a-Nova   Salvaterra do Extremo

Pedrógão Pequeno   Mosteiro   Sarzedas   A23,IP2   Ladoeiro   Zebreira   Segura   Ceclavín

Troviscal   Isna   Benquerenças   **Castelo Branco**   Piedras Albas

Sertã   Sobreira Formosa   Retaxo   Cebolais de Cima   Monforte da Beira   Rosmaninhal   Alcántara

Proença-a-Nova   Malpica do Tejo

Cardigos   Vila Velha de Ródão   Pérais   Cedillo   Parque Natural do Tejo Internacional

Amêndoa   Fratel   66   Montalvão   Santiago de Alcántara

Presa   Mação   Envendos   Monte Claro   115   Nossa Senhora da Graça de Póvoa e Meadas   Membrio

Mouriscas   Belver   Amieira do Tejo   Nisa   Salorino   Herreruela

Pego   105   Atalaia   Arez   Fadagosa   116 117 118   Beirã   Valencia de Alcántara   Sierra de San Pedro

Alvega   Gavião   119   Marvão   120

São Facundo   Tolosa   Alpalhão   Castelo de Vide   121   122   San Vicente de Alcántara

Bemposta   Comenda   Gafete   Vale do Peso   Alagoa   123

São Bartolomeu   Monte da Pedra   Flor da Rosa   Fortios   Parque Natural da Serra de São Mamede   **SPAIN**

Vale das Mós   Longomel   Aldeia da Mata   124   Crato   **Portalegre**

127   126   Torre das Vargens   Cunheira   125   Alegrete   La Codosera   Alburquerque

Ponte de Sôr   Vale de Açor   Chança   Urrá   Bagulho   Esperança

Valongo   Seda   Alter do Chão   Villar del Rey

Galveias   **ALENTEJO**   Assumar   Arronches

Benavila   130   Cabeço de Vide   Senhora do Rosário   Ouguela

Aldeia Velha   Fronteira   131   Vaiamonte   Monforte   Nossa Senhora da Graça dos Degolados

Avis   Ervedal   Santa Eulália   Campo Maior

Maranhão   Vale de Maceiras   Veiros   Barbacena   Caia

Cano   Sousel   Santo   São

Cabeção   132   Aleixo   Vicente   A6,IP7   Badajoz

Pavia   Casa Branca   Orada   Vila Fernando   Elvas

Brotas   Estremoz   Arcos   Terrugem   Vila Boim   Vila Viçosa

São Gregório   Vimieiro   133   135 134   São Romão   Borba   138

Sabugueiro   Santana do Campo   Vale do Pereiro   139 136   137

156   Gafanhoeira   Igrejinha   Évora-Monte   Bencatel   Juromenha

Arraiolos   Azaruja   140   141   Pardais   Olivenza

A6,IP2,IP7   Redondo   Alandroal   Mina do Bugalho   San Jorge de Alor   Valverde de Leganés

Terena   142   San Benito de la Contienda   Llanos de Olivenza

150-154   155   Santa Susana   Aldeia dos Marmelos   Táliga

Évora   Aldeia de Ferreira

3

6

Map 5

29

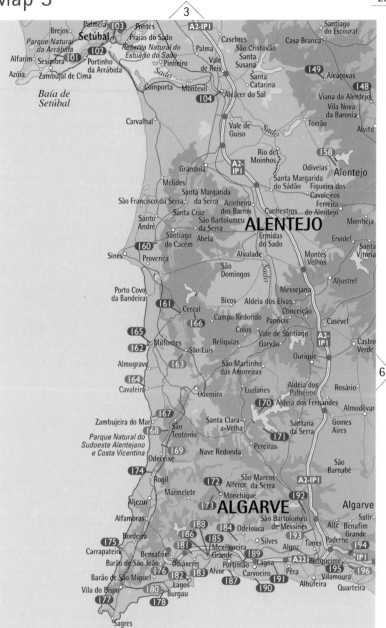

Map 6

4

Montoito
Caridade São Pedro Cheles Alconchel
147 São Manços Vendinha do Corval 143 144
Torre de Reguengos Monsaraz Villanueva Valle de
Coelheiros de Monsaraz 145 del Fresno Matamoros
Aguiar Campinho Mourão
São Bartolomeu do Outeiro Luz Zahinos Jerez de los
Oriola 146 São Marcos Granja Valencia Oliva de Caballeros
Santana Portel do Campo del Mombuey la Frontera Ardila
Alvito Vera Amieira Estrela
Vila de Cruz Alqueva Póvoa de Amareleja
Vila Frades São Miguel Santo Barrancos Encinasola Higuera
Ruiva Vidigueira Marmelar Ardila Amador la Real
Faro do Cuba Selmes Moura Safara
Alentejo Pedrógão Santo Aleixo Cumbres de
Trigaches São Matias Machados da Restauração San Bartolomé
São Brissos **ALENTEJO** Sobral
Beringel Beja Nossa Senhora Brinches Pias da Adica La Nava
159 das Neves Vale de Vila Verde Rosal de la Frontera Aroche Cortegana
Penedo Santa Clara Vargo de Ficalho Jabugo
Gordo de Louredo Quintos Serpa Almonaster la Real
Cabeça Gorda Salvada Vila Nova SPAIN Santa Ana
Trindade São de São Bento la Real
Brás Santa Santa Bárbara San
Albernoa Mosteiro Iria de Casa Telmo Valdelamusa
Vale de Açor Amendoeira Vales El Cerro de Andévalo
Entradas Parque Natural do Mortos Cabezas Silos de
Algodor Vale do Guadiana Corte Paymogo Rubias Calañas Calañas
Corte Gafo de Cima do Pinto
São Marcos Alcaria Mina de São Domingos Villanueva
da Ataboeira Ruiva Moreanes de las Cruces
Santa Bárbara Mértola Santana Puebla Tharsis Sotiel Coronada
de Padrões São João dos de Cambas de Guzmán Valverde
Senhora da Caldeireiros El del Camino
Graça de Padrões Pomarão Andévalo Alosno Beas
São Miguel do São Sebastião Espírito El Granado El Almendro
Pinheiro dos Carros Santo Sanlúcar Villanueva de
Santa São Pedro Giões de Guadiana los Castillejos San Bartolomé Trigueros
Cruz de Solis Alcoutim de la Torre
Martim Longo Pereiro Guerreiros Gibraleón A49
Ameixial Vaqueiros Zambujal do Rio San Juan
Cachopo **ALGARVE** Odeleite San Silvestre del Puerto
Vale de Guzmán Cartaya Aljaraque Moguer
da Rosa Azinhal Villablanca Huelva
Barranco Feiteira Peralva Junqueira Lepe El Rompido Palos de
do Velho Santa Umbrias Castro Marim Ayamonte La Antilla la Frontera
Querença Catarina de Camacho A22 Isla Cristina Punta Umbría
São Brás da Fonte 204 206 207 Vila Real de Santo António Mazagón
de Alportel do Bispo Santo Tavira Cabanas Reserva Natural do Sapal
Loulé 198 205 Estêvão 208 de Castro Marim Costa de la Luz
197 Estoi Moncarapacho 209 e Vila Real
Almansil 199 202 203 Santa Luzia de Santo António
Faro 200 201 Luz
Olhão Fuzeta
Parque Natural
da Ria Formosa

Scale: 1:1,200,000

Porto Moniz
214 São 215
Vicente Santana
Parque Natural
de Madeira
Calheta 213 Ponta Estreito Machico
do Sol de Câmara Santo
Ribeira de Lobos António Camacha Santa Cruz
Brava Câmara 211 Caniço 210
ARQUIPÉLAGO de Lobos **Funchal**
DA MADEIRA 212

5

Photo Laura Kinch

minho

minho

Minho is named after the river Minho which marks the border of Portugal with northern Spain

• Lush northwest province and birthplace of Portugal – Afonso Henriques was crowned the first King in **Guimarães** in 1179

• Ancient **Ponte de Lima** is a dignified market town clinging to the surrounding hills and named after its Roman bridge

• Sip a delicious glass of fizzy **vino verde** – green or young wine in the **Valença do Minho** fortress and gaze across to Galicia in Spain

• The **Peneda-Gerês National Park** – famous for wolves, megaliths, **espigueiros** (granite maize-drying houses), traditional culture and superb walking

• **Viana do Castelo**, a pretty seaside town, has heart-stopping views from the Cathedral and is known for its cheerful and pious festivals

• Visit **Braga**, the spiritual capital of Portugal. Climb the many steps to the important pilgrimage site of Bom Jesus do Monte

• **Barcelos**, home of Portugal's national symbol, the cockerel; wonderful weekly market, known for linen and pottery

Casa de Rodas
4950 Monção, Minho

Casa de Rodas is certainly a sight for (city) sore eyes; a long sweep of lawn bordering the main drive, then in the distance the low, clean-cut manor house with its chapel grafted onto one flank. This impressive home has been in the family for more than 400 years but your hosts are not pretentious about their aristocratic lineage: Maria Luisa's casual manner and her genuine friendliness are a lovely appetiser for the experience of being here. There are a number of reception rooms on the ground floor, each quite different from the next; they have marvellous wooden ceilings, stucco and panelling, trompe l'oeil marble and painted friezes. The overall effect is festive and fun. There are family antiques, portraits and photos; masses of books and comfy sofas to read them in, a grandfather clock, piano and games table. The bedrooms are just as memorable. Each one is different, most vast, each with its own dressing room. The newer rooms are beautiful too and have bigger bathrooms and their own balconies but less of a feel for the past. A most beautiful house. *Minimum stay three nights.*

rooms	Main house: 3 doubles, 1 twin. Outside: 4 suites; 2 pool suites occasionally available.
price	€80. Suites from €80. Singles €70.
meals	Good restaurants in village.
closed	Rarely.
directions	From Valença, arrive at roundabout to Monção. Straight on towards Melgaço. 500m on right at Turismo de Habitação sign. Gateway after 200m.

Senhora Maria Luisa Távora
tel   +351 251 652105

B&B

Map 1 Entry 1

Pousada de Valença do Minho

São Teotónio, Baluarte Socorro, 4930-619 Valença do Minho, Minho

The hillfort of Valença do Minho boldly stands on the north-western frontier with Spain, staring out at the fortress in Tui just metres from the river border. Enter crenellated gates clearly designed for horses and carts. Today the cobbled streets are wide enough for a car – just – and are merry with streetsellers, tourists and banter. Push through the throng to the far end of the fortress and you enter the peaceful haven of the pousada. The building is modern and not overly inspirational but we include it because of its position within this fabulous fortress – and its views. Bedroom furnishings are on the conservative side but no matter – they are very comfortable and have sparkling white bathrooms. Ask for a room with a view towards the south. The restaurant probably has the best choice of regional food within the city walls and the terrace and lounge buzzes around teatime. After dinner, retire to one of the lounges with sofas to sink into, modern art on the walls and gentle music. A great stop-off point if driving to or from the ferry in Santander.

rooms	18: 7 doubles, 11 twins.
price	€100-€150. Special offers available - see web site.
meals	Dinner, 3 courses, €26.
closed	Rarely.
directions	In Valença, follow signs for Fortaleza. Go into fortress walls & follow signs for Pousada São Teorónio.

	Senhor António Neiva
tel	+351 251 800260
fax	+351 251 824397
email	recepcao.steotonio@pousadas.pt
web	www.pousadas.pt

Hotel

Map 1 Entry 2

Os Bravos

Estas, Tomiño, 36730 Pontevedra, Galicia, SPAIN

Pluck fresh kiwi, peaches and nectarines for breakfast. Stroll around your walled garden – yes, you will feel proprietorial – before breakfasting on your bedroom balcony with its views to Portugal. Slipped into this unspoilt pocket of Spain, this is a genuine hideaway. Several notches above the average self-catering villa, the sprawling, five-bedroom, colonial-style house combines modernity with Galician charm. Locally-made chestnut furniture, sloping ceilings and splashes of chintz give a hint of 'country' while the modern sofas and owner's bold paintings add panache. The kitchen is so well-equipped you'll want to take it home. Couples or small families will be cosier in the nearby, but screened, stone cottage. Judith (English and the artist) and Karl (half-Galician) are warm, engaging, fun and know all the best beaches, walks and romantic ruins. But often it's just too tempting to do nothing but drift around the garden and pool, or perhaps sketch or paint (studio and materials available for budding artists). At night, you'll be hard pushed to hear anything more than the soft thud of an over-ripe peach.

rooms	4+2: 4 doubles. 1 cottage for 4; 1 villa for 8-10.
price	B&B €60. Villa £750 p.w. Cottage £450 p.w.; combined £1,000 p.w. (self-catering prices in sterling).
meals	Excellent restaurants nearby.
closed	Rarely.
directions	From Vigo N-550 for Tui. After sign for Tomiño, past Vilar de Martos, is a yellow bar, El Paso; next right for Estas. Through village for 2km. House on left (mint-green wall).

Karl Abreu & Judith Mary Goater
tel +34 986 623337
fax +34 986 623338
email huntingfordfarm@farmersweekly.net

Pousada de Vila Nova de Cerveira

Dom Diniz, Largo do Terreiro, 4920-296 V. Nova de Cerveira, Minho

Come in September and join in the harvest festivities. Eveyone carries their crop to the main square where villagers help to separate the corn heads; then the party starts – and lasts all weekend! Within the old town walls is a castle – whence great river views – then, up tiny cobbled streets, this 13th-century manor house, the pousada. It's comprised not of one grand building, but, charmingly, of several little converted houses, some with terraces, some with views. The young staff are friendly and helpful, happy to park your car and organise your baggage. Bedrooms have toile de Jouy fabrics with Portuguese scenes for bedcovers and curtains, and there are dried corn sheaves, still-life prints and blue and cream rugs for decoration. Sparkling bathrooms have deep tubs and thick robes. After dinner, settle down in the cosy bar with a drink and a game or two. The sea is 10km away but you can feel it, and there's a boat that will take you down the wide Minho river to the coast. There's a dizzy array of good things at breakfast – including champagne, should you be feeling celebratory.

rooms	29: 6 doubles, 18 twins, 2 triples, 3 suites.
price	€100–€145. Suites €120–€174. Special offers available - see web site.
meals	Dinner, 3 courses, from €20.
closed	Rarely.
directions	In Vila Nova de Cerveira, follow signs for pousada. Unload in front of hotel.

	Senhor Marco Santos
tel	+351 251 708120
fax	+351 251 708129
email	recepcao.ddinis@pousadas.pt
web	www.pousadas.pt

Hotel

Map 1 Entry 4

Casa de Esteiró
Vilarelho, 4910-605 Caminha, Minho

A magical old house that reflects the warm, outgoing personalities of owners José and Maria, the Casa de Esteiró is a rich experience from the moment you arrive. This late-18th-century house is extremely handsome and decorated with antiques and fine furniture – traditional Portuguese as well as finds from the owners' years abroad in the diplomatic service. The gallery is long, with masses of comfortable seating, beautiful cushions, porcelain and paintings, plus a lovely granite fireplace. The library is exquisite, and there is a small chapel off it (ask about the altar carried by Great Grandfather during the Peninsular War). The bedrooms too have both Portuguese and foreign furnishings, the suites are particularly special; all are fresh with garden flowers. Breakfast can be served either in the suites, the apartments or in the formal dining room, lined with beautiful ceramic dishes. Outside: a good pool and a garden with many specimen trees (planted by an earlier owner, Viscount Negrelos), which thrive in this Minho climate… and some delightful quiet areas for sitting and listening to the running water and birds.
Minimum stay 2 nights.

rooms	2 + 3: 2 suites.
	3 apartments: 2 for 4, 1 for 2.
price	€90-€100. Singles €65-€80.
	Apartment for 2 €80; for 4 €120.
meals	Available locally.
closed	Rarely.
directions	From Viana do Castelo to Valença on N13. In Caminha, right at 1st sign for the Centre & Turismo de Habitação. At T-junc. right at sign Casa de Esteiró. On right; ring bell.

	José Manuel & Maria Villas-Boas
tel	+351 258 721333
fax	+351 258 921356
email	casaesteiro@iol.pt
web	www.ciberguia.pt/casa-esteiro

Casa Santa Filomena

Estrada de Cabanas, Afife, 4900-012 Viana do Castelo, Minho

A grand entrance gate beckons you in to the Casa Santa Filomena, a solid, stonewalled building that was built in the 1920s. It is tucked into a quiet corner of an already quiet village; peace is assured. When we visited in early spring the old wisteria was a riot of tumbling lilac and mauve, as pretty a welcome as you could wish for. A high wall runs around the property; it girdles a small vineyard where vinho verde grapes are grown. Elsewhere the profusion of flowers is heady proof of the microclimate that this part of the Minho enjoys. It seems as if anything will grow here, and your breakfast juice will be from the oranges in the garden. Bedrooms are rather functional but perfectly clean and comfortable. Your hosts and their staff are extremely helpful; José himself has a passion for collecting and restoring carriages. When he's around, ask to see them: they are a delight. This is a charming and secluded spot, and good value. Among other diversions, a swimming pool and tennis courts are a kilometre away, and wonderful beaches not much further. *Minimum stay three nights.*

rooms	5: 4 twins/doubles, 1 suite.
price	€50–€55. Suite €60.
meals	Several good restaurants nearby. BYO.
closed	Rarely.
directions	From Valença to Viana, 1st left to Afife. From Viana 1st right. At square in centre of Afife turn inland/right (Estrada de Cabanas). House up hill on left at 1st fork.

José & Mary Street Kendall

tel	+351 258 981619
fax	+351 226 175936
email	soc.com.smiths@mail.telepac.pt

B&B

Map 1 Entry 6

Quinta da Bouça d'Arques

Rua Abreu Teixeira, Vila de Punhe, 4905-641 Viana do Castelo, Minho

In the grounds of the grand, 300-year-old manor are these modern apartments: the Abreu Teixeira family have lived here for centuries and have combined their talents to create a stylish conversion. Old stone walls, contemporary glass panels and modern art – sheer minimalist chic. Splashes of colour contrast with dark antiques – pink and red striped silk wall-hangings above fine old beds – while neutral colours blend beautifully with beams, tiles, terracotta floors, granite doorways and painted wooden shutters. Hunting prints, baskets, blankets and tall glass vases filled with petals add character, while bathrooms are luxurious with hand-painted tiles, deep baths and fluffy towels. A woollen cushion on a carved bench, a blanket on a sofa, burning inscense, a silk-clad mannequin – all contribute to the serenity of this place. Start the day with breakfast on your own terrace, or in the living room with its deep sofas; then move to the wooden loungers by the pool. And there are courtyards and vineyards to explore. A deeply relaxing place with surprising touches at every turn.

rooms	5 apartments: 4 for 2, 1 for 4.
price	€595-€1,050 per week.
meals	Good restaurants 7-12km.
closed	Rarely.
directions	IC1 Porto-Viana junc. 11 on N103 Braga-Barcelos. At r'bout N13 for Viana do Castelo. After 4km right N13 for Vila Verde & Baroselas. At blue sign for house, right, follow cobbled road; on left.

	Ana Luisa & João Magalhães Couto
tel	+351 226 179431
fax	+351 226 154765
email	joaomcouto@net.sapo.pt
web	www.boucadarques.com

Self-catering

Map 1 Entry 7

Casa do Ameal

Rua do Ameal 119, Meadela, 4900-585 Viana do Castelo, Minho

Casa do Ameal has been absorbed into the urban fabric of Viana do Castelo – but the moment you arrive in the entrance courtyard, with its gracious box hedging and gurgling fountain, the outside world feels far away. The stunning estate was bought in 1669 by the de Faria Araújo family whose numerous descendants still watch over the place; there are 84 family members who take it in turns to visit at weekends. The loveable, elderly Maria Elisa will proudly show off the collection of handicrafts and the family costume 'museum'; note the grandparents' christening robes and traditional Minho dress, still used for weddings and festivals. You choose between seven converted apartments – some have their own kitchenettes, others a shared barbecue/kitchen area, and there's a shared games room and living room. Pretty bedrooms are furnished in a simple, rustic style, some with mezzanines; beds have good linen. Continental breakfast is served in the dining room above the granite pool... wander at peace among fruit and nut trees in the gardens. *Minimum stay three nights.*

rooms	7 apartments: 3 for 4; 4 for 2.
price	€80 for 2; €130 for 4.
meals	For larger groups, by request. Good restaurants within walking distance.
closed	Rarely.
directions	From Porto, N13/IC1 for Viana do Castelo; right for Meadela. There, right at r'bout, then next right: Rua do Ameal. House on left.

	Senhora Maria Elisa de Magalhães Faria Araújo
tel	+351 258 822403
fax	+351 258 822405

B&B & Self-catering

Map 1 Entry 8

Casa de Arrabalde
Arcozelo, 4900 Ponte de Lima, Minho

Cross the Roman footbridge straight into town from this elegant, walled manor house. The young couple who run it are great fun, love meeting people and manage to juggle busy careers with family life; she is passionate about Portuguese literature, he is studying for his Doctorate in economics and they both teach. There's a pretty music room with a fabulous stucco ceiling, a wonderful well-stocked library, and the reception rooms are serenely relaxing. Generous bedrooms are furnished with carved antiques, red scatter rugs and Chinese pottery. For privacy you may prefer one of the self-catering apartments in the peaceful grounds next to the pool; they have functional interiors with simple, new Portuguese furniture, good views to the hills and are ideal for families. The Casa is an excellent spot from which to explore the area – but do book early: they get busy during the festivals. The market, held every other Monday, is a treat, villagers from all over gathering to sell their wares. Sociable breakfasts are served in the traditional dining room of the main house – you'll enjoy the lively atmosphere!

rooms	3 + 2: 1 double, 2 twins. 2 apartments for 4.
price	€80. Singles €76. Apartment €130.
meals	Restaurants within walking distance.
closed	Rarely.
directions	Cross bridge towards Lima. At roundabout, 1st right (Transito local); right after 50m. House on left after 300m.

	Doutor Francisco Maia e Castro
tel	+351 258 742442
fax	+351 258 742516
email	geral@casadoarrabalde.com
web	www.casadoarrabalde.com

B&B & Self-catering

Map 1 Entry 9

Casa de Pomarchão

Arcozelo, 4990-068 Ponte de Lima, Minho

Casa de Pomarchão dates all the way back to the 15th century but owes its present look to a rebuild of 1775 when a baroque chapel and veranda were added. The manor is at the centre of a 60-hectare estate of vineyards and thick pine forest. Your choice is between an apartment in the wonderful main building (every inch the aristocrat's residence) or your own solidly built house. Some are classical in style (Milho and Bica), others have a more rustic feel (Toca and Mato). What is special is their utter comfort; no corners have been cut. The houses all have hearths, top-quality sofas, warm curtains, paintings, good beds and well-equipped kitchens. French windows take you out to your own garden or terrace and the whole of the estate is yours for walking. You can swim in the huge old water tank, visit nearby Ponte de Lima and the beach is just a short drive away. This is a wonderful place to head for if you are planning a longer stay in Portugal. Frederico's wife well greet you with a warm smile, and she speaks excellent English.

rooms	8 self-catering apartments & houses.
price	For 2 €65–€70; for 4 €115–€130.
meals	Good restaurants a short walk.
closed	10-30 December.
directions	2km outside Ponte de Lima on N201 to Valença. Signed.

	Senhor Frederico Villar
tel	+351 258 741742
fax	+351 258 742742
email	frederico-vilar@clix.pt
web	www.casadepomarchao.com

Self-catering

Map 1 Entry 10

Casa da Várzea

Várzea, Beiral do Lima, 4990-545 Ponte de Lima, Minho

You'll see Casa da Várzea as you wind your way up from the valley below. It would be hard not to fall in love with the beauty of the place, cradled among terraced vineyards. It lay abandoned for many years, but Inácio Caldas da Costa, who was born here, took courage and after his retirement set about the restoration of the family seat. Várzea now has six big, light and charmingly decorated rooms. Family antiques are here for you to enjoy; you may find yourself in grandmother's or great-uncle's bed, made in cherry. Prints and framed embroidery, polished wooden floors and rugs are endearingly domestic. And in the public rooms wood-clad floors and ceilings lend warmth to grandeur — there's a lovely old chest with a secret drawer for hiding gold sovereigns. At breakfast there are long views from the airy dining room, plus homemade jams and fruit from the farm. There's a library, a pool-with-a-view and the old wooden 'drying house', now a second lounge/playroom — and a bar for tasting local vinho verde. Above all, Inácio and his wife will give you a genuine welcome.

rooms	6 + 1: 2 doubles, 2 twins, 2 family rooms. 1 apartment for 4.
price	€80. Singles €70. Apartment €100.
meals	Dinner sometimes available from €15.
closed	Rarely.
directions	From Porto-Valença m'way at Viana do Castelo, towards Ponte da Barca for 6km to S. Martinho Gandra. Right to Beiral for 2km, church on left; on left after 200m.

	Senhor Inácio Barreto Caldas da Costa
tel	+351 258 948603
fax	+351 258 948412
email	casadavarzea@iol.pt
web	www.sapo.pt/casadavarzea

B&B & Self-catering

Map 1 Entry 11

Adere Soajo

Associação para o desenvolvimento da região de Soajo, Bairros, 4970-653 Soajo, Minho

You are in a pretty village untouched by the outside world in the Peneda-Gerês National Park – known for its wolves, ancient history, broad rivers and spectacular plunge pools. The villagers have formed a cooperative and have created something remarkable: the old village tavern has been transformed by fine craftsmen and traditional materials into two rustic, self-catering houses. Expect low timbered ceilings, polished floors, hand-made country furniture, open fires, leather sofas with gentle colours, soft lights… and a mouthwatering array of goodies on arrival: ham, cheese, a homemade cake, fresh jam, milk, coffee. Wandering through the narrow streets, where old ladies in black chat contentedly to their neighbours, you will feel you have stepped back in time. Mountain bikes are provided, there's hearty dining in the restaurant nearby and excellent local wine and cheese. In the morning, fresh bread is tied to your door so you can breakfast when you please – and the breakfast varies a little each day. Authenticity at its simple best.

rooms	8 cottages: 4 for 6; 2 for 4; 2 for 2.
price	From €40 per night for 2; €80 for 4; €120 for 6.
meals	Two good restaurants in village.
closed	Never.
directions	From Ponte de Lima, take N203 past Ponte da Barca; continue until sign for Soajo; follow signs to village.

	Senhora Rosalina Araújo
tel	+351 258 576427
fax	+351 258 576427
email	turismo.adere-soajo@sapo.pt
web	www.casadesoajo.com

B&B & Self-catering

Map 1 Entry 12

Quinta do Convento da Franqueira
Carvalhal CC 301, 4755-104 Barcelos, Minho

This wonderful 16th-century monastery is hidden away among cork oaks, eucalyptus, cypress and pine trees. The cloister is thought to have been built with stones from the ruins of the castle of Faria. Certainly the brothers came here for the splendid isolation and the spring which now feeds a swimming pool, built above ornamental steps and with excellent views of house and church. Five centuries on, the granite buildings have been restored to their former grace by the Gallie family, a labour of love for 'how things were'; the results are delightful. Rooms are generously proportioned and have fine antiques, both English and Portuguese. There's a four-poster in one room, old prints, pretty bedside lamps and stuccoed ceilings. The snug, simple courtyard apartment is a fun hideaway with a roll-top entrance and terrace with gentle views. The estate produces its own vinho verde from vineyards that roll right up to Franqueira's walls; ask to be shown the winery. Children have swings in the gardens and a rocking horse in the play room. Visit nearby Barcelos market. *Minimum stay two nights.*

rooms	4 + 2: 2 doubles, 2 twins. 2 apartments: 1 for 2; 1 for 2 + child.
price	€100-€105. Singles €75. Apartments €560-€700 p.w.
meals	Good restaurant 4km.
closed	November–May.
directions	From Braga, N103 to Barcelos. 3rd right for Póvoa de Varzim. Right under bridge, 2nd left to Franqueira. Through village; middle road of 3 up hill into woods to bar. Right; left after church.

	Piers & Kate Gallie
tel	+351 253 831606
fax	+351 253 832231
email	piers@quintadafranqueira.com
web	www.quintadafranqueira.com

B&B & Self-catering

Map 1 Entry 13

Quinta do Tarrio

Tamel, Santa Leocádia, 4750 Barcelos, Minho

A farm with 300 years of history, this delightful place sits in gardens of lawns, flowers, orange, lemon, pear and plum trees and is surrounded by vineyards and a kiwi plantation. Owners Marine, who is Swedish, and George, who spent much of his early life in Norway, are informal and welcoming. The bright interior is full of interesting antiques and ancient farming artefacts and has lots of space; relax with a drink from the honesty bar in the *sala*, a room of tiled floors and rugs, with splendid views over the flower-filled patio garden and beyond. In colder weather open log fires and woodburning stoves are lit. Courtyard bedrooms encircle the old magnolia tree and are comfortable, quiet and have pretty curtains and cushions; beds are large, with twin beds zipped together to make doubles. Everything is on a grand scale, not least the breakfasts; the juice comes from their oranges and the homemade jams include kiwi. The grounds are full of variety and a safe place for children to explore; there's an attractive pool area, tennis court, a place to barbecue and space to play ball games. *Minimum stay two nights.*

rooms	5: 4 twins/doubles, 1 suite for 2-4.
price	€80. Singles from €65.
	Suite for 2 €80; for 4 €110.
meals	Excellent restaurant 1km.
	Cafe nearby. BBQ area here; BYO.
closed	November-Easter.
directions	From IC1 exit for Barcelos-Braga; follow N205 until N103; turn twice towards Viana do Castelo, until r'bout. On 50m & right to Tamel. 1km to Quinta.

	Marine & George Ennis
tel	+351 253 881558
fax	+351 253 882773
email	quintadotarrio@hotmail.com
web	www24.brinkster.com/tarrio

B&B

Map 1 Entry 14

Pousada de Amares

Santa Maria do Bouro, Mosteiro Sta. Maria do Bouro, 4720-633 Amares, Minho

A simple village, an austere exterior, a funky hotel. We love this place, with its minimalist interiors, modern art and big spaces – the monastery has been transformed. Architect Eduardo Souto Mouro has turned the colonnaded section of the ruins into a central feature, and mountain water still flows through the space; now the old irrigation channels run down to an oval-shaped marble pool, candlelit at night. Light streams in through every corner, some bedrooms have floor to ceiling windows with long views to the Serra de Cabrera, there are pencil sketches, rich hangings and even antique doors hung decoratively on walls. In the restaurant, vaulted ceilings, a stone chopping table laden with food, and ancient stone bread ovens at the back. A second dining room has a cavernous ceiling and contemporary low-hung chandeliers; people marry here, the speeches flowing from the high prayer balcony above. The old olive and wine room, an elegant spot for conferences, still has the high wooden doors for horses and carriages. Soak up the the views, the tranquillity and the simplicity of it all.

rooms	32: 14 doubles, 16 twins, 2 suites.
price	€73-€110. Special offers available - see web site.
meals	Dinner, 3 courses, from €25.
closed	Rarely.
directions	From Braga N103 for Póvoa de Lanhoso. At Geraz do Minho N205 for Amares. Pousada signed.

	Senhor Albino José Rolim Marques
tel	+351 253 371970
fax	+351 253 371976
email	recepcao.bouro@pousadas.pt
web	www.pousadas.pt

Hotel

Map 1 Entry 15

Quinta de São Vicente

Lugar de Portas, Geraz do Minho, 4830-315 Póvoa do Lanhoso, Minho

Dogs dozing in the shade set the pace; a flower-filled oasis, ideal for those who love peace and tranquility, country walks and birdsong. Teresa and Luís are delightful and will welcome you to their traditional bougainvillea-clad Minho farmhouse. This is an enchanting place: relaxed, solidly comfortable, and unostentatious. An enormous drawing room feels more like a conservatory with high windows opening on two sides, family photos, a woodburner and plenty of sofa space. The dining room is off to one end; at breakfast there will be a big spread and a chance to admire the large collection of old porcelain. In warmer weather you eat out under the orange trees with views of surrounding hills and the farm's kiwi fruit vines. And your sleep should be deep – only birdsong will rouse you. Bedrooms are manicured, large and filled with unusual antiques. Cor de Rosa has its own veranda, Amerelo is perfect for families, Azul is rather smaller, but pretty. Ask to be shown the unusual paintings in the Quinta's chapel (1623) and find time to visit the diminutive castle of nearby Póvoa do Lanhoso.

rooms	3 + 1: 3 twins/doubles. 1 self-catering house for 4.
price	€65. House for 2 €90; for 4 €130.
meals	Dinner with wine €17, by arrangement. Restaurants a short drive.
closed	Rarely.
directions	From Porto A3 north. Exit Braga Sul & Celeiros. Follow Braga Sul, Chaves & Póvoa de Lanhose (N103). Left for Amaraes; after 2km left for Turismo Rural. Signed.

	Senhora Teresa V Ferreira
tel	+351 253 632466
fax	+351 253 635377
email	info@quintasaovicente.com
web	www.quintasaovicente.com

B&B & Self-catering

Map 1 Entry 16

Pousada do Gerês-Caniçada / S. Bento

Caniçada, 4850-047 Caniçada, Minho

The mountains surround you and the top of the world feels close. These views are hard to beat – watch the sun reflect on the river far below as you sip your sundowner on the terrace. The chalet-style building is not old but looks perfect in this landscape; inside, a calm, peaceful atmosphere prevails. The lounge, with its high beamed celings and sofas to sink into, is a comfortable spot to curl up with a book, particularly in winter when the fires are lit. The restaurant serves a great selection of mountain dishes – the local cheeses are delicious, as are the Portuguese wines – and there's a cosy bar to retire to. Bedrooms have warm blankets on simple, wooden beds, some rooms have balconies, bathrooms are white and fresh. Take a dip in the flower-framed pool, wander the terraced gardens, try your hand at tennis. And there's plenty of fantastic trekking in the protected Peneda-Gerês National Park – friendly staff will tell you about the best routes. With its breathtaking views, this small hotel is a treat for lovers of the great outdoors.

rooms	29 twins/doubles.
price	€100-€155. Special offers available - see web site.
meals	Dinner, 3 courses, from €20.
closed	Rarely.
directions	From Braga N103 towards Póvoa de Lanhoso & Vieira do Minho. Follow signs to Caniçada. Pousada signed on left.

	Senhor Albino Rolim
tel	+351 253 649150
fax	+351 253 647867
email	recepcao.sbento@pousadas.pt
web	www.pousadas.pt

Hotel

Map 1 Entry 17

Casa dos Lagos
Bom Jesus, 4710-455 Bom Jesus, Minho

A calm, dignified welcome awaits you. The house was built by a viscount at the end of the 18th century on a wooded hillside which it shares with the Bom Jesus sanctuary; don't miss the extraordinary baroque staircase that zigzags up to the chapel, and visit on a weekday to avoid the crowds of pilgrims. Both the devout and the less so are welcome at Andrelina's home – a lesson in quiet elegance. Light floods in through the French windows of the sitting/dining room; at one end hangs a fine chandelier under which there will be cake for breakfast, at the other, a velvet sofa draws up to a large fireplace where you may sip a pre-dinner glass of port served from a decanter. The terrace gives onto a garden where stands of camellia break up the order of carefully clipped box hedges and ornamental fountains; the views from here are breathtaking. Only one bedroom is in the main house. It is large, elegantly corniced and has a fine antique furniture: a marble-topped dresser, a cavernous wardrobe, an ornately carved bed. Other rooms and the apartments are more modern, and are large and well-equipped.

rooms	3 + 4: 3 twins/doubles. 4 apartments.
price	€80. Singles €69. Apartment for 2 €80; for 4 €130.
meals	Good restaurants nearby.
closed	Rarely.
directions	From Braga, EN103 to Bom Jesus. House is signed on left.

	Senhora Andrelina Pinto Barbosa
tel	+351 253 676738
fax	+351 253 679207
email	casadoslagosbomjesus@oninet.pt

B&B & Self-catering

Map 1 Entry 18

Pousada de Guimarães - Santa Marinha
Costa, 4810-011 Guimarães, Minho

The peaceful presence of the Augustinian monks lingers and the place is bathed in music – gentle chants in the open courtyard, Bach's melodies rolling around the lofty dining room… their echoes in the old chapter hall stir the soul. Dona Afalda, wife of the first king of Portugal, gave the building to the church and it watches over the town in which Portugal was born. The original features of the monastery remain – its decorative façade, its ancient *azuelos* – yet a captivating modern hotel has evolved. Outside, plenty to explore – a lake, a fomal garden, a trickling stream and grotto. The new pool is set apart and has a bar, there's a huge square for aperitifs. Wide corridors lead to small double bedrooms made up of former monks' cells; you get great views from key-hole windows and bathrooms that sparkle. For atmosphere we prefer the old building to the new wing. An old-fashioned drawing room, modern art, entertainment for children, a fountained terrace, delicious *bacalhão* with corn bread for supper and breakfast fit for a king.

rooms	51: 20 doubles, 29 twins, 2 suites.
price	€73-€126. Special offers available - see web site.
meals	Dinner, 3 courses, from €26.
closed	Never.
directions	From Porto A3 towards Braga, then A7 Guimarães. In town follow signs for Pousada de Sta. Marinha to top of hill.

	Senhora Carolina Marafusta
tel	+351 253 511249
fax	+351 253 514459
email	recepcao.stamarinha@pousadas.pt
web	www.pousadas.pt

Hotel

Map 1 Entry 19

Casa de Sezim

Apartado 2210, 4810 Guimarães, Minho

Casa de Sezim has been in the family for more than 700 years. The first grapes were trod here in 1390! Today the estate's vinho verde is of prize-winning quality. The elegant portal in Sezim's rich ochre façade (the present building is mostly 18th century) strikes a properly welcoming note and this grand old house will seduce you with its understated elegance. You enter via an enormous, sober lounge with heavy old oak beams, granite floor and walls. The family coat of arms graces the hearth and forebears look down from their gilt frames – if only one could invite them down for a game of billiards! The fun really begins upstairs in the bedrooms. Some have four-poster beds, others have tapestried headboards, perhaps a writing desk; all have some antique pieces and rich patterns on wallpaper, bedspreads and curtains. But the gaily decorated panelling is their main joy. We'd probably sacrifice space and go for a tower room with a view. Also memorable are Sezim's panoramic paintings that date from the early 19th century with exotic scenes from the Old and the New Worlds.

rooms	10: 9 twins/doubles, 1 suite.
price	€60-€100. Singles €45-€78. Suite €92.
meals	Lunch/dinner €23, by arrangement.
closed	Rarely.
directions	From Porto, A3 for Braga; A7 to Guimarães. N105 for Santo Tirso. Right in Covas (after petrol station & Ford garage); house 2.2km further directly opp. 'Tecidos ASA'.

	Senhor António Pinto de Mesquita
tel	+351 253 523000
fax	+351 253 523196
email	geral@sezim.pt
web	www.sezim.pt

B&B

Map 1 Entry 20

Quinta de Cima de Eiriz

Lugar de Cima de Eiriz, Calvos, 4810-605 Guimarães, Minho

On a south-facing slope of the beautiful Penha mountain, this old Minho quinta has been completely restored. Marvel at the size of the granite lintels, flagstones and building blocks of the entrance hall; in the beamed and terracotta-tiled guest living room the old grape press has been transformed into an unusual raised bar – help yourself to a drink. The pillar-box red of the doors and windows lends a lighter note. Bedrooms are in the old stable blocks, updated with central heating and phones and sparkling marbled and tiled bathrooms. Most memorable of all are the views over the trimmed lawns and across the valley. Breakfast is a big meal: fresh orange juice, yogurt, several types of bread and cake and homemade jams. Afterwards you can stride straight out towards the wooded summit of Penha. In the warmer months cool off in the pool; there is also an excellent games room. The views are long and rural, and 10km away is ancient Guimarães with its narrow streets, castle and superb museum. Closer still: the Santa Marinha da Costa Monastery, the best preserved medieval building of the region.

rooms	4: 1 double, 3 twins.
price	€75. Singles €50.
meals	Good restaurants 5km.
closed	Rarely.
directions	A3 Porto-Braga. In Vila Nova de Famalaicão, A7 to Guimarães; towards Fafe & Felgueiras. After 4km, right for Felgueiras for 4km; right at sign Penha & Lapinha. After 2km, left at stone cross; signed.

	Doutor João Gaspar de Sousa Gomes Alves
tel	+351 253 541750
fax	+351 253 420559

B&B

Map 1 Entry 21

Pousada de Mesão Frio

Solar de Rede, Sta. Cristina Estrada Nacional nº108, 5040 – 336 Mesão Frio, Minho

A grand, palacial *solar* (country manor) from the 17th century that exudes elegance and prosperity. It's now a formal hotel, with doormen and butlers and furniture fit for a king. Antique blue and white *azulos* in the entrance hall show traditional Portuguese scenes; carved, high-backed chairs, huge flower displays and gold laquered furniture add a touch of decadence. Views from the bedrooms in the main house stretch far east and west along the river Douro, and the steep terraces grow the precious grapes for port; the hotel makes its own – buy some to take home. Bedrooms have antique furniture and pretty soft furnishings, and the main house suite is a dream. Several stone outbuildings have been agreeably converted into further suites; floral fabrics lend a country-cottage, almost English, feel. Most of these rooms have balconies or terraces and are delightfully secluded. Dine grandly in the old kitchen – or, equally grandly, in the dining room, where parties may gather around one big solid table and drink from silver goblets. A pretty chapel is attached – and there's a lovely pool with views.

rooms	29: 21 twins/doubles, 8 suites.
price	€125-€229. Singles €157-€174. Suites €179. Special offers available – see web site.
meals	Dinner, 3 courses, from €25.
closed	Rarely.
directions	N108 to Mesão Frio. Pousada signed on left.

	Senhor Joaquim de Sousa
tel	+351 254 890130
fax	+351 254 890139
email	solar.da.rede@douroazul.com
web	www.pousadas.pt

Hotel

Map 1 Entry 22

Casa da Lage

Gémeos, 4890 Celorico de Basto, Minho

A faded old manor that was once the family seat; now Berta has breathed new life into the old walls. She's an artist who teaches locally and has thrown herself into restoring the house to its former glory – wooden ceilings are painted red and green, and there are flowers on the bedroom ceilings. The garden does still need attention but the old fruit trees flourish, the birds are bountiful and the peace certain. Come to paint or draw, and don't expect great luxury. The tiny village is reached by tiny roads; with each turn you delve even deeper into the fabric of rural Portugal. The whole cavernous house can be let to a group, but if you go B&B, you'll enjoy the meals; traditional dishes are served by candlelight in the kitchen with open fire and old bread oven. Rooms are based around the bougainvillea-tumbled courtyard and have antique and modern furniture, good paintings, modern art and simple bathrooms. Feel at home in the bar with old piano and family pictures taken during the decadent 1920s, unwind in one of several lounges – or on the wide veranda out back. Lap up the peace.

rooms	6: 5 doubles, 1 single.
price	€75, including breakfast. Singles from €37.50. Whole house, self-catering, from €1,400 per week.
meals	Dinner, 3 courses, €20.
closed	Rarely.
directions	From Porto A4 towards Celonico de Basto. From Celorico de Basto towards Felguiras; 1st left. Follow road round; house up lane to right.

	Senhora Maria Berta Alvares de Moura
tel	+351 963 551202
fax	+351 258 733908

B&B & Self-catering

Map 1 Entry 23

Casa de Dentro 'Capitão-Mor'

Vila-Ruivães, C.180, 4850-341 Vieira do Minho, Minho

This was the home of Capitão-Mor de Ruivães who put the French to rout during the Peninsular War (the 'War of Independence' to the Portuguese). It sits proudly on one side of the valley that divides the Cabeira and Gerês mountain ranges, in the tiniest of hamlets amid terraced vineyards and deep greenery. Both hosts and home exude warmth and welcome. Ilda, a retired school teacher, relishes sharing her knowledge of this corner of the Minho: she has maps ready for your walks and will tell you about the region's fascinating mythology. We loved the sitting room with its low beams, granite hearth, old copper still and wall cabinets displaying the family china – just the place for nestling down with a good book. The bedrooms are as unassuming as the rest of Ilda's home; varying in size, they have antique beds and wardrobes, parquet floors, rugs and pretty bedside lamps. Breakfast is as generous as you'd expect: yogurts, homemade jams, fruit juice and Ilda's very special cake, *bola de carne folar*. All this and a tennis court, a pool-with-a-view and the Gerês National Park on your doorstep.

rooms	5 + 1: 4 doubles, 1 twin. 1 apartment for 6.
price	€63. Singles €50. Apartment €180-€190; €1,100 p.w.
meals	Good restaurants in village.
closed	Rarely.
directions	From Braga, EN103 to Ruivães. At sign, Turismo de Habitacão, right. House in centre of village, to right of church.

Senhora Ilda de Jesus Truta Fraga de Miranda Fernandes

tel	+351 253 658117
fax	+351 253 658117
email	casadedentro@clix.pt

B&B & Self-catering

Map 1 Entry 24

Photo Laura Kinch

douro

douro

*Douro is named after the River Douro (River of Gold) which rises
in Spain and snakes through the steep terraces towards the sea*

• **Porto**, the country's second largest city, historically linked to
Bristol. Colourful tall houses in the UNESCO World Heritage
Site, the Ribeira, with its lively nightlife and buzzing restaurants

• Wander around **Amarante** – a gracious town, where flower-
filled balconies overhang the river Tâmega. The collection of
Amadeo de Souza Cardoso's contemporary, futurist and cubist
paintings are on display

• Awesome pre-historic rock drawings in **Vila Nova de Foz Côa**

• Discover the process of making **port wine**. Tour one of the
grand lodges or try your hand at treading the grapes

• Travel up **river by boat** from Porto until the valleys steepen
and terraced vineyards spring up all around

• Explore the Douro valley by **steam train** from Porto to
Pocinho. Visit in September when the the vines turn rich red and
orange

Pestana Porto
Praça da Ribeira, 1, 4050-513 Porto, Douro

Facing the river Tejo in the Ribeira district are some of the most beautiful townhouses in the city. Merchants and traders used to live here, behind the muted red and ochre, balconied façades. Now six of these narrow frontages have been ingeniously converted into this single, three-storey, quirky-modern hotel – with glass-sided walkways bridging the gaps between. Look upwards to the differing heights of the houses, gaze down on the narrow cobbled streets. Gone are the days when old Oporto was a bustling port – now the tempting aromas of fresh fish pull in the tourists, and the boats bring the Douro grapes to the distilleries. Smartly-dressed doormen will welcome you, and staff are incredibly friendly. Bedrooms – in mulberry or sage – are luxurious: potions and lotions, fat fluffy bathrobes, crisp cotton sheets. Ask for a room at the front with a balcony and a river view. A cocktail before dinner? There are sofas in the restaurant – and the city walls run right through. Porto is a World Heritage Site – book in for several days.

rooms	48: 45 twins/doubles, 3 suites.
price	€140-€181. Singles €124-€163. Suites €252-€278.
meals	Lunch & dinner available.
closed	Never.
directions	Head to Ribeira area, next to river. Praça de Ribeira is next to the water; hotel is on corner.

	Senhora Mariana Lacerda
tel	+351 22 340 2300
fax	+351 22 340 2400
email	pestana.porto@pestana.com
web	www.pestana.com/PT/Hoteis/LisboaPortoCascais/Porto/

Hotel

Map 1 Entry 25

Pensão Avenida

Avenida dos Aliados, No. 141 4º 5º, 4000-067 Porto, Douro

Smack bang in the centre of Porto, this friendly, inexpensive guesthouse is run by the delightful João Brás and his wife. They also own Castelo de Santa Catarina (entry 25) and go the extra mile to make your stay special. On the fifth floor of a typical 19th-century townhouse, reached by lift, are these very simple, bright and spotlessly clean rooms. Breakfast is a good spread and is served in the light-filled cream breakfast room overlooking the square and the impressive government buildings. The odd antique is dotted around but the feel of this place is relaxed and unpretentious. Do ask for local maps; the S. Bento train and tube station is outside the door, as are excellent restaurants and cafés. Walk to monuments such as Torre dos Clérigos, Sé Cathedral, Palácio da Bolsa, to Ribeira and the famous Oporto cellars – or travel up the river Douro by boat; information is provided at reception. A simple place with a great welcome and terrific value for money. *Show your copy of Special Places to Stay and João will let you park free at the Castelo de Santa Catarina hotel nearby.*

rooms	15: 5 doubles, 8 twins, 2 triples.
price	€38. Singles €28.
meals	Excellent restaurants nearby.
closed	Rarely.
directions	Centre of Porto, opposite Town Hall & São Bento station, near Praça de Liberdade.

	Senhor João Brás
tel	+351 22 2009551
fax	+351 22 2052932
email	pensaoavenida@clix.pt
web	pensaoavenida.planetaclix.pt/

B&B

Map 1 Entry 26

Residencial Castelo Santa Catarina
Rua Santa Catarina 1347, 4000-457 Porto, Douro

This eye-catching building was built high up above Porto during the period which the Portuguese call the Gothic Revival. Even if the corner turrets and window arches don't remind you of Notre Dame, you can't fail to be intrigued by this tile-clad edifice – it stands like a folly, surrounded by tall swaying palms, in an otherwise conservative suburb. The interior décor is as extravagant as the exterior. Be regaled by gilt and stucco, chandeliers and mirrors, cherubs and lozenges, Tiffany lamps and roses, repro beds and cavernous wardrobes. It's showy, over the top, faded in parts, garish in others – and great fun. Your choice of carpet colour? Turquoise, lime green or navy paisley. There is the odd patch of peeling paint, the bathroom tiles are often out of step with the rooms but these things are part of the charm. The affable owner João is normally around in reception and with fluent English can answer all your questions about this whimsical building. Try to book the suite in the tower; it's worth it for the views. An enormously entertaining city hotel.

rooms	24: 21 twins/doubles, 3 suites.
price	€65. Singles €45. Suite €85.
meals	Restaurants nearby.
closed	Rarely.
directions	At top of Rua Santa Catarina, just below Plaza Marques Pombal. Follow signs.

	Senhor João Brás
tel	+351 225 095599
fax	+351 225 506613
email	porto@castelosantacatarina.com.pt
web	www.castelosantacatarina.com.pt

B&B

Map 1 Entry 27

Casa dos Esteios

Quinta do Ameal, 3 Miguel de Paredes, 4575-373 Penafiel, Douro

The granite farm buildings, encircled by kiwi plantations, have been beautifully converted. The wine cellar is now an open-plan living/dining room, the grape press the base for the woodburning stove, the old stables are luxurious bedrooms. No expense has been spared; it is fresh, bright, uncluttered - a happy blend of antique and modern. A stone bread oven rubs shoulders with a sleek, cream, Swedish-style fitted kitchen with granite work tops, where smiling Daniella, who was born here, makes tasty breakfasts. The dining room is deeply traditional with its dark wooden table and English and Portuguese antiques. Wooden floored bedrooms, set around the courtyard, have armchairs and more dark antiques, enlivened by fabrics patterned with English roses and pretty checks. New bathrooms are luxurious and sparkling. The pool has views to the hills and a small play area for children. Make time for the renowed spa town of Termas de São Vicente, and Porto, a short drive. This is a super place for a group of friends to rent, and an easy, relaxing spot for a few days' B&B.

rooms	7: 2 doubles, 5 twins. Whole house can be rented for a week.
price	€60. Singles €50. House €1,500 p.w.
meals	Good restaurants nearby.
closed	Never.
directions	From Porto IP4 to Penafiel. Exit for Nó de Guilhufe (Penafiel Sul & Entre-os-Rios) on N106 for 12km. Left to Rio de Moinhos on N312; right at sign for Casa dos Esteios.

	Senhora Maria Jorge Nogueira da Rocha
tel	Mobile: +351 96 2830701
fax	+351 21 7591894
email	nogueirarocha@netcabo.pt

B&B

Map 1 Entry 28

Casal de Aboadela
Aboadela, 4600-500 Amarante, Douro

You'll long remember arriving at Aboadela. Once you turn off the busy main road you twist and turn along the narrowest of lanes to this delightfully sleepy hamlet and its old farmhouse. There is many a treat in the rambling gardens: an old granite maize store, a bubbling spring, gourds and pumpkins drying in the sun, old millstones recalling the building's origins. There are roses and oranges and vines and, in among them, secluded places for contemplation. The bedrooms are in the main house, simply attired in cottage style with family furniture and lacking nothing; just to one side in a converted outbuilding is the 'stone little house' (sic) which is self-contained – with a barbecue – and would be just perfect for a longer stay. The guest sitting/dining room is similarly unpretentious: granite-walled with a tiled floor and potted plants. Home-grown wine is available. A French window gives onto a small balcony and lets in the morning light and the view; your attentive hosts will spoil you at breakfast. There are lovely rambles straight out from the house and the São Gonçalo monastery in Amarante is a short drive.

rooms	4 +1: 3 twins, 1 suite (twin & single). 1 house for 2.
price	€45. Singles €40. Suite €50. House €55.
meals	Picnics & light snacks on request. Good restaurants 3-10km.
closed	Rarely.
directions	From Amarante, IP4 for Vila Réal. 9km after Amarante, right to Aboadela; follow signs for Turísmo Rural; right at T-junc.; follow 'TR' sign to house.

	José Silva & Helena Rebelo
tel	+351 255 441141
email	srebelo@med.up.pt

Pousada do Marão / São Gonçalo

Serra de Marão, Ansiães, 4600-520 Amarante, Douro

The Marão mountain range awaits you, and you can gaze down the valleys from your bed. Smart tartan-dressed beds have headboards with carved hearts, there are balconies, fluffy bathrobes and lashings of hot water – a comfortable and comforting place to come back to after a long day's walk. You can even breakfast on your own terrace. This pousada has a small, intimate feel and the friendliest local staff. In the lounge is a winter-lodge atmosphere thanks to roaring fires, leather chairs, panelled ceilings, baskets, sisal mats on polished floors and red tartan armchairs. Amarante, the nearest town, is devoted to Saint Gonçalo who, according to legend, was the matchmaker patron saint. The atmosphere is intimate, and romantic – candlelit dinners at individual tables, then an aperitif in that cosy lounge. The exterior is not much to write home about but once inside you will fall under the spell of this dear little hotel. Do visit the Mateus Palace and the art gallery of Amadeo Sousa Cardoso – or just sit back and relish the views.

rooms	15: 6 doubles, 8 twins, 1 suite.
price	€100-€140. Suite €160. Special offers available - see web site.
meals	Dinner, 3 courses, from €26.
closed	Rarely.
directions	IP4 towards Vila Real, junc. 21. Pousada signed.

	Senhor João Amaral
tel	+351 255 460030
fax	+351 255 461353
email	recepcao@sgoncao@pousadas.pt
web	www.pousadas.pt

Hotel

Map 1 Entry 30

Casa da Levada

Travanca do Monte, Cx. 715, Bustelo, 4600 Amarante, Douro

The crenellated tower is visible as you come down the winding cobbled track into this ancient hilltop village, perched amid mountain views. Levada is really a small castle in a settlement built of rough-hewn, moss-covered granite blocks where people and animals still live cheek-by-jowl. Rough wooden doors open to reveal a goat, a pair of oxen, an old woman embroidering: scenes from centuries past. The house is a mountain refuge, and hosts Maria and Luís are wonderfully welcoming. She is an English teacher, he a humorous man whose family have lived here for 300 years. You'll sleep in bedrooms with granite walls, wooden ceilings, beams and sisal matting. The Tower Room has a separate bathroom across the landing and a balcony; the Poet's Room has a trapdoor down to the bathroom. The lounge is comfortable and the dining room barn-like, with a large oval table at which everyone eats together: food is traditional and the wine comes from Luís's mother's farm. Up the hill, pass granite water mills to a bleak hilltop with great boulders and dolmens. An amazing place.

rooms	4: 1 double, 2 twins; 1 twin with private bath.
price	€75-€90. Singles €60-€72.
meals	Dinner with wine, 3 courses, €25. Restaurants 2km-15km.
closed	Rarely.
directions	From south A4. After Amarante, exit 18 to Régua & Mesão Frio. Follow for 8km, then right for Turismo d'habitacão.

	Luís & Maria Vasconcelos do Lago Mota
tel	+351 255 433833
fax	+351 255 433833
email	casalevada@clix.pt

B&B

Map 1 Entry 31

Casa d'Além

Oliveira, Mesão Frio, 5040-204 Mesão Frio, Douro

The cheerful façade of Casa d'Além looks out across the stunning terraced vineyards of the Douro valley and reflects the optimism of the early 1920s. The public rooms are the most refined: the Rennie Mackintosh print on easy chairs, sofas and drapes is perfectly balanced by the delicate wrought-iron work of the balconies. Piano, card table and shining parquet create an atmosphere of old Portugal. Next door is a panelled dining room and, still more remarkable, a long painted corridor, a 'marbled sunburst', which leads to your bedroom. A feast of period pieces, there are rugs and marble-topped dressers, generous old tubs and wash stands. Rooms have heavenly views. Paulo and his wife speak excellent English and their marvellous staff will take care of you; ask Elisabete about personal trips along the Douro by boat or steam train, and visits to Mateus Palace in Vila Réal. Outside are views, pure air and a secluded pool area. Be sure not to miss dinner: perhaps a roast from their bread oven, homemade ice-cream and a chilled glass of the local wine. A very special place.

rooms	4: 1 double, 2 twins, 1 family room.
price	€75. Singles €60. Family room €80-€100.
meals	Lunch/dinner, 3 courses, from €17.50.
closed	Rarely.
directions	From Porto, A4 for Vila Réal. N108 to Régua. After Mesão Frio, on for 8km to Granjão. Under railway bridge, then right to Oliveira. Signed on right.

	Senhor Paulo José F S Dias Pinheiro
tel	+351 254 321991
fax	+351 254 321991
email	casadalem@clix.pt
web	www.casadalem.pt

B&B

Map 1 Entry 32

Casal Agrícola de Cevêr

Quinta do Pinheiro, 5030 Santa Marta de Penaguião, Douro

Grapes are still crushed by foot in this winery, on the western reaches of the Douro. Alice and son Filipe opened up their 19th-century house six years ago, while continuing to produce their own-label port and olive oil. All visitors are invited to tour the production areas and to sample the latest offerings. Rooms are comfortable and airy with up-to-the-minute bathrooms; for a small extra charge you can take the suite with its own little gallery. National Trust colour schemes combined with good 19th- and early 20th-century antiques create a mood that is calm and reasonably formal. Guests have their own sitting room with smart striped sofas and walls of books on what to do and see in this most beautiful region. There's a large basement games room with a pool table, too. For warm days there's a Roman swimming pool set on its own lawned terrace, against a backdrop of vines. Dinner in the family dining room is incredible value and includes wine, port and coffee. Very few English people have found their way here – a pity, as they are missing something special.

rooms	5: 3 doubles, 1 twin, 1 suite.
price	€80. Singles €67. Suites €90.
meals	Dinner with wine, 3 courses, €25, by arrangement.
closed	Christmas.
directions	From Porto A4 to Vila Real. Take Santa Maria exit onto N2. House clearly signed on right, just before entering village.

	Filipe Manta & Alice João Mergulhão
tel	+351 254 811274
fax	+351 254 811274
email	casalagricoladecever@casalagricoladecever.com
web	www.casalagricoladecever.com

B&B

Map 1 Entry 33

Quinta Bartol
Carrazeda de Ansiães - Beira Grande, Douro

Sit under ancient willows, gaze across to vineyard-cloaked hills and raise your glass to the good fortune that has brought you to Quinta Bartol. This 200-year old farmhouse, on the banks of the Douro, is the hub of one of the oldest family-run working farms in the region. Guests are welcomed as family into gracious, relaxed rooms comfortably dotted with antiques, chintzy sofas and piles of books. Large bedrooms are traditional country style and have wooden floors and shutters, dark antiques and embroidered bedcovers. Five share bathrooms; families might prefer to take the separate cottage. Breakfasts are jolly affairs in the big, cosy kitchen while summer dinners are enjoyed on the riverside terrace. Every meal is an occasion, and the fruit, vegetables, olive oil and wine are home-produced. Swim in the river, go fishing, take a boat trip or find a shady spot in the secret garden for a snooze. The peace, the views, the unhurried pace are the essence of Quinta Bartol. Mariluz and José love to look after you and will delight you with stories about the area.

rooms	6 + 1: 6 doubles. Cottage for 4.
price	€70-€80. Cottage €100.
meals	Dinner, 3 courses, by arrangement.
closed	Rarely.
directions	From Porto follow signs for Vila Real and then signs for Alijó, Tua, Carrazeda de Ansiães & Beira Grande. Owner will meet you here or at train station.

	Senhora Christina Pacheco
tel	+351 282 760624
fax	+351 282 422535
email	telopacheco@clix.pt

B&B & Self-catering

Map 2 Entry 34

Photo Laura Kinch

trás-os-montes

trás-os-montes

Trás-os-montes means 'beyond the mountains', referring to the Gerês, Alvão & Marão mountain ranges.

- The north-eastern, most remote province of Portugal. Known to be sleepy and friendly with a very traditional culture

- **Vila Réal** – visit the Palácio Mateus, this fantastical place is where the well-known Rosé is produced

- **Chaves** is a spa town with a Roman bridge dating back over 1900 years and the most delicious smoked presunto

- **Bragança** has a 3rd-century Citadella and its archeological museum is home to some 2000-year-old granite statues of boars, thought to be ancient fertility symbols

- **Parque Natural de Montesinho** – the 750 km^2 of grassland and forest which crosses into Spain has been populated since the Iron Age; subsidies ensure the sensitive restoration of buildings

- Step back in time at ancient festivals – during **Caretos of Podence** (near Macedo de Cavleiros) in February masked men rampage the streets, good-humouredly embarrassing anyone who comes into their path

Casa Cabrilho
5470-019 Lapela-Cabril, Trás-os-Montes

Chef Antonio is determined to put this mountain hamlet on the culinary map. He and his father make a good team: Antonio trained as a cook in Australia and London; Manuel, once a waiter on a cruise ship, tends the picturesquely sloped vegetable garden. So, you'll get more than rice and chips here. Expect the freshest vegetables, home-smoked ham and local *cabrito* (kid) and the heartiest soups and stews. Bedrooms, in contrast, are an afterthought: small, with cork floors, floral covers, bare ceiling bulbs, and the bathroom is shared (among members of the same party). Hardly a place for sybarites, then, but valuable for those seeking an insight into the 'real' Portugal. Hearty hikers wanting to spend a night in these remote hills would be as happy as Larry. Mention must be made of the balustrade-free steps up the rooms and the sheer-drop terrace: leave adventurous offspring at home! Spend the day in the hills in the beautiful Peneda-Gêres National Park, return for a splendid supper, play a round of billiards, turn in for a quiet night. A no-frills, peaceful place to stay miles from the beaten tourist track.

rooms	4 doubles sharing bathroom, let to same party only.
price	€40. Singles €30.
meals	Lunch/dinner €15.
closed	Rarely.
directions	From Braga, EN103 for 35km. Before Salamonde, turn off for Cabril for 21km to Lapela.

	Senhor António Goncalves
tel	+351 253 659260
email	res.cabrilho@sapo.pt

B&B

Map 1 Entry 35

Casa das Cardosas

Rua Central, Folhadela, 5000-103 Vila Real, Trás-os-Montes

A grand Trás-os-Montes manor in as bucolic a setting as you could hope to find – yet you are a mile from Vila Real. The Cardosa family has been here for 250 years and once made wine. The glorious gardens produce peaches, plums, cherries and raspberries, and there's a pool. Find time to let the warm-natured Maria Teresa tell you a little of the area's history over a chilled drink on one of her three terraces (what views!). Bedrooms are a step back in time, darkish but quiet, elegantly decorated without a hint of hotel. One has an ornate Bilros four-poster, the 'French' room has pretty fabrics and a chandelier, the back room, the smallest, leads enticingly to the terrace. The old stone dormitory for grape pickers has become a roomy winter sitting room with rugs on shining parquet, innumerable antiques, fresh flowers and family mementos – all add up to a mood of unaffected intimacy. Breakfast at Cardosas is a generous meal with homemade jams, juices and eggs; at dinner you may feast on roast beef, or hake from the wood-fired oven. Make sure you have time to explore the Alvão Natural Park.

rooms	3: 2 doubles, 1 twin.
price	€60. Singles €55.
meals	Lunch/dinner by arrangement.
closed	Rarely.
directions	In Vila Réal head to university. Turn right to village; signs to the house begin at the left of the main entrance to the university.

Senhora Maria Teresa Cardosa Barata Lima

tel	+351 259 331487
fax	+351 259 331487

B&B

Map 1 Entry 36

Quinta de la Rosa
5085-215 Pinhão, Trás-os-Montes

If port is your tipple, then stay at the Quinta de la Rosa. The family has been in the trade for 200 years; this factory estate matures its wines in-house and sells directly to customers. The choice here is between B&B and self-catering farmhouse. Of the B&B rooms, the newest share a terrace high above the river and railway, while those in the labyrinthine main house are right by the water. (Expect steep steps.) The suites are the best, with their faded English armchairs and painted corner cupboards; one has its own little lounge and a view of Pinhão. Of the two houses, each with a pool, we loved rustic Lamelas, tucked away at the top of the estate and approached through a forest. It is beautifully decorated and equipped for a group of six. Amerela, also lovely, is further down the hill. B&B guests are served breakfast at pretty tables in a sunny dining room with a river view; housekeeper Filomena looks after you well. But your first priority is a tour of the cellars and a tasting – followed, perhaps, by a swim or a canoe trip on the Duoro. September is harvest time – feel free to join in!

rooms	6 + 2: 1 double, 3 twins, 2 suites; 2 self-catering houses for 6-10.
price	€75. Singles from €60. Suite €95. Houses €660-€1,400 per week.
meals	Dinner, 3 courses, €25, except Sunday. Simple restaurants nearby.
closed	Never.
directions	Signed from Pinhão. Tricky parking down sloping drive.

	Senhora Sophia Bergqvist
tel	+351 254 732254
fax	+351 254 732346
email	sophia@quintadelarosa.com
web	www.quintadelarosa.com

B&B & Self-catering

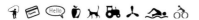

Map 2 Entry 37

Casa de Casal de Loivos

Casal de Loivos, 5085-010 Pinhão, Trás-os-Montes

Oh the views! Among the best in this book – or anywhere. This northern manor has been home to the Sampaios since 1733. The house is in the village, yet from the front you see few dwellings – and the mighty Douro far below. It is a marvellous sight and every room opens to it. Tradition, comfort and gentility are the hallmarks here. Manuel is a truly old-fashioned, charming gentleman, and attracts a cultivated clientele; he speaks perfect English, usually sports a cravat and likes you to dress for dinner. Traditional meat and fish dishes are created from old family recipes, and are always excellent. The dining room is simply beautiful, and dominated by its white-clothed table; dinner conversation should be stimulating. There's a comfortable sitting room that opens onto the breakfast terrace, then it's down to the pool. The view-filled bedrooms are gorgeous, elegantly furnished with good bathrooms. Fuelled by good food and wine, bewitched by the interplay of light, land and water, and pampered by Manuel and his courteous staff, you'll feel halfway between earth and heaven.

rooms	6: 3 doubles, 3 twins.
price	€90. Singles €70.
meals	Dinner €22.50, on request.
closed	1-25 December; January.
directions	From Pinhão to Alijó; 1st right & up through vineyards until Casal de Loivos. House on right at end of village.

Senhor Manuel Bernardo de Sampaio

tel	+351 254 732149
fax	+351 254 732149
email	casadecasaldeloivos@ip.pt
web	www.casadecasaldeloivos.com

B&B

Map 2 Entry 38

Casa do Visconde de Chanceleiros

Largo da Fonte, Chanceleiros-Covas do Douro, 5085-201 Pinhão, Trás-os-Montes

The lap of Douro luxury with hosts whose aim is to make you wish you need never leave. Welcome to a world of big comfortable beds, squashy armchairs, lovely bathrooms, thick fluffy towels, great views, space inside and out, and friendly hosts and dogs. Kurt and Ursula's home is a classic granite and white manor house on the edge of a hillside village, with vine-covered terraces on one side. Wide granite steps lead down to the terrace where there is a huge pool with a long-roofed *cabana* furnished with sofa, stereo and tables. There are wrought-iron sunbeds with plump cushions, a sauna in a port barrel and an outdoor jacuzzi. All is tasteful and stylish, informal yet not over-casual. Indoors, lots of strong, warm colours set off by terracotta, slate and granite, and a mix of antique and modern furniture. The large colour-themed bedrooms are like big bedsitting rooms (one on two floors, ideal for a family) and have beautiful hand-painted furniture and beds. Breakfasts are feasts, and don't miss the splendid three-course dinners. All this and masses to do: ping-pong, tennis, squash, billiards, boules...

rooms	9: 8 suites, 1 family room.
price	€95–€120. Singles €95.
meals	Lunch €20. Dinner with wine, €30, on request.
closed	Rarely.
directions	IP4 from Porto to Vila Real; exit for Chaves. At r'bout follow signs to Sabrosa. There, turn for Pinhão. There, follow signs for Chanceleiros.

	Kurt & Ursula Böcking
tel	+351 254 730190
fax	+351 254 730199
email	chanceleiros@chanceleiros.com
web	www.chanceleiros.com

B&B

Map 2 Entry 39

Casa de Vilarinho de São Romão

Lugar da Capela, Vilarinho de São Romão, 5060-630 Sabrosa, Trás-os-Montes

An old place with a young heart. Here is a fine combination of old and new, of warm sunny colours, light and space. The 17th-century house overlooks the Pinhão valley, and has a much older chapel at its entrance. Cristina gave up teaching art to concentrate on the house, and later she turned her attention to the vineyards – her ancestors, who came to Portugal from Holland, are an established port-wine family. All is harmony and light: white walls, pale floors strewn with kilims and rugs, enormous rooms, grand paintings, fine antiques. The lounge is huge, cool and contemporary, with matching sofas and plenty of books. One of the bedrooms has twin brass beds and solid granite window seats, another an ornately carved bed. Bathrooms are immaculate, some with walk-in showers. Outside is a shaded terrace where you may breakfast in summer (fresh juice and fruits from the farm), an inner gravelled courtyard with dolphin-spouting fountains and a serene pool. All this, lovely walks along old hunting tracks and, always, those long, long views across the Pinhão valley.

rooms	6: 2 doubles, 4 twins.
price	€79. Singles €64. Extra bed €17.
meals	Dinner €20, by arrangement.
closed	Christmas.
directions	From Vila Real to Pinhão through Sabrosa; in Vilarinho de São Romão, you will see green wood gateway & chapel on left. Through gate.

Senhora Cristina van Zeller

tel	+351 259 930754
fax	+351 259 930754
email	mail@casadevilarinho.com
web	www.casadevilarinho.com

B&B

Map 1 Entry 40

Quinta do Real
Matosinhos, 5400 Chaves, Trás-os-Montes

The façade is a masterpiece of understated elegance. Long, low and lovely, the house was built in 1697 for the Viscountess of Rio Maior. Pass through the portal, topped by its granite cross, to enter an enormous cobbled yard. Bedrooms are divided between the main house and the converted farm buildings. All are a good size (except the attic room) and prettily decorated with white crocheted bedspreads and gorgeous antiques; some have views across the valley and shower rooms are spotless. The rooms in the outbuildings give onto the courtyard and are more modest, but are lovely and private and perfect for families. And you have free run of the house kitchen. There are two sitting rooms, one cosy with a woodburner, the other much larger with a minstrels' gallery. The dining room is delightful, too, with its large table, chandelier and tallboy brimming with old china and glass. Your hosts are the charming Dona Celeste, who has lived here all her life, and her son Ramiro, who left a city career for this "paradise in the mountains". There are a pool and barbecue, and riding can be arranged.

rooms	9: 8 doubles, 1 twin.
price	€55-€65. Singles €50-€55.
meals	Packed lunch €17. Excellent restaurants nearby.
closed	Rarely.
directions	From Vidago towards Loivos, then right for Quinta do Real. Through forest to village of Matosinhos: through village, then follow signs to Quinta.

Senhor Ramiro José Guerra

tel	+351 276 966253
fax	+351 276 965240
email	quintadoreal@sapo.pt
web	www.micasarural.com

B&B

Map 2 Entry 41

Quinta da Mata

Estrada de Valpaços, Nantes - AP. 194, 5400-909 Chaves, Trás-os-Montes

Filinto found this 17th-century house, restored it beautifully, and opened up to guests. The food is a treat: for breakfast, miniature pasties, homemade bread, Chaves ham, smoked sausage; for dinner, served at a table for 12, a hearty *cozido* (stew) perhaps, and a good wine from Valpaços. Quinta da Mata's bedrooms are equally special. The chestnut floors, dark panelled ceilings, dressed stone walls and hand-painted tiles are the perfect backdrop for Arraiolos rugs, crocheted bedcovers and well-chosen antiques; cut flowers and the lingering scent of woodsmoke add yet more character. For space choose one of the suites, big enough to lounge all day in; one has a library/office, the other a whirlpool bath. In the well-tended gardens are two tennis courts (Filinto is a qualified coach) and a pool, there are bikes to borrow and peaceful walks through the thickly wooded slopes of the Brunheiro mountains. Filinto's charm is infectious and our inspector has happy memories of afternoon tea with him at a table groaning under cheese, jam, doughnuts and cake. *Light aircraft flights available.*

rooms	6: 4 doubles, 2 twins, 2 suites.
price	€55-€70. Singles €50-60. Suites €64-€75.
meals	Dinner €15.
closed	Rarely.
directions	Just outside Chaves; N213 to Valpaços, through Nantes. Quinta signed.

	Senhor Filinto Moura Morais
tel	+351 276 340030
fax	+351 276 340038
email	quintadamata@mail.telepac.pt
web	www.quintademalta.net

B&B

Map 2 Entry 42

Solar das Arcas

Arcas, 5340-031 Macedo de Cavaleiros, Trás-os-Montes

In this very lovely corner of Portugal, the Solar das Arcas has dignified the village for 300 years. Carved mouldings surround the windows and doors of the fine nobleman's house, with its coat of arms above the portal and private chapel, *sala de piano*, old panelled ceilings (one octagonal) and stone staircase. The owners are direct descendants of Manuel Pessanha of Genoa, who taught the Portuguese the art of navigation. Both the double room in the main house and the apartments in the outbuildings are excellent, with modern checked sofas and comfortable beds (no kitchens). You are surrounded by a large organically-run estate of fruit and olives – and there's a pretty pool in the walled courtyard. As for the food? Look no further than the brochure. "You will feel that you belong to a real Portuguese family when you sit on a footstool savouring a glass of wine and nibbling at a piece of a smoked delicacy before the fireplace where iron vessels boil and the revolving plate grills simple, but first-rate meals". The *vinho* is included in the price.

rooms	1 + 6: 1 double. 4 apartments for 2, 2 apartments for 4.
price	Suites for 2-4, €74-€120. Apartments €70.
meals	Lunch/dinner with wine €25-€30, by arrangement.
closed	Rarely.
directions	From Bragança, IP4 for Vila Réal & O Ponto-20. Exit for Macedo de Cavaleiros, right on N15 for Zoio. After 1.7km, left via Ferreira to Arcas. House in village centre.

Senhora Maria Francisca Pessanha Machado

tel	+351 278 400010
fax	+351 278 401230
email	solardasarcas@mail.telepac.pt
web	www.solardasarcas.com

B&B

Map 2 Entry 43

Pousada de Bragança

São Bartolomeu, Estrada do Turismo, 5300 – 271 Bragança, Trás-os-Montes

White and functional outside; confident, contemporary and light-filled within. The Pousada has bags of style and views that sweep over the walled city of Braganca and to the hazy Trás-os-Montes mountains… you could spend all day on your pretty balcony watching the sun glide across the scene. Below is the elegant pool; beyond, across the river Ferrenga, the towers of the city's 12th-century castle. Rooms are sleekly modern with pale wooden floors and panelling, clean-cut furniture, creamy rugs and colourful bedspreads. Bathrooms are smart in pink granite. The same polished mood is reflected in the main rooms of the hotel where plate-glass windows make the most of the light. And everywhere, bold splashes of modern art – paintings, ceramics, sculptures and tapestries. Staff are friendly, efficient and full of suggestions for day trips and walking or cycling routes in the nearby Montesinho Natural Park. Popular with families – there's a children's pool – and couples, the hotel has a relaxed, buzzy atmosphere. Bragança is lovely – a 25-minute walk downhill, a taxi ride back!

rooms	33: 5 doubles, 28 twins.
price	€100–€155. Special offers available – see web site.
meals	Dinner, 3 courses, from €26.
closed	Rarely.
directions	From Porto, IP4 to Vila Real, then continue to Braganca. There, follow signs for pousada.

	Senhora Maria Antónia C.M. Pereira
tel	+351 273 331 493
fax	+351 273 323 453
email	recepcao.sbartolomeu@pousadas.pt
web	www.pousadas.pt

Hotel

Map 2 Entry 44

Photo Laura Kinch

beira

beira

Beira means the border with the Douro, Trás-os-Montes, Spain, the Alentejo, the Ribatejo and Estremadura. The Beira is divided into three geographical areas:

Beira Baixa (lower) & Beira Alta (higher)
• **Parque Natural da Serra da Estrela** – Portugal's highest mountain range (up to 1993m). Skiing here January-March. Stunning area for walking with well-mapped and marked hiking trails, and bird-watching May-October

• **Quejo de Serra** – a delightful local cheese, slice off the top and spoon out the delicious soft interior; sold at regional markets November-April

• Includes **Guarda**, Portugal's highest city, known for its chilly climate and **Viseu**, home of the velvety full-bodied red Dão wines

Beira Litoral (coastal)
• **Coimbra** – famous University town, 'the Oxford of Portugal' where students dress in black robes and wear top hats for graduation. Many learn Fado and there are great places to listen to male vocalists

• **Coinbriga** – Roman ruins where decorative mosaic tiles are still intact

• **Aveiro** sits at the mouth of a large netwok of wetlands – an area of saltpans, fishing and seaweed drying. Wonderful cultural festivals

Quinta da Ponte
Faia, 6300-095 Guarda, Beira

On the valley edge of the Serra da Estrêla, beside an old Roman *ponte*, is this 17th-century manor – a place of quiet dignity and good manners. At one end of the elegant façade is the Quinta's frescoed chapel – ideal for weddings. Choose between B&B in the old house or self-catering in a new apartment overlooking the swimming pool and the park beyond. Each apartment has a twin room plus two beds disguised as sofas in its sitting room; the kitchenettes are tiny but there is an extra shared living room with an open fire and games. In the main house the bedrooms have a period feel with their lovely carved wooden beds, immaculate fabrics and gleaming tiles. The old stable block is the dining room; the granite feeding troughs may still be in place but breakfasts are served on starched white tablecloths and excellent china. The little box garden was modelled on Versailles, and there are wild paths to explore and plenty of hide-and-seek nooks for children, of whom Dona Joaquima is very fond. And there are pretty walks along the river that runs alongside the grounds. Delightful.

rooms	2 + 5: 2 doubles/twins. 5 apartments for 4.
price	€90. Singles €84.80. Apartment for 2 €100 (min 2 nights).
meals	Lunch/dinner available locally.
closed	October-March, except New Year & Carnival.
directions	From Lisbon on IP5; exit 26 onto EN16 for Porto da Carne then Fara. House signed to right; follow road down to river & house (signed Turismo de Habitação).

	Sociedade Turistica Historia e Jardins, LDA
tel	+351 271 926126
fax	+351 271 926839
email	quintadaponte@oninet.pt
web	www.quintadaponte.com

B&B

Map 2 Entry 45

Quinta da Timpeira
Penude, 5100-718 Lamego, Beira

A cool, calm home close to the Sanctuary of Nossa Senhora dos Remédios, where pilgrims still climb the 700 steps on their knees. The immaculate, post-war house clings to the hillside and is bordered by a topiaried box hedge; below are terraces, pool, tennis court and orchard – space for alfresco lunch. Opposite are the Meadas mountains, behind are the vineyards that supply the nearby Raposeira sparkling wine factory. The house is comfortable in an uncluttered way and manageress Senhora Edite looks after you warmly. Bedrooms are not particularly roomy but are excellently decorated with a mix of old and new. Two on the lower floor share a bathroom and are next to a sitting room with games – good for families. Bathrooms are smart. The split-level sitting/dining room is striking with its long curved wall and spectacular views from its vast window and balcony. Dinner at the crisply laid table is traditional Portuguese, accompanied by Timpeira wines. There's a small 'shop' downstairs where you can buy local handicrafts, and a bar, a wine cellar and a ballroom!

rooms	7: 3 doubles, 2 twins, 2 suites.
price	€70. Singles €57. Suite €120.
meals	Lunch/dinner with wine €20, by arrangement.
closed	Rarely.
directions	From Lamego N2 for Viseu. Quinta da Timpeira is 2.5km after Raposeira sparkling wine factory, on left.

	Senhor José Francisco Gomes Parente
tel	+351 254 612811
fax	+351 254 615176
email	quintadatimpeira@portugalmail.pt
web	www.quintadatimpeira.com

B&B

Map 1 Entry 46

Casa Campo das Bizarras

Rua da Capela 76, Fareja, 3600-271 Castro Daire, Beira

Drive through the apple orchard to the fine old granite farmhouse where a corner of old Portugal has been lovingly preserved. Cool in summer, the house has bags of rustic character with heavy oak beams, stone floors and a cobbled wine cellar. There's a delightful reading room and an upstairs drawing room crammed with family treasures and mementos of farming life. The long, low kitchen has a large inglenook fireplace, bread oven and a marble-topped table for breakfast: do try the homemade cheese and compotes and ask about nearby excursions. There are two bedrooms in the main house and three in an adjoining wing. Dark antique furniture contrasts with creamy curtains and counterpanes, many edged with the regional lace. All have private bathrooms (some just across the corridor), with delicate Art Nouveau tiled mirrors. Apartments are in a cluster of farm buildings and have basic cooking facilities; there's also a communal kitchen, and a barbecue. The pretty raised pool has Roman steps and terracotta tiles. Jacó, a truly human-sounding parrot, and the elderly donkeys in the garden amuse visiting children.

rooms	5 + 4: 5 twins/doubles. 4 self-catering apartments for 2-5.
price	€54-€62. Singles €42-€48. Apartments for 2-4, €434-€466 per week; for 5 €628-€660 per week.
meals	Lunch/dinner €16, by arrangement.
closed	November.
directions	From Castro Daire to Fareja. In Fareja left at sign for Turismo Rural. Past church, up narrow cobbled lane, Bizarras on right.

	Senhora Marina Rodrigues Moutinho
tel	+351 232 386107
fax	+351 232 382044
email	casa.das.bizarras@mail.telepac.pt
web	www.casa-das-bizarras.web.pt

B&B & Self-catering

Map 1 Entry 47

Casa Grande de Casfreires

Ferreira de Aves, 3560-043 Sátão, Beira

Annette has lead an extraordinary life and it's fun to share her awe-inspiring manor house. She runs the place with her son, Francisco, and looks after her two teenage grandchildren and her visitors with the same kindness. The sitting room has an enormous granite fireplace and photographs from Annette's past: of her as a child with her family in Phnom Phen, as a young woman shooting in Africa, and in France, in a classic car. The house and its outbuildings have been cleverly converted from cowsheds to luxury apartments, from pigsties to sparkling bathrooms! There are now seven apartments (each with two bedrooms) plus three delightful rooms in the main house. The bedrooms have high doorways and ceilings, window seats, stripped wooden floors and crisp white linen. Views stretch down across fields and woodland to the valley below. The house, built in 1753, manages to combine a stately home atmosphere with the modern world. Some of the bathrooms have massage baths and power showers. Annette spoils you with homemade scones and chestnut jam for breakfast. Wonderful.

rooms	3 + 7: 3 twins/doubles; 7 self-catering apartments for 4.
price	€75. Apartments €100.
meals	Lunch/dinner by arrangement.
closed	Occasionally.
directions	From Viseu, N229 to Sátão. Then follow signs to Lamas de Ferreira & on to Casfreires.

	Senhor Francisco Oliva
tel	+351 914 030807
email	casa-grande@casfreires-oliva.com
web	www.casfreires-oliva.com

B&B & Self-catering

Map 1 Entry 48

Quinta da Comenda
3660-404 São Pedro do Sul, Beira

The lovely group of buildings is softened by a rampant camellia which lends swathes of colour when in flower. Lovers of organic wine may know this quinta for its prize-winning whites and rosés; what you may not know is that the first king of Portugal, Dom Afonso Enriques, did battle nearby, broke a leg and came to recuperate: this was his uncle's place. Guest rooms match expectations: polished parquet floors, elegant antique beds and pretty tiles in the bathroom. Lounge and dining room double up in a huge *salão* which leads to the old wine cellar, and you are treated to a real feast at the breakfast table. Details such as the fruit basket and bottled water in your room show how much the da Rocha family care. Swim or play table tennis in the gardens, meander along the river in a row boat and under the Roman bridge, wander through the vineyards and orchards, stock up on wine and chat with your charming hosts. On most Saturdays in summer there are wedding parties in the ivy-clad chapel. *Minimum stay two nights.*

rooms	6 + 1: 6 twin/doubles.
	1 self-catering apartment for 2.
price	€80. Singles €69.
	Apartment €800 per week.
meals	Breakfast €5. Restaurants nearby.
closed	Rarely.
directions	From Viseu, IP5 for S. Pedro do Sul on N16. A few km before S. Pedro follow Agro Turismo sign; Quinta on left, signed.

	Senhora Maria Laura Cardoso da Rocha
tel	+351 226 179889
fax	+351 226 183491
email	quintadacomenda@sapo.pt
web	www.quintadacomenda.com

B&B & Self-catering

Map 1 Entry 49

Casa da Calle

3400-487 Nogueira do Cravo, Beira

Built in 1743 of the local granite, this handsome house has been in the Tinoco family ever since. Its rooms tell the history – there are collections of everything from books and portraits to decanters and vine scissors. The effect is not remotely museum-like, partly because of the light that floods in through the generous windows and partly because of the warm personality of your hostess. Bedrooms are traditionally furnished with antique beds and wardrobes. Two have splendid *maceira* ceilings. All are given a modern edge with fresh sprigged curtains and covers; new bathrooms have sparkling white tiles. When we visited, Isobel was thoughtfully distributing chocolate and biscuits (as well as a bar list) to the rooms. There are two comfortable sitting rooms – or head out to the camellia lawn where barbecues are served on summer evenings under the weeping pines. Close to the mountains of the Serra da Estrela, you are in wonderful walking and riding country – try a guided horse trek. Three beautiful horses are kept for visitors' use and equipment is available – what a spot to explore!

rooms	3 twins.
price	€60. Singles €40.
meals	Dinner by arrangement. Good restaurants nearby.
closed	Christmas.
directions	A1 from Lisbon; IC6 & N17 towards Oliveira do Hospital. Left at traffic lights in Vendas de Galizes following signs to Nogueira. House on left exit of r'bout.

Senhora Isabel Tinoco

tel	+351 238 604878
mobile	+351 914 5400768
email	info@casadacalle.com
web	www.casadacalle.com

B&B

Map 1 Entry 50

Casa das Ribas

Lugar do Castelo, 4520-220 Santa Maria da Feira, Beira

The 'house of the steep banks' is perched on a hill with views to the Atlantic; the charming cobbled old town lies below. The 16th-century house with 'new' 1820 wing was originally a religious foundation; enter another age. In the entrance hall, a family coat of arms: this B&B is a stately home. There are several drawing rooms, polished parquet, chandeliers, religious icons, flagged kitchen with vast inglenook and a preponderance of dark wood. The atmosphere, however, is easy, and Dona Maria Carmina is the most solicitous, family-welcoming hostess; nothing is too much trouble. Bedrooms are relatively simple after the profusion of downstairs – fresh and spotlessly clean, with fine beds, firm mattresses and up-to-date bathrooms. The large, L-shaped Bishop's Room has seven shuttered windows, while the more rustic Casa do Caseiro, in the delightful grounds, makes a special holiday cottage. Maria has the greenest fingers; there's a box-hedged courtyard and masses of untamed space for children. And there are a library, a *sala da musica* with grand piano, a games room and a beautiful 16th-century chapel.

rooms	6 + 1: 5 twins/doubles, 1 suite. 1 self-catering house for 4-6.
price	€60-€75. Singles €50. Suite €75. House €100.
meals	A wide selection of restaurants nearby.
closed	Rarely.
directions	Exit Lisboa & Porto m'way at Feira & follow signs for Castelo; you can see castle in trees on way into Feira; house next to castle.

	Senhora Maria Carmina Vaz de Oliveira
tel	+351 256 373485
fax	+351 256 374481

B&B

Map 1 Entry 51

Pousada da Murtosa-Torreira/Ria

Torreira – Pico de Muranzel, 3870-301 Torreira, Beira

You could be at the end of the world. Perched on the skinny isthmus that separates the Atlantic from the lagoon of the Aveiro, the road ends just south of the pousada. Overlooking the water and backed by dunes, it has a dreamy setting that is perfect for anyone seeking walks, birdlife or the simple play of light on water. It is a 1060s building of a low-rise, open-plan design, its acreage of glass making the most of those mesmerising watery views. Reception rooms are cool and airy with slate floors and pale colours while bedrooms have a breezy New England beach-house flavour: cream painted furniture, marine blue fabrics, crisp tiled bathrooms. Stand on your balcony and watch the fish gliding through the lagoon below. The waters are unsuitable for swimming but you can watch, or join, the fishermen in their bright, gondola-style *moliceiros*. Take a dip in the pool and watch the sun rise over the dunes; hire a bike and cycle to São Jacinto, at the end of the isthmus, for Atlantic sunsets. Return to supper: shellfish, grilled bream, or, if you dare, eel stew.

rooms	19 twins/doubles.
price	€100-€165. Special offers available - see web site.
meals	Dinner, 3 courses, from €25.
closed	Rarely.
directions	From Lisbon IP1 north. At junc. 17 follow signs for Murtosa on N109. Continue over river; south on N327 for Torreira. Pass town & continue south. Pousada signed.

	Senhora Ana Sequeira
tel	+351 234 860 180
fax	+351 234 838 333
email	recepcao.ria@pousadas.pt
web	www.pousadas.pt

Hotel

Map 1 Entry 52

Casa de Sol Nascente

Rua de Alagoa, Taipa, Requeixo, 3800-881 Aveiro, Beira

East meets west in 'the house of the rising sun'. The architecture is the work of Ian's Japanese wife Chizu, whose paintings hang in many rooms (and in the Tokyo National Gallery). Enter to a column of glass around which curves a flight of stairs; light pours in. More curved walls, and graduated shadows, to "bring nature into the living room and soften the mood." Soothing downstairs bedrooms contain an immaculate blend of pieces from around the world, along with satellite TV; the suite on the upper floor has a glamorous bathroom, and a terrace. Chizu and Ian are welcoming and well-travelled, as easy with city slickers as with young families; the mood is gentle and relaxed. Meals from Chizu are superb and span a wide range of Portuguese and Japanese cooking; in the summer there are wonderful barbecues under the bamboo pergola, resplendent with vines and kiwi fruit, and a large lush garden. Breakfasts are mighty, snacks are on request. Nearby are the gorgeous Aveiro lagoons, full of birdlife, and sandy beaches are 10km away. Ian is a qualified meditation instructor: ask about weekend retreats.

rooms	4 + 1 : 2 doubles/twins, 2 suites. Apartment for 6.
price	€45. Suite €78. Apartment €930 per week.
meals	Lunch/dinner by arrangement.
closed	Rarely.
directions	A1; EN235 for Aveiro; immed. right to Mamodeiro; at 1st café, 1st junc. right to Requeixo. On to Taipa. Road bends down to right; at bend take smaller road going up on right; last house, 800m.

	Ian M Arbuckle
tel	+351 234 933597
fax	+351 234 933598
email	arbuckle@mail.telepac.pt
web	www.solnascente.aveiro.co.pt

B&B & Self-catering

Map 1 Entry 53

Casa da Azenha Velha

Caceira de Cima, 3080 Figueira da Foz, Beira

Once a flour mill (*azenha*), this large house is now much more: the decorative flourishes above doors and the large rooms suggest a grand history. After Maria de Lourdes and her dog have met you, you will find that the grounds teem with other creatures: deer, ostriches, cows, horses and peacocks. Bedrooms surround a pretty garden and flowers grow up around your windows; they are huge with large wooden beds and pretty coordinating bedcovers, flowers and tiles. Pamper yourself with a soak in the sunken bath – heaven. You breakfast in the large kitchen of the main house; rail-sleepers support the roof bricks, and farming equipment decorates the walls. A lounge in the old stable block has an honesty bar, comfy sofas, open fire and board games. There are also a pool, a tennis court, a snooker table and a barbecue; experienced riders may borrow a horse. A short walk from the main house is the new, rustic-style Azenha restaurant where you eat regional and international dishes. A perfect spot for families, couples or groups, and great in winter and summer. Excellent value.

rooms	6 +1 : 2 doubles, 4 twins; 1 apartment for 4.
price	€75–€100. Singles €65. Apartment €115.
meals	Restaurant dinner from €10.
closed	Rarely. Restaurant closed on Mondays.
directions	From Coimbra, N111 for Figueira da Foz. Shortly before Figueira turn for Caceira; immed. left following signs Turismo Rural. After 2km right for 500m; right again. House on left.

Senhora Maria de Lourdes Nogueira

tel	+351 233 425041
fax	+351 233 429704
web	

B&B & Self-catering

Map 3 Entry 54

Quinta das Lágrimas

Santa Clara, Apart. 5053, 3041-901 Coimbra, Beira

Quinta das Lagrimas has a place among the most remarkable hostelries in Portugal. The Palace is 300 years old but was rebuilt after a fire a century ago. Wellington stayed here and was captivated by the place and the legend that the tears (*lágrimas*) of the name were those shed by Dona Inês when put to the dagger by the knights of King Alfonso. Come to see 10 acres of wonderful gardens – some of which have been taken up by the golf school; many species have been brought from all over the world. The elegance of the double sweep of staircase leading to the main front is mirrored within. The dining room is stuccoed, panelled and chandeliered; dignitaries are international but the food is Portuguese and accompanied by fine wines from Lágrimas's large cellars. Bedrooms are fit for kings (a number have stayed here); ask for one in the old house, elegant and deeply luxurious with rich fabrics, vast beds and marbled bathrooms. The new building has minimalist rooms in neutral colours, a restaurant with a modern twist and a spa – the couples' massage the ultimate treat.

rooms	Main house: 18: 5 doubles, 9 twins, 4 suites. New building: 15: 14 double, 1 suite. Garden rooms: 21 twins.
price	€149-€189. Singles €121-€152. Triples €300. Suites €300-€375.
meals	Lunch/dinner €35-€50.
closed	Rarely.
directions	A1 to Coimbra; exit for Coimbra south. Head to city centre; signs for Portugal dos Pequenitos on left; Quinta signed.

	Senhor Mario Morais
tel	+351 239 802380
fax	+351 239 441695
email	geral@quintadaslagrimas.pt
web	www.quintadaslagrimas.pt

Casa O Nascer Do Sol

Largo da Eira Velha, Vale da Carvalha, 3360-034 Penacova, Beira

Lucy and Hans are delightful hosts and cannot do enough for you. They are Belgian and speak fluent Portuguese as well as French, English, German and Dutch. You'll be greeted with a local drink and Hans can arrange trips to wine cellars and around the local area. The shuttered bedrooms are all beige, simple and comfortable, with dark wooden beds, fans and side tables. The house is modern with a lovely beamed lounge/dining room; Flemish paintings, old antiques and leather sofas give a grand but comfortable feel. This is a peaceful village so you can eat outside to birdsong. Breakfasts are generous and delicious with fresh bread cooked in a wood-oven – locals pop in daily to drop off the freshest produce. Hans will take you to a typical, local restaurant on your first evening if you like, and give advice on good treks from the house. The garden has a small pool, potted geraniums and palms; there are pines, olive trees and eucalyptus all around. If you want to be truly looked after, this is the place to come. *Minimum stay three nights.*

rooms	8: 5 doubles, 1 family room, 2 suites.
price	€60-€70. Singles €50-€55. Suites €70-€80. Child's bed €15.
meals	Restaurants nearby.
closed	Rarely.
directions	Exit A1 Lisbon-Porto at Coimbra-Norte; IP3 for Viseu & Guarda; exit 12 for Porto de Raiva & Miro. Left under IP3 & wait by Stop sign. Hans will meet you there.

	Hans & Lucy Ghijs de Voghel
tel	+351 239 476871
fax	+351 239 476872
email	npp72198@mail.telepac.pt
web	www.casaonascerdosol.com

B&B

Map 3 Entry 56

Quinta do Rio Dão
3440-464 Santa Comba Dão, Beira

Perfect for lovers of the great outdoors – the setting is a dream. The house hides in a stand of old oaks on the banks of the small lagoon. Dutch owners Pieter and Juliette live here with their two boys – bought up on the farmstead when it stood in ruins – and have sensitively restored it in traditional Beira style. They are excellent, multi-lingual hosts, and give you the choice of B&B in their house or self-catering apartments and cottages. A traditional Portuguese look marries with a clean, uncluttered approach to space, and there's nothing too showy to detract from the natural beauty of the place. Bedrooms are not large but have a sunny feel; bathrooms are modern, there are lots of verandas and captivating views down to the river. In summer, life is spent mostly outdoors; birdsong at breakfast, and, at night, the lights of Santa Comba Dão twinkling across the water. With canoes, a rowing boat and a windsurfer for guests to borrow, this would be an idyllic place for a sporting holiday. Almost the feel of a mini holiday village – and great value. *Minimum stay two nights.*

rooms	4 + 5: 4 twins/doubles. 2 apartments for 2-4; 3 cottages for 4-8.
price	€52-€64. Apartments €50-€60. Cottages €90-€180.
meals	Various restaurants 5-10km.
closed	Rarely.
directions	From Lisbon, A1 for Porto. After Coimbra, IP3 for Viseu. 500m before Santa Comba Dão turn to Vimieiro. Follow sign Agro Turismo for 4.5km to Quinta.

Pieter & Juliette Gruppelaar-Spierings
tel   +351 232 892784
fax   +351 232 892372
email quinta@quintadoriodao.com
web   www.quintadoriodao.com

B&B & Self-catering

Map 4 Entry 57

Solar do Ervedal

Rua Dr. Francisco Brandão 12, 3405-063 Ervedal da Beira, Beira

Though architectural styles come and go, this noble, granite-built, 500-year-old
village residence has never left the hands of the descendants of Diogo Braz Pinto.
High walls surround the estate and you enter through elegant wrought-iron gates
– another world. A cobbled courtyard with pots of geraniums fronts the house;
behind are acres of organically farmed orchards and a stand of 200-year-old oaks.
Children are encouraged to explore and there are animals to fondle. Guest
bedrooms are in the south wing, the oldest part of the manor, and the house is
grand and peaceful. The large sitting room has an unusual octagonal ceiling and
gothic door arches of local granite; two burgundy sofas pull up to the hearth. The
dining room is just as delightful and we recommend you eat in: roast duck with
rice is a speciality, desserts are delicious and wines are local and good. Bedrooms
are grand, with ornate beds and other fine antiques, enhanced by polished
parquet, stuccoed ceilings and window seats. The present Viscountess Maria
Helena is a kind, gracious hostess – you'll be reluctant to leave.

rooms	6: 2 doubles, 2 twins, 1 family room for 3, 1 suite with 2 doubles.
price	€90. Single €80. Family room €120. Suite €125.
meals	Lunch/dinner €25, by arrangement.
closed	November & Christmas.
directions	Just before Oliveira do Hospital centre (off N17 Coimbra-Guarda), right just after VW garage to Ervedal da Beira. 16km to village. Solar signed from village centre.

	Senhora Maria Helena de Albuquerque
tel	+351 238 644283
fax	+351 238 641133
email	solardoervedal@mail.telepac.pt
web	www.solardoervedal.com

B&B

Map 1 Entry 58

Estalagem Casa D'Azurara
Rua Nova 78, 3530-215 Mangualde, Beira

In a quiet corner of a sleepy town, a swish place to unwind. Built by the Counts of Mangualde in the 17th century, now a small, luxurious hotel, it has two large lounges downstairs – one with a vast stone fireplace, the other with French windows and flamboyant drapes. There are framed etchings, potted palms, books, cut flowers and immaculate fabric on sofas and chairs. Carpeted corridors, and a lift, lead to the rooms, where furnishings are a mix of antique and repro; rich fabrics adorn windows and beds. Our choice would be suite-like 206, with its sloping ceiling, Dona Maria beds and romantic French windows. Note that the rooms at the back are the quietest, though Mangualde is not a noisy place. Breakfast includes a choice of breads, cheeses and cold meats while the dinner menu has a regional bias: fish dishes and duck are a speciality. Don't miss the gardens for their ancient magnolias, hortensias and camellias. The staff are caring and can organise wine tastings at nearby *adegas*. A place that pampers business people, couples and families – but not for those who like shabby chic!

rooms	15: 14 twins/doubles, 1 suite for 4.
price	€109-€120. Singles €87-€107. Suite €128-€143.
meals	Lunch from €15. Dinner from €20.
closed	Rarely.
directions	From Porto, IP5 for Guarda. Exit for Mangualde. House in town centre, signed. (Do not confuse with 2nd modern Estalagem at town entrance.)

	Senhor & Senhora Teixeira Bastos
tel	+351 232 612010
fax	+351 232 622575
email	reservas@azurara.com
web	www.azurara.com

Hotel

Map 1 Entry 59

Quinta das Mestras

Nogueira do Cravo, 3400 Oliveira do Hospital, Beira

A stream runs between the rambling stone buildings of the quinta and the *cabanas*. The old farmstead in its hillocky seven acres is surrounded by pine forests and olive groves; the Serra da Estrela rises nobly beyond. Dutch-born Rob and Australian Leondra – he a designer and cartoonist, she a translator – are engaging hosts whose B&B is as vibrant as they are. Bedrooms are named after the colour of each of their delightfully sloped wooden ceilings: Green, Yellow, Pink. Green is perhaps the nicest, with its own terracotta bathroom and ochre-painted wrought-iron beds. Pancakes, omlettes, fruit – something different for breakfast each day (included in the B&B price) is served on suitably rustic plates on a shady terrace or in the decoratively cluttered kitchen. Up on the hill, sharing a bathroom, are two self-catering *cabanes* – simple and private. You are two miles from the charming little town of Oliveira do Hospital, river canoeing and swimming are not much further, and fabulous walks start from the door. A fun, arty place to stay in one of Portugal's prettiest green corners.

rooms	3 + 2: 2 doubles, 1 twin. 2 self-catering cabins.
price	€32.50–€47.50; €200–€330 p.w. Cabins €30; €200 p.w. Use of kitchen €10.
meals	Breakfast €5. Dinner by arrangement.
closed	Rarely.
directions	From Coimbra for Seira; N17 for Oliveira. Before Oliveira, exit for N. do Gravo. Between Nogueira & Bobadela. Just off road, signed.

	Leondra Wesdorp
tel	+351 238 602988
fax	+351 238 602989
email	info@quintadasmestras.com
web	www.quintadasmestras.com

B&B & Self-catering

Map 4 Entry 60

Pousada de Vila Pouca da Beira

Convento do Desagravo, Calçada do Convento, 3400-758 Vila Pouca da Beira, Beira

The Convento do Desagravo was built on the orders of the bishop and a count, Dom Francisco de Faria Pereira, during the last quarter of the 18th century. It is a beautiful building, with a fine bell tower and dozens of arches. The restoration has been a complete success and it is now a peacefully stylish hotel. Hallways have creamy walls, earth-coloured cushions, stone floors and wrought-iron furniture. The central courtyard, flanked by stone pillars, has a natural pool in its centre. In the living rooms are bold red sofas on terracotta-tiled floors, local furniture and antique pieces from the convent including some stunning carved gilt work – now hung artistically on the walls. Bedrooms too use neutral and bold colours to great effect with red and cream bedspreads and red and gold latticed headboards. The views are best from the enormous bedroom terraces at the back: the Serra da Estrela enfolds before your eyes. The restaurant is quite large and serves the best local produce, and there's a pleasant bar, too. After dinner, meander down the vineyard path to the pool and drink in the peace.

rooms	24: 8 doubles, 12 twins, 4 suites.
price	€175-€190. Singles €163-€178. Suites €210-€228. Special offers available - see web site.
meals	Dinner, 3 courses, from €26.
closed	Rarely.
directions	From Coimbra, IC3 for Penacova, then IC6 to Vendas de Galises. Follow signs for Vila Pouca de Beira; signposted.

	Senhora Maria de Jesus Patrão
tel	+351 238 670080
fax	+351 238 670081
email	recepcao.desagravo@pousadas.pt
web	www.pousadas.pt

Hotel

Map 4 Entry 61

Hotel rural Quinta da Geía

Aldeia das Dez, 3400-214 Oliveira do Hospital, Beira

Aldeia das Dez in the foothills of the Serra da Estrela is an old hamlet to which the 21st century seems only to have given a passing glance. From the outside you'd never guess that the house is several hundred years old: Dutch owners Frenkel and Fir have completely renovated the place. Life centres on the lively, relaxed bar and restaurant – stained wooden tables and chairs, bright tablecloths, paintings by local artists – and is well frequented by the local folk who obviously approve of the cooking: traditional Portuguese food with Italian/French slant. Eat on the terrrace and enjoy the dreamy views of the mountains and tree-filled landscape. Large, bright bedrooms are beautifully finished: pine floors, stone walls, interesting angles, neutral colours. A suite or apartment would be perfect for families. Your hosts have mapped out the best walks in the area – follow Roman pathways through forests of oak and chestnut; the two dalmations might join you. An exceptional place, now with two large conference rooms.

Mininimum stay in apartments three nights; one week in summer.

rooms	11 + 4: 9 twin/double, 2 twins. 4 apartments for 2-6.
price	€65-€85. Singles €55-€75. Suite €90-€100. Apartments €100-€125; €600-€775 per week.
meals	Lunch/dinner from €22.
closed	2-22 January.
directions	From Coimbra, IP3 to intersection with IC6. 4km before Oliveira, at Vendas de Galizes, right signed Hotel Rural for 14km.

	Fir Tiebout
tel	+351 238 670010
fax	+351 238 670019
email	quintadageia@mail.telepac.pt
web	www.quintadageia.com

Hotel

Map 4 Entry 62

Pousada de Manteigas

São Lourenço, Penhas Douradas, 6260-200 Manteigas, Beira

One of the first pousadas to be built, it has the character of a mountain lodge with lots of rustic wood about the place and open fires. Pinch yourself to check you're still in Portugal as you encounter the gift shop selling fur capes and leather hats. You are in the Serra da Estrela Natural Park and the seasons are clearly defined. The smallish bedrooms have stout, county-style wooden furniture with cream woolly rugs scattered over dark stained floors. Curtains and covers are of jolly red and green tartans. The public rooms offer snooker, chess and somewhere comfy to read a book. This is the kind of place where guests strike up conversations with each other after a hard day's walking, fishing or skiing. The mountain community take huge pride in their pousada. It is perhaps the only one with a song written about it – ask at reception and they'll play it for you! Staff will also arrange picnics for walkers and, for the more adventurous, trips to the glacial valley of the Zezere. Try the famous Serra, the local soft cheese – delicious.

rooms	21: 11 doubles, 7 twins, 3 family rooms.
price	€130–€135. Special offers available - see web site.
meals	Dinner, 3 courses, €26.
closed	Rarely.
directions	From Lisbon, A1 to Torres Novas then A23 towards Guarda. Exit for Belmonte, then follow signs for Mantiegas. Pousada 13km above town. Signed.

	Senhora Maria José Garces
tel	+351 275 980050
fax	+351 275 982453
email	recepcao@slourenco@pousadas.pt
web	www.pousadas.pt

Hotel

𝑅 🐟 🗡 🗄 💬 🍷 👤 ⚲ 👞   Map 2 Entry 63

Pousada de Belmonte

Convento de Belmonte, Serra da Esperança, Apt. 76, 6250 Belmonte, Beira

The founding fathers of the medieval monastery chose themselves a remote rocky hill-side with open views across the plain; now rows of hazelnut trees and olives lead the eye to the pine- and eucalyptus-clad peaks of the Serra da Estrela. The ruins of the original *convento* have been cleverly incorporated into a modern hotel, offering 21st-century comfort and an ecclesiastical flavour. The main lounge occupies the original chapel with a galleried sitting area replacing the choir. The small cloister has been rebuilt as a sheltered place to sit or stroll. Two modern bedroom wings flank the old core – not particularly beautiful on the outside but extremely stylish within. A neutral palette has been adopted, with notes of ochre and terracotta. Rooms are all different, some with elegant wrought-iron light fittings or unusual wooden chairs. The honeymoon suite has an over-sized modern four-poster and its own rooftop terrace for romantic breakfasts. Outside, in a sheltered corner, is a small pool with Atlantic-blue tiles. In town is the family home and last resting place of Pedro Cabral, discoverer of Brazil.

rooms	24: 4 doubles, 19 twins, 1 suite.
price	€190. Singles €178. Special offers available - see web site.
meals	Dinner, 3 courses, from €26.
closed	Rarely.
directions	From Lisbon A1 to Torres Novas; A23 towards Guarda. Exit for Belmonte & folllow signs for Pousada.

	Senhor José Pedro Florindo
tel	+351 275 910300
fax	+351 275 910310
email	pousadadebelmonte@mail.telepac.pt
web	www.pousadas.pt

Hotel

Map 4 Entry 64

Casa do Castelo Novo

Rua Nossa Senhora das Graças - 7, 6230-160 Castelo Novo, Beira

The garden is simple, flourishing, the views are wonderful and the whole place is, according to one reader, "a joy." The Casa is a 17th-century home on the slopes of the Serra da Gardunha, an amphitheatre that leads down to the winding lanes of the village. The granite stonework front of this elegant house is deceptive: you cannot guess how the house is built up the steep rock, nor that the garden is at the level of the first floor. The ground floor is a sitting room for guests, where there are sofas, a wall of rock, and carpets from the Minho and Morocco. Up a wooden staircase and you find the main living room; here are sofas, a granite fireplace, bookcases cut into the stone walls, displays of ceramics, antiques and a shell-like wooden *maceira* ceiling. The dining/breakfast room is cosy, in 19th-century style. In the main house are a bedroom and suite, both with Dona Maria beds – the latter has the best view in the whole house. A few steps across the garden and you have a choice of a painted Alentejan double or a romantic twin. Alice and Manuel are very friendly and welcoming and prepare truly delicious Portuguese food.

rooms	4: 3 twins/doubles, 1 suite.
price	€60. Singles €45. Suite €70.
meals	Lunch/dinner with wine €20–€25, by arrangement.
closed	Rarely.
directions	A23 to Fundão. 10km south of Fundão, signs to Castelo Novo. Enter on R. de São Brás; at Largo da Bica right along R. da Gardunha, around castle, till R. Nossa Senhora das Graças; signposted.

	Senhora Alice Aleixo
tel	+351 275 561373
fax	+351 275 561373
email	castelo.novo@clix.pt
web	www.castelonovo.web.pt

B&B

Map 4 Entry 65

Casa Lido

Monte da Portelinha, Silveira, 6030-021 Fratel, Beira

This pretty cluster of Beira cottages is on the edge of a village frozen in time: old ladies wash lettuce at a shared tap and bake bread in an oven just opposite. Your hosts' design talents are reflected in their gorgeous self-catering cottages — they are also restoring an olive mill close by. All houses have traditional wooden ceilings and roughly-rendered white walls; the biggest house, for four, has a roof terrace and chairs and carved beds made by a local carpenter to their design. All rooms are beautifully lit; even the fruit bowl has been artistically placed. The cottage has a spiral iron staircase, a wood-burning stove and views over soft countryside towards the river from both courtyard and terrace. The converted barn, also for two, has a mezzanine, a huge window and a flower-filled terrace with a pergola. All have kitchens or kitchenettes and there's a delightful courtyard pool and barbecue to share. Lise and Udo can tell you everything you need to know, from when the bread and fish men come to the best local *festas* and restaurants. They also run occasional gourmet food weeks and art courses.

rooms	3 houses: 2 for 2, 1 for 4.
price	From €60; €192–€560 per week. B&B also available.
meals	Excellent restaurants nearby.
closed	Rarely.
directions	IP2-A23, exit 16 Silveira. Right Riscada-Juncal; under dual carriageway; left at T-junc. for Silveira. Pass Riscada exit; on until sign for Silveira. In village, follow road round to right; Casa at end.

	Lise & Udo Reppin
tel	+351 272 566393
mobile	+351 914 111469

Self-catering

Map 4 Entry 66

Hotel Residencial Casa do Outeiro

Largo Carvalho do Outeiro 4, 2440-128 Batalha, Beira

This small modern guest house is right in the centre of Batalha, its hillside perch ensuring that some bedrooms have views across the town's rooftops to the colossal Abbey. The Abbey was built in gratitude for Dom João's victory over the Castilian army in 1385 and is a masterpiece of Portuguese Manueline art, its exterior all carved pinnacles, columns and buttresses; the innards, especially the cloisters, are exceptionally beautiful too. If you come to visit the Abbey do stay at Casa do Outeiro even if at first appearance it is a rather unexciting place. José and Odete are the best of hosts; both combine careers in the town with attending to their guests. Their bedrooms are roomy and functional; all have modern pine furniture and own baths but their private terraces lift them into the 'special' league, while the wooden floors and ceilings add warmth. Most of the area to the rear of the building is given over to the swimming pool. The ever-helpful owners will advise you where to dine out and, in the morning, treat you to a generous breakfast that includes five or six homemade jams. Great value.

rooms	15: 10 doubles, 5 family rooms.
price	€40-€65. Singles €35-€55. Family rooms €55-€80.
meals	Restaurants nearby.
closed	Rarely.
directions	In Batalha, follow signs for centre. Hotel signed.

	Senhor José Victor Pereira Madeira
tel	+351 244 765806
fax	+351 244 768892
email	geral@casadoouteiro.com
web	www.casadoouteiro.com

Hotel

Map 3 Entry 67

Challet Fonte Nova

Rua da Fonte Nova P.O.Box 82, 2460-046 Alcobaça, Beira

Fabulous ceilings, elegant damask curtains at French windows, classical beds, glass chandeliers, antique dressers – what bedrooms! Equally delightful are the lofty stucco ceilings of the entrance hall, the oriental rugs, the stuffed red ottomans, the green and red couches and the Venetian-style chandeliers. This 19th-century chalet-style house is close to town yet peaceful – and a two-minute stroll from the Alcabaça Monastery World Heritage Site. In recent years a modern annexe has been sensitively added. These newer bedrooms are crisply and elegantly attired, one with a vast marble bathroom. Maria João lives nearby with her young family and is a kind hostess. The overall feel is one of turn-of-the-century graciousness and charm, you almost feel you are on a stage set – great fun. The garden has some formal terracing and beds brimming with agapanthus in summer; indoors are a bar and a snooker room. The hotel is a perfect launch pad for Batalha, another World Heritage Site, and the sweet little fishing village of Nazaré.

rooms	10: 8 doubles, 2 singles.
price	€110. Singles €85.
meals	Meals occasionally available, by arrangement. Restaurants nearby.
closed	24 December–1 January.
directions	200m from Alcobaça Monastery. Head towards the city 'Caldas da Rainha', 1st road on right.

Senhora Maria do Carmo e Adão Lameiras

tel	+351 262 598300
fax	+351 262 598430
email	mail@challetfontenova.pt
web	www.challetfontenova.pt

B&B

Map 3 Entry 68

PRIMAVERA

Photo Laura Kinch

estremadura

estremadura

*Estremadura means 'farthest from River Douro' named by the
Christians after defeating the Moors*

• **Lisbon** – the capital city with **Castelo São Jorge** in the
medieval Alfama district (the best views to the River Tejo and a
great place to get your bearings). Eat while listening to Fado,
the Portuguese 'blues'

• **Sintra**: a leafy paradise 40 minutes by train from Lisbon, with
two National Palaces, **Monserrate** and **Pena** parks (said to be
enchanted), a Capuchin monastery, a ruined castle, fairy-tale
villas, a suprising modern-art museum and long views to the sea

• Wonderful seafood restaurants and world championship
surfing in **Guincho**; and good surf in **Eirceira** and **Costa da
Caparica** too. The lively, cosmopolitan seaside resort of **Cascais**

• **Sétubal**: castle, fishing, fantastic seafood; the Sado Estuary
teems with dolphins. Visit the immense stretch of white sand on
the **Troia Peninsula**

• **Parque Natural de Sintra–Cascais** which stretches from Sintra
itself to Cabo de Roca, mainland Europe's most westerly point

• **Batalha** and **Alcobaça Monasteries** – Gothic and Manueline
architecture – both World Heritage Sites

Casa da Padeira

EN8 - S. Vicente 19, Alcobaça, 2460-711 Aljubarrota, Estremadura

Casa da Padeira takes its name from the baker's wife of Aljubarrota who, so legend has it, single-handedly dispatched seven Spaniards. A frieze of *azulejos* on the bar in the lounge shows her thwacking one of the septet into the bread oven. Several centuries on, a more gentle reception awaits you at this quiet B&B run by Lina and Nuno. The house is not old but the bedrooms on the first floor have an antique style thanks to ornately turned Bilros beds and furniture. The self-contained apartments (some with wheelchair access) are well furnished; bedrooms are a good size; sometimes there's an additional sofabed, and some of the bathrooms are brand new. The lounge has a stone fireplace and capacious yellow-striped armchairs and sofa. You breakfast well, with a selection of bread, cake, cheese and meat, and there is an excellent restaurant in nearby Aljubarrota. When you return after forays, visit the games room, with cheerful yellow-orange walls, a pool table and other diversions. The garden has a pleasant swimming pool bordered by plants, with sunloungers, tables and chairs aplenty.

rooms	8 + 6: 8 twins/doubles. 6 apartments for 2-6.
price	€50-€70. Singles €40-€55. Apartments €85-€120.
meals	Restaurant nearby. Self-catering in apartments.
closed	Rarely.
directions	Along EN8 from Alcobaça for Batalha. House signed on left on leaving Aljubarrota.

	Senhora Lina Pacheco
tel	+351 262 505240
fax	+351 262 505241
email	casadapadeira@mail.telepac.pt

B&B & Self-catering

Map 3 Entry 69

Casa da Reserva de Burros

Estrada das Grutas de St. António, Porto de Mos, 2480-034 Alvados, Estremadura

Gentle, friendly Paulo set up this unusual donkey sanctuary many years ago; he breeds them, too. He adores these creatures and will take you on day trips into the mountains. The rustic self-catering apartments are in a large granite cottage in the middle of the rugged hills. Bedrooms are simple with wide views, colourful bedspreads, freshly painted walls and carved wooden bedsteads. Paulo has added special touches – a stone trough sink here, a porcelain bowl on a pretty washstand there – to give a contemporary slant to the décor. Watch local weavers making beautiful striped rugs and bedcovers; buy wild herbs and honey. The cavernous restaurant – sometimes used by coach visitors who come for the day to experience this wonderful place – has a central free-standing oven and hay-bale seating which fits perfectly. Paulo knows the surrounding Natural Park area like the back of his hand and is always happy to advise. Visit the nearby caves, walk in the spectacular mountains, hire a bike nearby or revel in the serenity of the landscape. Poppies grow everywhere and the sunsets are inspiring.

rooms	3 self-catering apartments for 2-4.
price	€50; €231 per week.
meals	Restaurant & snack bar.
closed	Christmas & New Year.
directions	A1 exit 7 (Torres Novas) & follow signs for Grutas & Serra de Santo António. In Moitas Venda, left & keep following same signs.

	Senhor Paulo Araújo
tel	+351 966 229408
fax	+351 249 841166
email	info@reserva-de-burros.com
web	www.reserva-de-burros.com

Self-catering

Map 3 Entry 70

A Colina Atlântica

Quinta das Maças, Travessa dos Melquites 3, Barrantes, 2500-621 Salir de Matos, Estremadura

A friendly place which works its magic on many levels and a good place to come if you want to unwind in tranquil surroundings. The house is surrounded by apple orchards and there's wonderful walking nearby. Ineke and Ton, both social workers, have travelled a good deal in India and Asia, and soon make you feel at home. They create a special atmosphere – their company is good and the mood is relaxing. The bedrooms, in what once were the stables, have tiled floors and wooden ceilings; they are simple, uncluttered and comfortable. The house's huge loft is now a beautiful relaxation room with a wood-lined roof, cotton rugs and futons – you can join a 'guided meditation' class before breakfast if you feel like it. Or unwind with nurturing reiki, a gentle form of healing. Most nights there are delicious communal 'world cuisine' dinners in the dining room that opens onto a pleasant garden with tinkling chimes. If you need a knowledgeable escort, Ton will take you to the monasteries of Alcobaça and Batalha, to Óbidos and Nazaré. There's plenty to see locally, from hot springs to markets..

rooms	4: 3 doubles, 1 single.
price	€40-€45. Singles €25-€30.
meals	Dinner with wine €12, on request. Restaurants within walking distance.
closed	Nov-April (open Christmas & New Year).
directions	From Caldas da Rainha for Alcobaça. After 6km, at Tornada, right to Barrantes. At end of village, fork left to Valado; after 100m right opp. new house. 50m on left.

	Ineke van der Wiele
tel	+351 262 877312
email	info@a-colina-atlantica.com
web	www.a-colina-atlantica.com

B&B

Map 3 Entry 71

Casa do Casal do Pinhão

Bairro Sra. da Luz, 2510 Óbidos, Estremadura

Close to the medieval gem that is Óbidos, on the surrounding agricultural plain, is this long 1970s house. The set-up here is a mixture of *turismo rural* and stud farm – take a peek at the arch-necked Lusitanian horses in the stables nearby. Light, carpeted bedrooms lead onto a long veranda that overlooks pergola and pool; they have wooden beds, *alcobaça* bedcovers and matching table runners and curtains. Mini-fridges contain a small bottle of port – a nice touch. Self-service breakfast costs extra. The apartments are more functional and a little tired in feel; with basic divan-beds in the living rooms, they would be suitable for a couple or a young family of four. Crawl out of bed, throw open the French windows, and take a dip in the pool that waits outside (and there's a separate shallow one for little children). There are loungers on the grass and an honesty bar in the lounge. The scrubby garden is fringed by umbrella pines, eucalyptus and gingeiras – its fruits end up in the local *ginja*, or cherry wine. Not a sound, just sheep, dogs, goats and birds. *Further apartments 1km at neighbouring quinta.*

rooms	8 + 2: 8 twins/doubles. 2 self-catering apartments for 2-4.
price	€60-€80. Apartments €80 for 2, €90 for 3, €100 for 4.
meals	Restaurants nearby.
closed	Rarely.
directions	EN8 to Caldas da Rainha. Look for blue signs to house from Óbidos.

	Senhora Maria Adelaide
tel	+351 262 959078
fax	+351 262 959078
email	casal.pinhao@iol.pt
web	www.mundo.iol.pt/casal.pinhao/turismo

B&B & Self-catering

Map 3 Entry 72

Casa das Senhoras Rainhas

Rua Padre Nunes Tavares, No. 6, 2510-070 Óbidos, Estremadura

An almost palpable sense of history lingers on every corner of Óbidos. It is a preserved village, tourist-filled but a delight. This very special little hotel, below the castle's corner, has teased generous space out of an old building – wisely resisting the temptation to cram in too many rooms. It is subdued, tasteful, light and airy, with a little garden, a restaurant and attractive common space – an appealing combination of intimacy and luxury. You are greeted with a drink, or tea, and fresh biscuits. Refreshingly uncluttered bedrooms have handsome soapstone floors, dark wood and cane headboards, bowls of fruit, generous toileteries. Most of them have balconies. The restaurant, in ochre and red, looks out onto the little patio and the castle walls. The food goes one step better than the usual 'salt, pepper and olive oil' of Portuguese seasonings: a delicious local sea bream with browned butter and capers, for example. You can retreat to the old fig tree in the patio for a quiet read… but the whole place is a retreat, and a deeply soothing one.

rooms	9: 8 doubles, 1 suite.
price	€144–€165. Tower suite €159–€186. Singles €132–€151.
meals	Restaurant in hotel.
closed	Rarely.
directions	Once in Óbidos, call for detailed directions.

	Senhora Mariana Palma
tel	+351 262 955 360
fax	+351 262 955 369
email	info@senhorasrainhas.com
web	www.senhorasrainhas.com

Hotel

Map 3 Entry 73

Casa de S. Thiago do Castelo

Largo de S. Thiago, 2510-106 Óbidos, Estremadura

Don't miss hilltop Óbidos, a beguiling maze of cobbled streets softened by blue and ochre washes and romping stands of bougainvillea and jasmine. The 'house of St James' has been in the family for over a century; more recently Carlos opened for guests, and there's a cheery French housekeeper to welcome you. From outside you could not guess the extent of this old house; a warren of corridors leads to the rooms. Decoration has been meticulously studied and carefully crafted. Bedrooms, not large, have dark panelled ceilings and massively thick walls. Some windows have the original *conversadeiros*, or gossiping seats! There are wrought-iron bedsteads, floral curtains and bedspreads, smart bathrooms and the occasional detail you'd expect of a large hotel, such as logo-ed writing paper and envelopes. Retire to the small lounge with open hearth and bar (try a glass of the local cherry liqueur, *ginjinha*); there's a billiard room too, and, in the lee of the castle battlements, a colourful, walled, Arabesque patio. Carlos is a loquacious host who loves having guests. *Overflow extension up road.*

rooms	6: 5 doubles, 1 twin.
price	€85-€90. Singles €70-€75.
meals	Good restaurants nearby.
closed	Never.
directions	Enter Óbidos through main gate. Continue to end of street. House on right, below castle.

	Senhor Carlos Lopes
tel	+351 262 959587
fax	+351 262 959587

B&B

Map 3 Entry 74

Pousada de Óbidos/Castelo

Paço Real, Ap. 18, 2510-999 Óbidos, Estremadura

This pousada has one of the most spectacular positions in Portugal – set inside the 14th-century castle at the pinnacle of walled, whitewashed, hilltop Óbidos. A small cobbled garden with sculpted bushes leads to reception; walk out on the ramparts and you look straight down onto dappled ochre rooftops and winding streets. Swags of bougainvillea and ivy spill over dazzling white walls into secret gardens where cats stretch in the sun; enticing alleys lead through ancient stone archways. Beyond, the surrounding plain reaches to the sea. We think the incomparable views more than compensate for the mauve hues and stainless steel of the décor, and the slight touch of the institutional about the food and the staff. Breakfast is enjoyed in the light and airy dining room with its marvellous outlook fromy stone-pillared windows; dine in, or head off into town for the rest of your meals. If you're into medievalism, the split-level tower rooms will appeal: vertiginous stairs lead up from each small (windowless) hall and bathroom to a tiny stone bedroom with arrow slits for windows and a superb four-poster bed.

rooms	9: 4 doubles, 2 twins, 3 suites.
price	€165-€250. Singles €153-€238. Special offers available - see web site.
meals	Dinner, 3 courses, from €26.
closed	Rarely.
directions	From the motorway follow signs to Óbidos & then Pousada.

	Senhora Costa Sousa
tel	+351 262 955080
fax	+351 262 959148
email	recepcao.castelo@pousadas.pt
web	www.pousadas.pt

Hotel

Map 3 Entry 75

Quinta de Santa Catarina

Rua Visconde da Palma d'Almeida, 2530-166 Lourinhã, Estremadura

If style, elegance, comfort and service are high on your list of hotel essentials then Quinta de Santa Catarina is your place. It was built in the 16th century, rebuilt in the 18th and embellished by various illustrious forebears of the Almeida Braga family; they even escaped collectivisation during the Revolution. The expanding suburbs of Lourinhã have brought new neighbours but the building still looks out across wooded grounds where the tallest of palm trees (you'll find them on the family coat of arms too) increase the sensation of coming across a genuine oasis. You may be met by a uniformed maid who will lead you to your room via elegant reception rooms where ancestral portraits, gilded mirrors and chandeliers, brilliant polished tables and dressers, candelabras and flowers would provide a wonderful backdrop for the grandest of weddings. In the bedrooms are polished antique beds, dressers and occasional tables, more cut flowers, deep-pile carpets and captivating views out to the palm trees. Teresa teaches English and has a gift for making you immediately unwind.

rooms	5 twins/doubles.
price	€78-€90. Singles €63-€80.
meals	Snacks by the pool. Dinner available locally.
closed	Christmas.
directions	From Lisbon, A8 for Porto. Exit junc. 9 to Lourinhã. There, at roundabout with fountain, take Rua Adelino Amaro da Costa, past restaurant D. Sebastiao. Entrance on right.

	Senhora Teresa Maria Palma de Almeida Braga
tel	+351 261 422313
fax	+351 261 414875
email	quinta.santa.catarina@netc.pt

B&B

Map 3 Entry 76

Quinta do Salvador do Mundo

2590-211 Sobral de Monte Agraço, Estremadura

The Quinta of the Saviour of the World once belonged to the bishopric of Évora and is a large farmhouse near a Roman-Gothic church of the same name. This is an area of vineyards, rolling hills and windmills, and the farm overlooks a vast valley with views to the Serra do Socorro. The quinta has been stylishly rebuilt, a stunning blend of old and new. It has grand furniture, a Steinway, chandeliers, silver, family antiques and lots of glass and pine – all in a light and airy building. The furniture includes English, French, Portuguese and Indo-Portuguese pieces. Moroccan mosaic tables stand on a terrace outside the magnificent breakfast room which has windows along one side and views of the valley and ruined church. Four bedrooms are in a separate building; they too are roomy and comfortable, each with antique beds and desks. Enjoy the luxury you'd expect from a top hotel, the grandeur of a *casa nobre* and a beautifully designed modern setting. Teresa is gracious, friendly and well-travelled. *Five bedrooms in main house not generally available.*

rooms	9 doubles.
price	€105-€130. Singles €90-€115. Extra bed €35.
meals	Restaurants nearby.
closed	20 October–15 November.
directions	From A8 exit junc. 6, left at Pero Negro; left again, then right, follow signs for Salvador (7km from motorway).

	Senhora Teresa Sucena Paiva
tel	+351 261 942880
fax	+351 261 943199
email	quintasalvador@ip.pt
web	www.quintasalvador.com

B&B

Map 3 Entry 77

Casa do Paço de Ilhas

Santa Isidoro, 2640-068 Ericeira, Estremadura

Arty, funky, quirky - and a short walk from a beautiful surfing beach with courses. Margarida has lived here for years and her bohemian spirit fills the space. The walls in the bar are choc a bloc with posters, photos, prints, plates and paintings – some her own – and other eclectic but tasteful clutter; the mood is happy, young, unpretentious. Miguel, who is half-English, rustles up the freshest and most delicious meals with a meditteranean/Portuguese slant: fish from the sea, herbs from the garden. Casa do Palheiro is perfect for families or surfing friends with its mezzanine bedroom; it has cobbled floors and a jolly kitchen with the *alambique* where firewater was once distilled. In Casa do Celeiro you may cook in the simple kitchen or on the little open fire; then eat out on the sweet terrace. Tiny Casa dos Azores has a multicoloured celing and is a delightful place for a couple. Outside, a shared barbecue area and space to cook and eat, a saltwater pool, shady spots in the garden and Zorro, the donkey. And there's a B&B room to which you may retreat for a flower-filled bath – bliss.

rooms	1 + 3: 1 double. 3 self-catering apartments: 1 for 4, 2 for 2.
price	€30-€40; €150-€200 p.w. Apt for 4: €63-€90; €350-€500 p.w; for 2 €50-€70; €280-€400 p.w.
meals	Breakfast on request. Dinner, 3 courses, €30-€40.
closed	Rarely.
directions	On road between Ribamar & Santo Isodoro, north of Ericeira on road next to sea.

	Senhora Margarida Ferreira Carrasco
tel	+351 261 864962
mobile	+351 916 363830
email	pacodilhas@iol.pt

Self-catering

Map 3 Entry 78

Pensão Residencial Sintra

Quinta Visconde de Tojal, Travessa dos Avelares 12, 2710-506 Sintra (S.Pedro), Estremadura

We loved the air of faded grandeur enveloping this family-run B&B. It was built on a thickly-wooded hillside as a viscount's summer retreat in the days when fashionable Sintra was a hill station to local and international gentry – and became a B&B in 1958. An original bannistered staircase winds up to the bedrooms. These are enormous with high ceilings, wooden floors and rather dated furniture and fittings; it all has a distinctly out-of-time feel; modern rooms are more functional. Ask for a mountain view. Downstairs is an enormous dining room/bar where snacks are available, but we'd prefer to sit out on the wide terrace (with tea and cakes in the afternoon) with its beguiling views up to the fairy-tale Moorish castle. And the garden is a delight: dripping with greenery, it has some old, old trees, a swimming pool lower down and a small play area for children. Multi-lingual Susana is a young, bright and caring hostess. The village centre with its numerous restaurants and shops is a short stroll away; for the more energetic, attractive paths lead steeply up to Sintra's castles and palaces.

rooms	15: 7 twin/doubles, 8 doubles. Extra beds available.
price	€50-€90. Singles €45-€85.
meals	Snacks available all day, from €3. Good restaurants nearby.
closed	Rarely.
directions	From Lisbon, IC19. Exit for Sintra & São Pedro & follow signs to São Pedro & historical centre. Hotel signed on right as you exit S. Pedro, towards historic centre of Sintra.

	Senhora Susana Bezold Rosner Fragoso
tel	+351 219 230738
fax	+351 219 230738
email	pensao.residencial.sintra@clix.pt

B&B

Map 3 Entry 79

Casa Miradouro

Rua Sotto Mayor 55, PO Box 1027, 2710-801 Sintra, Estremadura

The gaily striped walls make this an easy place to find as you wind down from Sintra. The present owner left a successful career in Switzerland to launch himself into restoring this light, elegant and airy home with views on all sides. Pass through a palm-graced porch, and a handsome bannistered staircase leads you to the bedrooms. Here antique beds and wardrobes stand on sisal matting; ceilings are high and have the original stucco mouldings. It feels fresh and uncluttered, helped by the size of the rooms, the two in the attic included. Views are to the sea or to the hills. The sitting room has a similarly unfussy feel; here the sisal balances the flounced curtains. There is a bar with several different ports, and a hearth for sitting round in the colder months. Further downstairs is a modern breakfast room, simply decorated with four round tables and giving onto a large terrace. Classical music accompanies breakfast: cereals, cheeses, juices, yogurts, fresh fruit, savoury and sweet breads. Frederic is a gentle-mannered, attentive and truly charming host, his home as well-kept as any of Portugal's best.

rooms	6: 4 doubles, 2 twins.
price	€95-€125. Singles €80-€112.
meals	Excellent restaurants nearby.
closed	Mid-Jan-mid-Feb.
directions	From Lisbon, IC19 to Sintra. Follow brown signs for Centro Histórico. At square by palace, right (in front of Hotel Central) & on to Tivoli Hotel. Down hill for 400m. House on left. Street parking outside.

	Frederic & Janda Kneubühl
tel	+351 219 107100
fax	+351 219 241836
email	mail@casa-miradouro.com
web	www.casa-miradouro.com

B&B

Map 3 Entry 80

Lawrence's Hotel

Rua Consigliéri Pedroso 38-40, Vila de Sintra, 2710-550 Sintra, Estremadura

Founded in 1764, it is the oldest hotel on the Iberian Peninsula. Everyone who was anyone wanted to stay here, and did – after Lord Byron's visit in 1809. He wouldn't recognise the stylish modern 'restaurant with rooms' that it has become. "The guest comes first, last and is everything," is Dutchmann Jan Bos's philosophy and service is perfect without being ingratiating. (A waiter who worked here as a boy was absolutely delighted to return 40 years later, the day the hotel reopened!). Furnishings are elegant and comfortable yet refreshingly uncluttered. Bedrooms have wooden floors, firm beds, country-fresh fabrics and a romantic feel; bathrooms are top-notch, the best sporting hydromassage baths. And then there's the restaurant. The menu is Portuguese rather than international, the food is impeccable and the wines the nation's best. Sintra is Portugal's pastry-capital – you will not be disappointed by your strawberry and raspberry *millefeuille* on its wild berry coulis. Breakfasts, too, are exquisite. One of the most beguiling – and friendly – hotels, bang in Sintra's historic heart. *Good pool nearby*

rooms	16: 11 twins/doubles, 5 suites.
price	€171-€235. Singles €139-€182. Suites €299-€347.
meals	Dinner from €40.
closed	Rarely.
directions	Hotel in Sintra city centre. Call for details on booking.

	Jan Bos
tel	+351 219 105500
fax	+351 219 105505
email	lawrences_hotel@iol.pt
web	www.lawrenceshotel.com

Hotel

Map 3 Entry 81

Quinta das Sequóias

Casa de Tapada, Estrada de Monserrate, 2711-801 Sintra, Estremadura

Hidden in its deep forest, this house is steeped in seclusion, rich flora and dream-like views of palaces and castles. This long, two-storey white Quinta, dating from 1870, is full of delights. Candida, warm and joyful, has a home of remarkable beauty inside and out. Corridors and walls are adorned with paintings and sculptures from some of Portugal's foremost artists, alongside fascinating older pieces from all over the world. Bedrooms are individual, with carved beds and polished mahogany furniture, rugs on tiled floors and carpets. The two bedrooms in the towers have beamed ceilings. The living room is long with comfy sofas, and overlooks the garden. Nearby is a library, and a comfortable lounge with games and lots of light. The breakfast room has a large open fireplace and tables large and small, and of course you may eat outside: Sintra is all slopes, and in front of the house the garden descends on lawned terraces, with pergolas and lush foliage, a burbling stream below and a swimming pool with views for miles. The people, the morning mists and sunsets are very special. *Minimum stay two nights.*

rooms	5: 2 doubles, 3 twins/doubles.
price	€120-€145.
meals	Excellent restaurants a short drive. Salads from €12.50. Cheeseboard for 2, €20.
closed	Christmas.
directions	From Sintra, follow signs past the Tourist Office to Palácio de Seteais. Continue for 1km; Sequóias signposted on left, up 2km through forest.

	Senhora Candida Gonzalez
tel	+351 219 230342
fax	+351 219 106560
email	candigonzalez@hotmail.com
web	www.quintadasequoias.com

B&B

Map 3 Entry 82

Casa no Ar

Rua Monte de Lua, Penedo, 2705-055 Sintra, Estremadura

The name means 'house in the sky' – you can see why. The views reach to the sea and the hills, far from the hubbub below. And this is a fun place to be, especially for families. The lived-in feel means you settle right in; children will adore their 'secret' bedrooms under the eaves and the special spot with rocks and plants growing inside. Your open-plan farmhouse kitchen is decorated with farming artefacts and has everything you could possibly need. There's a large barbecue and outdoor kichen too, a pool, floodlit at night, and a pretty garden and a lounge with terrace and views. Mezzanines with space for a futon, sofabeds in the lounge... this is a higgledy-piggledy, flexible sort of place. There's also a separate hideaway next to the pool: a studio for couples or teenagers seeking privacy. Bedrooms are simple, no-fuss spaces but no matter; there's so much to keep you entertained you won't mind a bit. Jane, who lives up the road, is just as relaxed; this was her and her children's home for many years. Great local walks, beaches and palaces and the Natural Park, the Serra da Sintra, to explore.

rooms	House for 6 + 4 children.
price	€1,000–€1,500 per week.
meals	Many restaurants nearby.
closed	Rarely.
directions	From Sintra head for Colares. At Church Square left for Penedo. Through 3 arches, sharp left after 4th arch; through village left into Rua Monte de Lua. 2nd on right.

	Jane Doody
tel	+351 219 291304
email	janedoody@hotmail.com
web	www.janedoody.com

Casal das Giestas

Rua do Alto da Bonita 112, Ranholas, 2710-185 Sintra, Estremadura

Plants with vibrant orange flowers climb all over this pretty cottage and there are plenty more in the walled garden too. A jasmine- and wisteria-covered pergola overlooks the most fragrant setting for breakfast. Your hostess is a mine of information about Portuguese society and history and enjoys having guests to stay. Her house, built in the 1890s, has something of an English B&B feel: an old kitchen dresser in the dining room filled with English and Portuguese porcelain, an oval dining table, silver candelabra, old prints. Bedrooms are comfortable with good linen, wooden floors and rugs, dark antique furniture and plenty of books. The gardens are quiet, calm and child-friendly with layered terraces, lush plants, magnolias and old trees; at night you may hear the hoot of an owl. Relax on the quiet lawn in the day; the chocolate, white and honey-coloured labradors will keep you company. When you go out in the evening babysitting can be arranged: there's an abundance of fascinating places to visit in Sintra, only a mile away. And it's very close to those marvellous Atlantic beaches.

rooms	3 twins.
price	€90.
meals	Excellent restaurants nearby.
closed	Rarely.
directions	From Lisbon, IC19 to Sintra, to Ranholas, then uphill. Right after large house with blue & white tiles. House on left.

	Senhora Neilma Williams Egreja
tel	+351 219 234287
email	casal.giestas@oninet.pt
web	www.casaldasgiestas.pt.vu/

B&B

Map 3 Entry 84

Quinta Verde Sintra

Estrada de Magoito, 84, Casal da Granja/Varzea de Sintra, 2710-252 Sintra, Estremadura

A modern house midway between Sintra and the beaches, set well back from the road, with distant green hills all around. This is a family home where Cesaltina, her husband Eugénio and sons Miguel and André create an easy, friendly atmosphere. Nature is bountiful; the house wrapped around by honeysuckle, palms, bay trees, cedar and succulents – breathe in the peace and quiet. Apartments have large sitting rooms, some with open fires and well-equipped kitchens and are set apart from the main house. Bedrooms have a mixture of wooden and metal beds, some antiques, pretty lights, matching fabrics on drapes and bedspreads, crisp white linen and tiled floors softened with small rugs. Bathrooms sparkle. Breakfast is taken at the rattan tables-for-two in the new conservatory breakfast room, or, on summer mornings, out on the terrace, next to the pool, with views of the lush Sintra hills. See if you can pick out the Moorish castle, Pena Palace, Monserrate house, the Quinta da Regaleira and Palácio de Seteais. It's a short drive to great beaches; fish restaurants too.

rooms	5 + 2: 3 doubles, 2 twins. 2 apartments for 4.
price	€70-€100. Singles €60-€90. Apartments €100-€150.
meals	Dinner, by arrangement, €12.50-€15. Light meals available.
closed	Rarely.
directions	From Sintra for Ribeira de Sintra; to x-roads, pass tram lines to Café Miranda. 1km, right for Magoito. After r'bout, left, then right. At V. de Sintra, after 1.5km, on right.

	Senhora Cesaltina de Sena
tel	+351 219 616069
fax	+351 219 608776
email	mail@quintaverdesintra.com
web	www.quintaverdesintra.com

BtB & Self-catering

Map 3 Entry 85

Casa do Celeiro

Pé da Serra, Colares, 2705-255 Serra de Sintra, Estremadura

It's wild and inspiring up here in the Serra de Sintra, a lushly wooded National Heritage site. The farm buildings sit serenely on their hill with views of azure Atlantic waters and sunburnt fields. Mary and Alan are friendly and relaxed. They teach small groups on painting holidays and exhibit their own work in Lisbon. They are also the architects responsible for the stylish renovation and extension of their 17th-century farmhouse. Upstairs a two-story conservatory which can be used for painting; below Alan's acrylic jewellery workshop. Above the house is a high pool built on an *eira* (stone threshing circle) with panoramic views. But it's not just the architecture that makes this place special, it's also the bohemian feel: sculptures in the courtyard, paintings in every corner, books on art and design, easels, brushes, dozens of plants and quirky bits and pieces. Rooms are simply comfortable, with those views. Meals are communal with plenty of fresh Portuguese food, wine and conversation; there's also a basic shared kitchen. And you don't have to paint to stay here – find your own space and relax. Heaven.

rooms	4 doubles.
price	€70. Singles €45. 10-day painting courses £900-£1,000 (full board).
meals	Good restaurants 2km. Dinner for 3 or more, by arrangement.
closed	December–January.
directions	Lisbon-Cascais; signs to Sintra via Azoia on coast road to Pé da Serra. Approaching Pé da S. fork, yellow wall on right & small turning circle. Back towards Cascais & immed. left up steep road.

	Alan & Mary St George
tel	+351 219 280151
fax	+351 219 282480
email	asgmsg@mail.telepac.pt
web	www.portugalpainting.com

B&B & Self-catering

Map 3 Entry 86

Quinta do Rio Touro

Caminho do Rio Touro, Azóia, 2705-001 Sintra, Estremadura

Luxuriate in sea views from the top bedrooms of this tropical oasis. The lush organic gardens have masses of fruit – peaches, bananas, grapefruit, oranges, apples, plums, strawberries and, above all, limes. Feel free to pick your own. Scented jasmine tumbles over the entrance and other fragrant bushes tempt you into the gardens day and night. Your hosts are great travellers: having worked in the diplomatic field for many years their library reflects their travels, from Norway to Spain, Japan to Portugal; Senhor Reino likes nothing more than to help you plan your own journeys. The main house has an amazing collection of artefacts: Roman pots, Moroccan stone carved tables, antique fans and art pieces from all over. Choose between the rooms in the main house with their balconies, suites and Portuguese tradition, or go for a more private room in the little house at the foot of the garden. The locally sourced and organic breakfasts are outstanding: home-laid eggs, local pastries, fresh cheeses, their own honey, ginza jam and pumpkin chutney. *Minimum stay two nights.*

rooms	6: 2 doubles, 2 suites for 2+2, 2 suites.
price	€120-€200. Singles from €110.
meals	Restaurants within walking distance. Dinner occasionally available.
closed	Rarely.
directions	A5 towards Cascais, junc. 12 for Malveira. Right; on for 8km; left for Azoia. 70m on left again, follow signs. Past 1st house; stone wall with wooden door.

	Maria Gabriela & Fernando Reino
tel	+351 21 929 2862
fax	+351 21 929 2360
email	info@quinta-riotouro.com
web	www.quinta-riotouro.com

B&B & Self-catering

Map 3 Entry 87

Casa Buglione

Estr. Nova, 95 - Azóia, 2705-001 Colares, Estremadura

Giampiero and Paul are a delightful pair and you'll feel at home the moment you arrive. They designed the semicircular house themselves to make the most of the stunning sea views; the breakfast room is the best place to drink them in. Breakfasts and dinners are delicious – your hosts ran a restaurant and know what they're about. Paul and his sister were also the figure skating champions of Switzerland: a picture on the mantlepiece shows their graceful dance on a frozen lake. The house is full of extravagent things from all over Europe, there are Louis XIII and XIV chairs in bedrooms, sumptuous bedlinen, thick bathrobes, bedroom doors hand-painted by Jean-Pierre, gorgeous antique mirrors and beautiful paintings from Italy, France and Switzerland. The village has some excellent restaurants and a friendly snack bar in its beautiful old windmill. Walk to the most westerly point of Europe, take off to the beach or stretch out on a lounger next to the sheltered pool. *No smoking in bedrooms. Wine appreciation available.*

rooms	3: 1 double, 2 twins. Can be let as interconnecting suite for 4.
price	€80-€90.
meals	Dinner, 3 courses with wine, €20, by arrangement. Excellent restaurants nearby.
closed	Rarely.
directions	In Azóia head to centre. There, in front of Refugio da Roca restaurant, right up Estrada Nova. House, number 95, 150m on right.

	Giampiero Pedruzzi
tel	+351 219 280369
fax	+351 219 289545
email	casabuglione@sapo.pt
web	www.casabuglione.com

B&B

Map 3 Entry 88

Convento de São Saturnino

Azóia, Cabo da Roca, 2705-001 Sintra, Estremadura

Deep in Azóia's valley something magical has happened. On the site of a ruin these talented owners designed a series of buildings based on a 12th-century convent. Whitewashed, inter-connecting spaces, curved roofs, winding steps, sparkling sea glimpses and a trickling spring – a place to lose yourself in. Bedrooms are decadently stylish, fabrics are rich, bathrooms are pampering. In the large lounge are squidgy sofas, coffee-table books, an old library and a collection of scrolls and artifacts found on the site. Help yourself to a drink from the honesty bar, then retreat to the high-ceilinged, candlelit dining room where the food is home-cooked and delicious (we loved the chilled melon soup with parma ham). Pad around the house, scramble down to the sea or recline on a rock and breathe it all in; the Convento feels restorative and spiritual. Add to this a shiatsu massage and your bliss should be complete. The atmosphere is more small hotel than private home but the staff are perfect and the beds with sea views are out of this world. Enchanting.

rooms	9: 3 doubles, 3 twins, 3 suites.
price	€180-€200. Singles from €150.
meals	Lunch snacks sometimes available. Dinnerwith wine, 3 courses, €30.
closed	Rarely.
directions	A5 Lisboa-Cascaís, exit Malveira - Aldeia do Junto. 4km after Malveira da Serra, left for Cabo da Roca. At Moinho D. Quixote bar round to right until you see house signs.

	John Nelson Perrie
tel	+351 219 283192
fax	+351 219 289685
email	contact@saosat.com
web	www.saosat.com

B&B

Map 3 Entry 89

Fortaleza do Guincho

Estrada do Guincho, 2750-642 Cascaís, Estremadura

The crest at this 17th-century cliff fortress reads 'Where the earth ends the sea begins'; as you are almost surrounded by the crashing Atlantic waves you tend to agree. This ochre-coloured oasis is metres from the most westerly point in Europe – walk to the other end of Guincho beach and you're there. There's an enormous, balconied, courtyard entrance with a high glass ceiling, suits of armour, modern chandeliers, leafy plants and tiled floors; follow the red carpet to the rooms upstairs. Bedrooms have watery views; in the suite you can watch or listen to the waves from bed – or close the double-glazed windows to the turbulent ocean. Bedrooms have archways, soft colourings, smart bedcovers, duckdown duvets, the heaviest curtains, the thickest bathrobes and every hotel luxury imaginable, from Nina Ricci soaps to treats on the pillows. The contrast between the hotel-style luxury inside the building and the wild windy turbulance on a blowy day outside is part of the thrill. You can play at being rugged on that dramatic headland and then retreat for a slap-up dinner.

rooms	27: 24 twins/doubles, 3 suites.
price	€170-€485. Singles €160-€405. Suites €295-€415.
meals	Lunch/dinner up to €46.
closed	Never.
directions	From Lisbon, A5 to Cascaís, then EN91. At 1st r'bout follow signs for Birre; over 2nd r'bout following signs for Areia to Guincho Beach. Left at x-roads for 500m. Fortress on right, signed.

	Senhora Isabel Ferreira Froufe
tel	+351 214 870491
fax	+351 214 870431
email	reservations@guinchotel.pt
web	www.guinchotel.pt

Hotel

Map 3 Entry 90

Estalagem do Forte Muchaxo

Praia do Guincho, 2750-642 Cascais, Estremadura

Guincho is a long, curving sandy surf beach, backed by the Serra de Sintra – a perfect place from which to watch Atlantic sunsets. One of the best views is from Tony Muchaxo's inn, perched at one end of the beach. It's full of character, a fantastic combination of ocean liner and Neptune's grotto, with stone, cork pillars and strange wooden ceilings; floors are of *calçada*, parquet, slate, terracotta and marble, often sloping to adjust for the fact that it was all built on the ruin of an old fort. The restaurant has great ocean views and the building is arranged around an inner courtyard where sea birds land among the succulents; there's plenty of peeling paint, too, but then the ocean is fierce. Take a dip in the saltwater pool instead. In the bar find a wishing well with running water, rock 'booths' and tree-trunk tabletops and pillars. Bedrooms are large and comfortable; pay the extra for the sea views. You feel you're almost in the brine, and you hear the raging waves all night – an extraordinary mixture of wild nature, marble floors and beds with vinyl-padded bedheads. Eat in, or out in Cascais.

rooms	60 twins/doubles.
price	€65-€145. Singles from €55.
meals	Dinner from €25.
closed	Rarely.
directions	In Cascais, follow signs to Guincho. Along coast wide beach as road turns inland. Forte Muchaxo on curve on left, a little below road.

	Senhor António Muchaxo
tel	+351 214 870221
fax	+351 214 870444
email	info@muchaxo.com
web	www.muchaxo.com

Hotel

Map 3 Entry 91

Pousada de Queluz/Lisboa

D. Maria I, Lg. Palácio Nacional de Queluz, 2745–191 Queluz, Estremadura

You dine in the magnificently baroque Royal Summer Palace – 'Portuguese Versailles'. The pink pousada is on the other side of the courtyard, in the old *torre do relógio* – the clocktower – and has been beautifully renovated and revived. A dear little theatre, which would have been used for private performances, is now a space for occasional impromptu entertainment – truly charming with a gilded balcony and armchairs. Bedrooms have dark wooden furniture and raspberry and gold bedcovers; bathrooms are generous. Downstairs are a lounge, comfy with open fire, oil paintings, writing desk and bar, and a buffet-breakfast room, where tables are laid for two. Formal dining takes place in the Palace's grand old kitchen with its magnificent stone table and enormous central bread oven. Gold curtains hang at tall windows, there are bronze artefacts, sparkling, candle-dressed tables and a harp. A 20-minute taxi ride from the centre, the Pousada is not in the best area of Lisbon, but is worth the stay just for the Palace.

rooms	26: 24 twins/doubles, 2 suites.
price	€125-€195. Suites €179. Special offers available - see web site.
meals	Dinner, 3 courses, from €30.
closed	Rarely.
directions	From Lisbon, IC19 for Sintra; follow signs for Queluz & Pousada de Queluz.

	Senhor António Casa Nova
tel	+351 214 356158
fax	+351 214 356189
email	recepcao.dmaria@pousadas.pt
web	www.pousadas.pt

Hotel

Map 3 Entry 92

Pálacio Belmonte

Páteo Dom Fradique 14, 1100-624 Lisbon, Estremadura

A massive EU-subsidised restoration has pulled the 600-year-old palace into the 21st century. Frédéric Coustols, the owner, is a specialist in sustainable development, and has won an award for his use of natural materials. The magical palace hides down a cobbled passage at the top of one of Lisbon's hills (picture shows view). Each understated but richly decorated suite is as big as a house and has a balcony or terrace with superlative views. The Bartolomeu de Gusmão suite is at the top of one of the Moorish towers, its octagonal sitting room, bedroom and bathroom on three levels, reached via a spiral stone stair. The Padre Himalaya suite is bliss for honeymooners, with circular views of Lisbon from its Roman tower. There are wild silks in warm colours, heated terracotta tiles, original masonry, lovely antiques and baskets of herbs and spices to perfume the rooms; some have delicate frescos, all have white marble bathrooms. Lime mortar gives walls a soft patina, corridors are polished stone: luxury at its simple best. The pool is heavenly – black marble with wooden decking, fringed by orange and lemon trees.

rooms	10 suites.
price	€300-€1,200.
meals	Catering for groups and special requests only. Good restaurants nearby.
closed	Rarely.
directions	At the foot of Lisbon Castle, just outside walls.

Senhor Fernando Malveiro

tel	+351 218 816600
fax	+351 218 816609
email	office@palaciobelmonte.com
web	www.palaciobelmonte.com

B&B

Map 3 Entry 93

Solar do Castelo

Rua das Cozinhas, 2 (ao Castelo), 1100-181 Lisbon, Estremadura

The setting is spectacular – high up on the hill this new hotel sits within the pedestrian precinct of St Jorge's Castle overlooking the river Tejo and the centre of Lisbon. The building housed the kitchens of the first Royal Palace 800 years ago. It surrounds an inner courtyard and gardens and has ruins – such as the cistern – to explore. Décor is mainly modern with a beautiful mix of materials: marble, tiles, textiles, wood. Walk down corridors and see wooden floors, walls tiled in the Pombal star/flower/star pattern, wicker armchairs and chunky blue and grey pottery. Bedrooms are pristine, with marble bathrooms; large beds have wicker headboards. Some have exposed brick and timber walls, some stone and they all have rich textured fabrics, with linens, kilims and throws in natural colours: blues, terracottas, browns. The mansard bedrooms in the old part of the building have the best views. The courtyard garden is very pretty and you can breakfast here on wooden tables scattered in fresh flowers. There's a lovely tiled arch, water and patio pots – a haven in the city.

rooms	14: 4 doubles, 10 singles.
price	€182-€290. Singles €170-€260.
meals	Breakfast €14. Lunch & dinner available locally.
closed	Never.
directions	Arriving by car, go to Largo Menino de Deus entrance, where security guard will tell you what to do. Hotel in car-free precinct above city.

	The Cardoso & Fernandes families
tel	+351 218 806050
fax	+351 218 870907
email	solar.castelo@heritage.pt
web	www.heritage.pt

Hotel

Map 3 Entry 94

As Janelas Verdes

Rua das Janelas Verdes 47, 1200-690 Lisbon, Estremadura

In the old city, just yards from the Museum of Ancient Art, is this old, aristocratic townhouse; the great 18th-century novelist Eça de Queirós lived here. It is a perfect place to lay your head when in Lisbon, and from the moment you are greeted by the smiling Palmira you feel like an honoured guest. To one side of the reception is the lounge, with marble-topped tables (for breakfast in winter), a handsome fireplace, piano and comfortable chairs. Breakfast in summer (or have a candlelit aperitif) on the patio. Enormous ficus and bougainvillea run riot, a fountain gurgles and wrought-iron tables stand on dragon-tooth cobbling. A grand old spiral staircase leads you to the rooms, some of which have views of the river Tejo (book early if you want one). They are furnished with repro beds, flounced curtains and delicate pastel colours. Dressing gowns and towels are embroidered with the JV logo. And instead of a 'do not disturb' sign there's a hand-embroidered little pillow that says 'shhh!'. A delectable small hotel, enlarged to include a library on the top floor with impressive views of that river.

rooms	29 twins/doubles.
price	€182–€290. Singles €170–€260.
meals	Breakfast €14. Lunch & dinner available locally.
closed	Never.
directions	A2 m'way over river Tejo, then exit for Alcântara. Over r'bout; follow tram route for approx. 500m. Hotel on right, close to Muséo de Arte Antigo.

The Cardoso & Fernandes families

tel	+351 213 968143
fax	+351 213 968144
email	janelas.verdes@heritage.pt
web	www.heritage.pt

Hotel

Map 3 Entry 95

Residencial Alegria

Praça da Alegria 12, 1250-004 Lisbon, Estremadura

This family-run B&B could hardly be in a better position, yards from the street life of the Avenida de Liberdade yet in a quiet palm-fringed square which belies its inner-city status. It's all been freshly-painted on the outside and you should approve of your room, too: "bright, cheerful, clean and basic" is how our inspector describes her favourite Lisbon digs. For the moment there is not much in the way of public space but Felix, the Alegria's likeable owner, has extended the ground floor into a larger breakfast room. The antique dresser groans with the weight of the crockery and the fresh coffee is good. Some room are a shade drab with rather tired-looking bathrooms. Try to book our favourite room, number 114, which has been redecorated in a jolly mix of blues and yellows (see photo). The double-glazing is good news for light sleepers; the corridors have been painted in cheerful yellow and this and the shining parquet floors give the place a friendly feel. An inexpensive and central address, close to restaurants and the capital's attractions – ideal for those on a tight budget.

rooms	35: 20 doubles, 11 twins, 3 triples, 1 suite.
price	€38-€48.50. Suite €68.
meals	Excellent restaurants nearby. Light snacks from €2.50.
closed	Rarely.
directions	Turn off Avenida de Liberdade into Praça de Alegria. House between police station & 'bombeiros', behind Hotel Sofitel. Nearest metro: Avenida. Underground car park nearby, from €18 per day.

	Senhor Felix Santos
tel	+351 213 220670
fax	+351 213 478070
email	mail@alegrianet.com
web	www.alegrianet.com

B&B

Map 3 Entry 96

Hotel Métropole

Praça D. Pedro (Rossio) no. 30, 1100-200 Lisbon, Estremadura

You couldn't be more central – Hotel Métropole stands in Lisbon's main square, in the old town, walking distance from the central train station and with great views of Castelo de São Jorge and the Alfama. Built in 1917, the hotel has been carefully restored so as not to lose its youthful charm. Black and white checked floor tiles, cream walls with a green stripe, swagged curtains and retro lamps in the lounge add a touch of glamour; there are comfortable chairs in pinks, greens and creams and the feel is relaxed and unpretentious. At the far end of the lounge is the bar – a great spot for a post-prandial drink before hitting the town. Bedrooms at the front have suitably 20s furniture, French windows and balconies; you may breakfast here if you wish. Bathrooms have a new tiles in the old style and look sensational. A fun place to come and feel nostalgic about the old days. There's a huge choice of restaurants nearby and fantastic shopping. Staff are very friendly and happy to provide a map, a cup of tea or whatever you need.

rooms	36: 12 doubles, 20 twins, 4 triples.
price	€90–€180. Singles €80–€170.
meals	Excellent choice of restaurants a short walk away.
closed	Rarely.
directions	From airport, take shuttle bus (91) to front door or taxi (approx. €15).

	Senhor Alexandre de Almeida
tel	+351 213 21 9030
fax	+351 213 469166
email	metropole@almeidahotels.com
web	www.almeidahotels.com

Hotel

Map 3 Entry 97

Mouraria

Castle Hill, Lisbon, Estremadura

A little home in Portugal's great capital and good value. It has a well-lived-in family feel – Ken and Carole happily brought up their children in this friendly neighbourhood. Your first floor flat has large windows and a mellow lounge decorated in neutral colours perfect for evening relaxation. But don't expect grand luxury: bedrooms – three interconnecting – are simple, fresh and functional, and there's a single bathroom to share. The kitchen/family room is well-equipped with a washing machine, coffee percolator and microwave, a dining table and sofas. You are on the third floor yet your French windows open straight into the walled garden – an oasis of calm. A family friend who speaks English and lives downstairs is very welcoming and will show you the street's shop and small bar. It's a hilly spot: up takes you to the castle, down takes you to the shops and restaurants of the centre. Leave the car behind! All sorts of information has been thoughtfully provided; there's so much to see and do in Lisbon and it's a short train ride to the palaces of Sintra. A good spot for families or groups of friends. *Minimum stay three nights.*

rooms	1 apartment for 3-5.
price	£390-£550 per week. Weekends from £250. .
meals	Good restaurants nearby.
closed	Never.
directions	Taxi from Lisbon airport (€15) or go to Largo Martim Moniz. Walk up Escadinhas da Saude. Left at top, house 30m on left.

	Ken Parr & Carole Young
tel	+351 245 964465
fax	+351 245 964465
email	parryoung@pomarv.jazznet.pt
web	www.pomarv.jazznet.pt

Self-catering

Map 3 Entry 98

Antiga Casa do Castelo

Rua do Espírito Santo, 2, 1100-224 Lisbon, Estremadura

Your own slice of Portuguese life – complete with outside washing rails so you can meet the locals. And it's right inside the Castelo de São Jorge: a short stroll and you have the best view in town. At sunset you might just find a fado singer. In the evenings the tourists head down the hill and you have the place to yourself – along with the local kids who love to play hide and seek in the nearby square. This place is absolutely perfect for an independent couple wanting to visit Lisbon for a weekend. Your hosts thoughtfully leave a delicious welcome hamper for you, the kitchen's stocked with essentials and there's a tiny grocer's down the narrow streets where you can buy fresh bread morning and evening. It's absolutely gorgeous inside – tiny, but with everything you need. An open-plan living room and kitchen, a leaf table for two, a small study and a bedroom in the eaves. Marsha and Tom have a flair for design – the flat is neutral, textured and beautifully decorated with soothing fabrics and soft lighting. Stay longer than just a few days and explore the area. *Minimum stay three nights.*

rooms	1 apartment for 2.
price	€255 for 3 nights; €575 per week.
meals	Good restaurants nearby.
closed	Occasionally.
directions	From Lisbon airport táxi to Castelo São Jorge, Rua Espírito Santo, Numero 2. From Lisbon in Praça Figueira no. 37 bus to last stop, Castle entrance, & walk though castle arch up Rua Santa Cruz do Castelo to house.

	Tom & Marsha Grigg/Smith
tel	+351 245 964006
fax	+351 245 964006
email	antigacasa@yourhomeinlisbon.com
web	www.yourhomeinlisbon.com

Self-catering

Map 3 Entry 99

Pestana Palace

Rus Jau, 54, 1300-314 Lisbon, Estremadura

The hotel is in the former Valle Flór Palace that dates back to the 19th century; the main building is a National Monument. The pretty façade is painted yellow and the whole place has been painstakingly restored after years of neglect. Careful, detailed craftsmanship has worked its magic – today's reception rooms are splendidly, outragiously over-the-top. Be seduced by chandeliers, golden pillars, stucco, tall leafy palms, hand-painted ceilings of cherubs and fantastical scenes. Madonna reputedly stayed in one suite – a haven of decadence and exquisite antiques. If you can't afford to stay in the main house, at least book dinner in the decorative dining room – the food looks as good as it tastes – or take a drink in the lounge bar. Modern bedrooms in the new annexe are conventionally appealing with large beds and swagged curtains; some have French windows that open to the gardens, glorious with established plants and trees and circular fountained pool. The old chapel is just next door, staff are perfect and there are a gym, two pools and a luscious spa. Extraordinary.

rooms	190: 173 twins/doubles, 17 suites.
price	€430-€2,600. Special offers available - see web site.
meals	Dinner, 3 courses, from €38.
closed	Never.
directions	From Lisbon take a taxi to Pestana Palace.

	Senhor Paolo Dias
tel	+351 213 615600
fax	+351 213 615601
email	reservations.cph@pestana.com
web	www.pestana.com

Hotel

Map 3 Entry 100

Quinta de Santo Amaro
Aldeia da Piedade, 2925-375 Azeitão, Estremadura

Looking out to the Arrábida mountains, this gracious quinta was the family's summer house; now Maria lives here and opens her doors to guests. Bedrooms and apartment have a deliciously homely feel, and children will love the attic with its three rooms. In 'the middle house' are planked floors, panelled ceilings and attractive wooden beds. In the apartment, oil paintings and open hearths (a winter fire lit on arrival), period bathrooms and a piano. The lovely garden has shady walks and a discreet pool. It's the sort of place you won't want to leave. Breakfast is a help-yourself feast of homemade breads, jams, cheeses, eggs and bacon, Maria's oranges and the neighbour's strawberries – in season... But what makes it all so special is Maria herself, a lady with boundless enthusiasm and energy; she places a welcoming bottle of wine in your room and is full of ideas on where to eat and what to do. Lisbon is an easy drive, the beaches of the Setúbal peninsula are nearby, and the local Fonseca wine cellars are well worth a peek. *Minimum stay two nights.*

rooms	3 + 1: 2 doubles, 1 twin. 1 self-catering apartment for 6.
price	€85. Apartment €240; €1,585 p.w.
meals	Good restaurants nearby.
closed	Rarely.
directions	From Lisbon, m'way for Setúbal. Exit for Azeitão, then Sesimbra; route 378 to r'bout at Santana; left to Azeitão on route 379 for 6km. At Café Estrela dos A., right for Estrada dos A. House at end.

	Senhora Maria da Pureza O'Neill de Mello
tel	+351 212 189230
fax	+351 212 189390

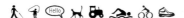

Map 5 Entry 101

Pousada de Setúbal

São Filipe, Castelo de S. Filipe, 2900-300 Setúbal, Estremadura

Climb up though ancient archways framed by old tiles to the 1590 fortress, built by King Filipe II of Spain. Setúbal Castle has the best views of the city below, but you can also see much further – across the bay to the long white stretches of sand on the Tróia peninsular. Climb giant stone steps to the top and ask to see the old chapel with stunning old *azulejos*. The pousada has been cleverly done and feels intimate and friendly. Rooms have been beautifully decorated in greens and golds and are all individual – one has its own sitting room on a mezzanine, while the suite has a view-filled balcony and a fresh fruit platter. There's antique carved furniture in the bedrooms and some lovely old wooden dressers in the hallway. The restaurant serves local seafish and regional food and has more fantastic vistas across the Sado estuary. Staff are friendly and happy to advise on the best things to see and do, from boat trips to golf – and it's an easy hop to Lisbon. The Arrábida mountain range and natural park are also close by.

rooms	16: 8 doubles, 7 twins, 1 suite.
price	€125–€195. Special offers available - see web site.
meals	Dinner, 3 courses, from €26.
closed	Rarely.
directions	From the A2 follow signs for Sétubal. There, follow signs for Pousada.

	Senhor Miguel Castilho
tel	+351 265 550070
fax	+351 265 539240
email	recepcao.sfilipe@pousadas.pt
web	www.pousadas.pt

Hotel

Map 5 Entry 102

Há Mar Ao Luar

Casa do Mar e Moinho do Mar, 3114 Setúbal, Estremadura

The vibrant Brazilian dancers in the paintings sum it up: this place is fun. And funky. Stay in the windmill whose staircase, hugging the curved wall, winds up from the circular living space to bed. Or take the beach *cabana* – French windows pull the sea views into the open-plan bedroom/dining room downstairs, there are twin beds in the attic for the children and colouful ribbons hanging from the doors. It's the kind of place where you won't mind getting sand everywhere. Happy summer holidays will be spent here and everything has been designed with the sea in mind – pictures of lighthouses, colourful tiling on the bathroom floors, hanging rails for tea towels, updside-down painted fish and buckets, whale-tail door handles, lobster pots and more. Breakfast waits in the fridge, fresh bread is attached to the door in the morning. White-sand views, peace, sea air – inspirational. Pretty gardens too and a lovely pool to cool off in. It's good value and you're very close to beautiful beaches, dolphins, boat trips – and, of course, the big city.

rooms	3 + 5: 1 double, 2 twins. Windmill for 2; house for 2; cabana for 4; 2 apartments for 2.
price	€50-€90. Small twin €50-€90. Windmill €90-€105. Cabana €75-€90.
meals	Seafood restaurants nearby.
closed	Rarely.
directions	From A2 for Sétubal centre; follow signs for Pousada de São Filipe. Up hill until sign for Há Mar auo Luar; 2nd on right.

	Senhora Maria Pereira Caldas
tel	+351 265 220901
fax	+351 265 534432
email	hamaraoluar@iol.pt
web	www.hamaraoluar.com

B&B & Self-catering

Map 5 Entry 103

Pousada de Alcácer do Sal

D. Afonso II, Castelo de Alcácer, 7580-123 Alcácer do Sal, Estremadura

One of the finest of the pousadas, a Moorish castle that dominates this rice-paddied valley. There was once a convent within its ruined walls; now the cloister has gone minimalist and the mood is more luxurious than ecclesiastical. This stupendous conversion combines generous spaces and plentiful reminders of the building's origins with deep modern comfort. Patches of gilded carved wood, antique pieces, kilims and oriental carpets float on a sea of cream marble against white walls and modern art – it is a magnificent blend of modern and medieval, Moorish and baroque. It's cosy too, with huge red and blue suede sofas to sink into, and, in winter, a big fire in the bar. The bedrooms, all with views, have contemporary wooden furniture and delightful textured fabrics for bedspreads and curtains. All 35 rooms fit beautifully into the old castle ramparts, yet there's still room for a pool and a little lawn – and a terracotta terrace on which you dine. A last dash of style: many of the doorways are of warm speckled stone, remnants from the ancient castle walls.

rooms	35: 6 doubles, 27 twins, 2 suites.
price	€125-€190. Suite €179-€256. Special offers available - see web site.
meals	Dinner, 3 courses, from €25.
closed	Rarely.
directions	From Lisbon A2, exit for Alcácer. Follow signs for pousada.

	Senhor Agusto Rosa
tel	+351 265 613070
fax	+351 265 613074
email	recepcao.dafonso@pousadas.pt
web	www.pousadas.pt

Hotel

Map 5 Entry 104

Photo José Manuel – thanks to Icep Portugal www.imagesofportugal.com

ribatejo

ribatejo

Ribatejo means 'Tejo Riverbank'. A small province with plains where wheat, vegetables and olives are grown

• **Tomar** is known for the Convento de Cristo – the former home of the Knights Templar, the mystical religious order powerful between the 12th and 16th centuries,

• **Santárem** is the main town, known for festivals and bullfights; the Archaeological Museum is worth a visit

• **Fátima** – in 1917 three girls saw an apparition of the Virgin; now 100,000 pilgrims return twice a year to commemorate this extraordinary occurrence

• Natural parks of **Serras d'Aire** and **Candeeiros**, a limestone range riddled with caves

• **Castelo de Almouril** – this fabulous medieval castle has a spectacular setting on an island in the Tejo River

• The famous horse fair of **Feira de São Martinho** is held in Golegã during the first half of November. Colourful parades, running bulls, Lusitano horses, competitions, wine and chestnuts

Solar de Alvega
EN 118-km149, Alvega, 2205-104 Abrantes, Ribatejo

The Marquês de Pombal built it in the 18th century and it is as imposing as ever, with views to the stream, tall walnut trees a waterfall and countryside beyond. Maria Luiza and her English husband Paul met in Africa and bought the house in 1998. Since then they have restored it to its former grandeur and introduced interesting juxtapositions of English and Portuguese antiques: Staffordshire figures cheek-by-jowl with blue and white *faience*, an English grandfather clock ticking to an old Portuguese flag. Maria has restored many of the antiques and other *objets* herself, from antique letter-scales to Art Nouveau lamps and intricate furniture. Sumptuous bedrooms have polished parquet floors and antique beds with elaborate wooden headboards; all are different – one room in the tower has five windows and access to the *mirante*, the roofed balcony; another opens onto a beautiful little chapel. They may do weddings here soon and the bridal suite has the only original bathroom: cool pink and black marble. And do try the *jardineira* stew: mixed meat and vegetables with potatoes and peas – delicious.

rooms	5 + 4: 5 twins/doubles; 4 apartments for 3-4.
price	€80-€90. Apartments €100; €550 per week.
meals	Lunch €15. Dinner €20, by arrangement.
closed	Rarely.
directions	A1 Lisbon-Porto. Exit Torres Novas; east on A23; exit Mouriscas. Signs for Castelo Branco & Portalegre. House 5km after exit from A23.

	Senhora Luiza Mallett
tel	+351 241 822913
fax	+351 241 822915
email	solaralvega@yahoo.co.uk
web	www.solardealvega.com

B&B

Map 4 Entry 105

Quinta do Troviscal

Alverangel - Castelo de Bode, 2300 Tomar, Ribatejo

If you love water, you'll love Troviscal. The modern villa looks over the vast reservoir at Castelo de Bode... such peace. Vera and João are an engaging couple with two teenagers and a pair of golden labs. Their house, on a secluded inlet at the end of a dusty winding track, is surrounded by pines, poplars and eucalyptus. The façade is the traditional yellow and white, the proportions are good, and the décor a smooth blend of new and traditional Portuguese. There is a harmonious use of materials: American oak ceilings, slate floors, hand-painted St Anna bathroom tiles. Beds are comfortable, rooms light and fresh, and glass-paned doors open onto a wonderful veranda where good breakfasts are served (homemade cake, fruit, yogurt, coffee or tea). The stone house has a cheery lounge and a pretty terrace with furniture, pergola and barbeque. Laze by the lovely pool, or stroll down the terraces and through the shaded pergolas – one a tunnel of wisteria, bliss in the spring – to the private floating pontoon; swim in the turquoise waters, bask on the sunlounger, slip off in the row boat. Special. *Minimum stay two nights at weekends.*

rooms	3 +1: 1 double, 1 twin, 1 suite; 1 house for 4/6.
price	€85. Suite €100. House €150 per day. Extra bed €20.
meals	Good restaurants a 15-minute drive.
closed	Rarely.
directions	From Tomar or Lisbon follow signs to Castelo de Bode. Straight on for 6km & follow signs for Quinta do Troviscal & Turísmo Rural; after 2km sign points to a track to right. Follow track to Quinta.

	Senhora Vera Sofia Sepulveda de Castel Bran
tel	+351 249 371318
fax	+351 249 371862
email	vera@troviscal.com
web	www.troviscal.com

B&B

Map 3 Entry 106

Casa da Avó Genoveva

Rua 25 de Abril 16, Curvaceiras, 2305-509 Tomar, Ribatejo

What strikes you on arrival is the serenity of the place. Huge old palm trees and pots of geraniums in the courtyard, a soft salmon and white façade – heaps of southern charm. José or Manuela usher you through to public rooms which are plush yet homely. In the living room are a large open hearth, comfy couches, a piano, a card table, family photos and books; in the dining room, dark antique dressers and a huge breakfast table – perfect *turismo de habitação*. In the music room guests can take their pick from classical and fado to play; and the snooker room doubles as a library. There's also a small bar, well-stocked with Portuguese wines. And what bedrooms! Dark panelled ceilings, family antiques, good old paintings, stunning crochet; the doubles are up the old stone staircase, the lovely apartments are in a converted granary across the way. There are also tennis, bikes to borrow and a serene pool. You're off the beaten track yet minutes from historic Tomar, and near a reservoir with boats. Your hosts are kindly, educated people who delight in sharing this lovely, tranquil home.

rooms	3 + 2: 2 doubles, 1 twin. 2 self-catering apartments: 1 for 2, 1 for 4.
price	€70. Apartment for 2 €80, for 4 €130.
meals	Restaurants nearby.
closed	Rarely.
directions	From Lisbon A1, junc. 23 for Tomar. 8km on left for Curvaceiras.

	José & Manuela Gomes da Costa
tel	+351 249 982219
fax	+351 249 981235
email	avogenoveva@sapo.pt

B&B & Self-catering

Map 3 Entry 107

Pousada de Ourém/Fàtima

Conde de Ourém, Largo João Manso-Castelos, 2490–481 Ourém, Ribatejo

King of the castle is how you feel gazing from the windows and terraces of this hilltop retreat. In the heart of walled, medieval Ourém – a sleepy town of narrow streets and hidden gardens - the pausada commands peerless views over rolling countryside. Hiding behind the small, bougainvillea-hung courtyard, the hotel is a conversion of three medieval buildings, including a hospital and servants' quarters. The mood inside is unexpectedly light and modern. Bedrooms have a Scandinavian feel – sleek lines, pale colours, birch wood furniture; bathrooms are plushly marbled. The light from the large windows makes each room a soothing haven. (Ask for a veranda and a view.) Fruit, chocolates and towelling robes add to the comfort. Reception rooms are cool and simple and include a small bar and a café-style dining room. But outside is where you'll long to be. There's a reading nook in a converted chapel and a pool dramatically sited beneath the castle wall. Staff are professional but friendly, making this a perfect place to recover after a hectic day discovering the delights of Fàtima.

rooms	30: 12 doubles, 17 twins, 1 quadruple.
price	€100-€150. Singles from €88. Special offers available - see web site.
meals	Dinner, 3 courses, €25.
closed	Rarely.
directions	From Fátima follow signs for Ourém. There, follow blue signs to Castelo & pousada.

	Senhora Conceicão Costa Sousa
tel	+351 249 540920
fax	+351 249 542955
email	recepcao.ourem@pousadas.pt
web	www.pousadas.pt

Hotel

Map 3 Entry 108

Quinta de Alcaídaria - Mór

2490 Ourém, Ribatejo

The wisteria-clad manor has been in the family for 300 years and is every inch the grand country house: stately cedar-lined drive, box-hedged gardens, 14th-century chapel. The main house is a cool, gracious building – light streams into lofty, elegant rooms with marble floors, arches and delicate plasterwork. Don't miss the chance to dine (inexpensively) around the enormous table; the chandeliers and china may inspire you to dress for dinner. An attractive self-catering house is just up the hill, while the B&B rooms are in the main building – and very special they are, too. Expect antique dressers, beds, comfortable chairs, perhaps a grand bathtub with clawed feet… there are beautiful moulded ceilings and big bathrooms generously tiled and marbled. Add to this great views, a peaceful pool and the natural kindness of your English-speaking host (Teresa may invite you to join her and her son for a glass of fine port) and you begin to get the measure of this charming place. Don't miss hilltop Ourém – a gem.

rooms	6 + 3: 6 twins/doubles. 1 house for 4; 2 apartments for 4-6.
price	€90-€115. House & apartments €115-€125.
meals	Dinner, €17.50, on request. Light snacks available.
closed	Rarely.
directions	From Ourém, towards Tomar. After 2km, road curves right, left at Turismo de Habitação sign.

	The Vasconcelos Family
tel	+351 249 542231
fax	+351 249 545034
email	geral@quintaalcaidaria-mor.pt
web	www.quintaalcaidaria-mor.pt

B&B & Self-catering

Map 3 Entry 109

Casa do Patriarca

Rua Patriarca D. José 134, Atalaia, 2260-039 Vila Nova da Barquinha, Ribatejo

The Casa has been in the family for five generations; the Archbishop of Lisbon was born here in 1686. You'll be greeted by Manuel's son, daughter or wife, and friendly dog. The lounge has French windows opening to a walled garden; it's a long, low room, lined with sofas, comfortable not grand, a cool retreat. Just off here is a small kitchen for guests – excellent news for families not wanting to eat out. The long breakfast table is beautifully laid with home-grown fruit and delicacies, and juice fresh from their own oranges, and there's 'full English' if you prefer. Ground-floor bedrooms are homely and individually themed. Quinta has great-great-grandfather's bed; Oriente has lamps and cushions from India; Almirante is nautical in feel; Sana Sana evokes Mozambique – your hosts spent their honeymoon there. The much-loved gardens are a pleasure; an enormous date palm towers above the pomegranate, medlar, orange and fig trees, there are shady spots in which to sit and relax, and a pool edged by trees. Manuel and his family gently care for their guests and it's a treat to stay in this quaint little town.

rooms	6: 4 doubles, 2 twins.
price	€50–€75.
meals	Self-catering option.
closed	Rarely.
directions	From m'way, exit 1 for Torres Novas, then IP6, then IC3 for Tomar. After 1500m signed for Atalaia & house.

	Luisa & Manuel d'Oliveira
tel	+351 249 710581
fax	+351 249 711191
email	mop59265@mail.telepac.pt
web	casadopatriarca.pt.vu

B&B

Map 3 Entry 110

Casa do Foral

Rua da Boavista 10, 2040 Rio Maior, Ribatejo

A pretty 19th-century townhouse in an oasis-like garden. Inside comes as a surprise: the owner's passion for collecting has turned the Casa into a mini museum. Penknives, tankards, plates, fox-hunting prints, walking sticks: there are collections at every turn. It's peaceful here and you are looked after by the young housekeeper, Rosa. Out of season guests may use the big old-fashioned lounge/dining room, delightful with its many chesterfields, large fire, blue and white tiled panelling and hunting trophies on the walls. The breakfast room is cafeteria-like comparison, with wicker chairs, glass tables and a modern glass wall that looks onto an interior courtyard and pretty pepper tree. In the garden are palms, oleanders and tumbling bougainvillea, a rose pergola for shade, and a small but inviting swimming pool. Bedrooms are comfortable, light and roomy, with floral covers on new pine beds, and bathrooms in lime green; one room has a glass wall and four have mezzanines – fun for kids. This is a house of character, in a quiet street surrounded by semi-urban sprawl. An excellent stopover.

rooms	6 twins.
price	€65. Singles €48.
meals	Excellent restaurants nearby.
closed	Rarely.
directions	From A1 Lisbon-Porto or from A15 Santarém-Caldas da Rainha: exit Rio Main. In Rio Maior house signed.

	Senhor Carlos Higgs Madeira
tel	+351 243 992610
fax	+351 243 992611
email	moinhoforal@hotmail.com

B&B

Map 3 Entry 111

Quinta da Ferraria

Ribeira de S. João, 2040-511 Rio Maior, Ribatejo

It stands amid vineyards and olive groves; a channel cut from the river powered the mill and ran a turbine powerful enough to light up the rooms before electricity arrived. Now the whole farm has been thoroughly renovated to create a handsome and professionally run small country hotel. Planned with both business and holiday visitors in mind, its exceptionally green and tranquil setting – and the abundance of water – ensure its appeal for both types of guest. Bedrooms have new pine floors and ceilings, coordinated fabrics and repro furniture. Pine is also the theme of the sitting room, while sisal matting, rugs and open hearth add warmth to the huge space. The restaurant, by contrast, feels functional, due to its wedding-banquet dimensions. But this would make a good stopover when travelling from north to south – especially for families, with its riding stables, bicycles, educational farm museum and excellent pool. You can take a peek at the original olive-milling machinery, too.

rooms	13 + 2: 12 twins/doubles, 1 suite. 2 self-catering apartments.
price	€82-€99. Singles €70-€83. Suite €89-€115. Apts €121-€147.50.
meals	Lunch/dinner €21, by arrangement.
closed	Christmas.
directions	From Lisbon, A1 north for Porto. A15 for Rio Maior; exit 5 for Rio Maior. Left at r'bout for Ribeira de S. João. Signed on right.

	Senhora Teresa Nobre
tel	+351 243 945001
fax	+351 243 945696
email	quinta.ferraria@mail.telepac.pt
web	www.quintaferraria.com

B&B & Self-catering

Map 3 Entry 112

Quinta da Cortiçada
Outeiro da Cortiçada, 2040-173 Rio Maior, Ribatejo

Few settings are as peaceful. The gorgeous, pale pink building, reached by a long poplar-lined avenue, sits in the greenest of valleys. As we arrived a heron rose from the lake and flapped slowly away, a graceful welcome to a gracious place. Inside the silence feels almost monastic – birdsong instead of vespers. There are two elegantly pristine living rooms; one, dignified by the family *oratorio* (altarpiece), has a games table and high French windows on two sides, the other leads to a big wide veranda with colonial-style wicker tables and chairs. Cortiçada feels most sociable and homely at breakfast and dinner (both a treat) when all gather round the huge antique oval table. Large, serene bedrooms lie off the marble corridor and have old beds, antique dressers, thick rugs on polished pine. Bathrooms are impeccable, while sensitive lighting and carefully chosen fabrics make each room feel special. Outside, a peaceful lawn with a pool and willows for shade; vineyards surround you. You can sample wines in their winery, swim, play tennis and, like that heron, fish in the lake.

rooms	8: 3 doubles, 3 twins, 2 suites for 4.
price	€88-€113. Singles €77-€101. Suites €107-€132.
meals	Lunch/dinner with wine €21, by arrangement.
closed	Christmas Day.
directions	From Lisbon A1 north for Porto. Exit at Santarém on EN114 for Rio Maior. In Secorio, Quinta signed on right. After 12km (2km after Outeiro), pink farm in valley.

	Senhora Teresa Nobre
tel	+351 243 470000
fax	+351 243 470009
email	quinta.corticada@mail.telepac.pt
web	www.quintacorticada.com

B&B

Map 3 Entry 113

Casa da Alcáçova

Largo da Alcacova 3, Portas do Sol, 2000-110 Santarém, Ribatejo

Sleep above stone ramparts with drop-dead views to the Tejo river plain below. Equally stunning are the rooms of this 17th-century manor house tucked into Santarém's 13th-century walls – sumptuous! Although adorned with rich furnishings, the house has an easy atmosphere, thanks to these young, engaging, gracious hosts. Flowers in the bedrooms, contemporary art on the stairs, books and magazines in the living room. Bedrooms are unashamedly spoiling with gleaming antiques, real fires, magnificent bedheads and crisp, embroidered bedlinen. The Garette room has a jacuzzi for two, the Bocage room (reputedly he wrote erotic sonnets while staying here) has a fine bed. Bathrooms are pure luxury. The annexe rooms, overlooking the pool, would be ideal for families. Breakfast on the patio beside the fountain, relax underneath shady trees, sip coffee on the terrace with those ravishing views. You might want to dress up for dinner in the elegant dining room; Claúdia gives fresh twists to local dishes while Sérgio has a passion for the local wines. *Minimum stay two nights at weekends.*

rooms	Main house: 5 doubles, 1 twin. Poolside: 2 doubles.
price	€119-€169.
meals	Lunch €29. Dinner €39.
closed	Rarely.
directions	A1 north; exit for Santarém. Follow signs to centre & then to Portas do Sol. House on left side of Portas do Sol square.

	Senhora Maria Claúdia Coutinho dos Santos
tel	+351 243 304030
fax	+351 243 304035
email	info@alcacova.com
web	www.alcacova.com

B&B

Map 3 Entry 114

Photo Ben Ross

alentejo

alentejo

Alentejo means 'beyond the river Tejo' and covers almost a third of the country

Baixo Alentejo
- Stretches from the Algarve to south of Évora. Gently undulating landscape with olive, cork and eucalyptus forests

- Includes **Beja** the agricultural centre of the region, known as the Golden Plain. Visit on a Saturday when the morning market encircles the Castle

- The smart seaside town of **Vila Nova de Milfontes** has great restaurants and sensational beaches known for their surfing. **Zambujeira do Mar** is a quieter beach

Alto Alentejo
- Known for its hill-forts and walled cities rising from the plains: **Évora, Portalegre, Elvas, Estremoz, Marvão, Castelo de Vide** and **Monsaraz**

- Visit the 'white', or marble towns of **Serpa, Moura, Vila Viçosa** and **Borba**. Vila Viçosa is also the centre of the wine growing area for the delicious Alentejo reds

- The newly-built **Alqueva** lake, near Monte Saraz on the border with Spain is a wonderful place to cool off when the heat is on

Quinta da Bela Vista
7320-014 Póvoa e Meadas, Alentejo

Surrounded by gently undulating hills planted with cork and olive and long views you are wonderfully remote here. This working farm sits on the edge of the tiny village, and the family have been here since the 1930s; Dona Maria's uncle built the local dam. This is a genuine Portuguese home. In spite of lofty reception rooms and fancy chandeliers, books, magazines, photos, piano and dried flowers create a mood of intimacy. Of the old-fashioned bedrooms we liked Rosa best (no numbers here, insists Maria), with its own veranda and olive grove views. All the bedrooms are a good size and are blissfully quiet, most with views of the Castelo de Vide. The self-catering houses are more functional, and well-equipped. Your hostess is warm and friendly and it all feels a bit like staying with a favourite aunt. You'll eat well – on meat from the farm and their own eggs, wine and *aguardente* (grape brandy). A relaxed place for a family: snacks are available at all times of day and children will love the big games room and the farm animals. And there are tennis courts, bikes and a pool, too.

rooms	4 + 3: 4 twins/doubles.
	2 houses for 4-6; 1 loft apt for 2.
price	€80. Singles €65. Extra bed €20.
	Houses €130-€170. Apartment €75.
meals	Lunch/dinner €18, by arrangement.
closed	5-20 January.
directions	From Lisbon, A1 to Torres Novas; IP6 to Saida. From Saida IP2, then N118 to Póvoa e Meadas. Signed.

	Senhora Maria Teresa Monteiro dos Santos
tel	+351 245 968125
fax	+351 245 968132
email	belavista@mail.pt

B&B & Self-catering

Map 4 Entry 115

Casa do Parque
Avenida da Aramenha 37, 7320 Castelo de Vide, Alentejo

In a beautiful backwater of the Alentejo, surrounded by stands of chestnut and acacia, the hilltop town is girt around with its 13th-century wall. Steep cobblestone alleys run through the old Jewish *call* to the castle above; down the hill, near the leafy Praça Dom Pedro V, is this gaily canopied, cheap but cheerful hotel. The family are proud of their *hospitalidade portuguesa* and the sense of homeliness spills over into the bedrooms. These are darkly furnished and spotlessly clean, and while bath and shower rooms are on the small side, comfortable mattresses should gently lead you into the arms of Morpheus. In winter, hot-air heating warms the rooms in minutes. Don't miss dinner in the restaurant downstairs and the *migas alentejanas*, or one of the roast dishes; the dining room is a large, functional affair and you may be the only stranger among locals. Guests can enjoy a pool a kilometre away, at the owners' country property. Casa do Parque is a favourite with ramblers; the walking locally is marvellous.

rooms	25 twins/doubles, 1 suite.
price	€45–€55. Singles €30–€40. Suite €58–€65.
meals	Lunch/dinner €14.
closed	Rarely.
directions	From Portalegre E802 for Marvão, then left on E246 to Castelo de Vide. Into centre, then right along top of park; hotel at end on left.

	Senhor Victor Guimarães
tel	+351 245 901250
fax	+351 245 901228
email	casadoparque@mail.pt

Hotel

Map 4 Entry 116

Casa Amarela

Praça D. Pedro V, n.11, 7320-113 Castelo de Vide, Alentejo

Rough granite, wonderful old wooden doors and spacious, pretty rooms – a successful restoration of this sunny yellow house. The rooms are beautifully done with the occasional Portuguese clash of patterns: Arraiolos rugs alongside checked hotel-style armchairs, the odd touch of kitsch. A blue toile de Jouy print enlivens the ground floor bedrooms; by the time you reach the top, it's turned to pink. Bathrooms, with their yellow, marble-like ceramics, are stunning. The breakfast room looks out onto the city wall: you're on the central square of Castelo de Vide, one of those delightful old castellated Portuguese towns. Guarded by a castle, it has narrow cobbled streets and a collection of churches guaranteed to return stray medieval wanderers to the fold. Stands of chestnuts and acacias dotting the surrounding hills and valleys invite exploration on foot or horse. Owners Teresa and Victor will be on hand to look after your needs - but note that they don't live on the spot, so the character and feel here is more hotel than B&B. *Good pool 1km.*

rooms	10: 8 twins/doubles. 2 suites.
price	€100. Suites €150.
meals	Good restaurants nearby.
closed	Rarely.
directions	In centre of Castelo de Vide, opposite church.

	Senhor Victor Guimarães
tel	+351 245 901250
fax	+351 245 901228
email	casaamarelath@mail.pt
web	www.rtsm.pt/casa-amarela

B&B

Map 4 Entry 117

Rua Relógio
Number 7, Castelo de Vide, Alentejo

A lovely little house inside the castle walls of the medieval town of Castelo de Vide. It's in the most privileged position. You park surprisingly nearby, then walk up a cobbled street, past some food shops and bars, and there you are, looking at a very special medieval residence. Inside it's been refurbished in a Danish style. The shower room and a bedroom are on the ground floor, the kitchen, living room and second bedroom on the first floor. Small children may find the open stone steps linking the levels a little challenging. The small, lower twin-bedded room has a terracotta floor, wooden beds and is well lit. The upstairs bedroom has a masonry based double bed, with a foam mattress cut to accommodate a serious curve in the wall. It too is small. The living/dining room is surprisingly roomy, and has a great view across Castelo de Vide, over the castle walls towards Marvão. Its furnishings, which include hi-fi and books, are simple but comfortable. The small galley kitchen sports a tiny sink, but is well designed and equipped. It's a good house for a family with older children, or two couples. *Minimum stay four nights.*

rooms	1 house for 4: 1 double, 1 twin.
price	€65 per day. €415-€515 per week.
meals	Several restaurants nearby.
closed	Rarely.
directions	Folllow signs to Castelo. Up cobbled street, park inside castle wall & walk up through 1st gateway. Right; house 50m on left.

	Henrik Anderson
tel	+351 245 993814
email	fanand1@hotmail.com
web	www.castelo-de-vide.com

Self-catering

Map 4 Entry 118

Quinta da Saimeira

Vale de Rodão, bl2-cx3, 7330-151 Marvão, Alentejo

The setting is peaceful, there's a beautiful view of Marvão, and on clear days to the Spanish mountains. At noon Bonelli's eagles appear from their nest in the rocks above to soar in the warm air, and throughout the day, you can hear birdsong and the tinkling of goats' bells. Choosing the right epithets to describe this place is tricky: top-quality, minimalist, lavish, impeccable, stylish... Two delightful old houses, rebuilt and expanded, make up the accommodation. An enormous effort has been made to achieve high standards and style; in the kitchens everything is brand new, work surfaces are polished granite, hobs are ceramic. Bedrooms are simple and roomy, with wooden beams and very comfy, long, purpose-built beds, covered in big fluffy duvets. Michiel's big black and white photos adorn the walls. He's a professional photographer and will run workshops for two to four people. Through a busy planting programme, Magreet is creating soft garden spaces around the buildings. A highlight here is the sense of swimming to Spain in the infinity swimming pool. *Minimum stay 3 nights; 7 nights in summer.*

rooms	3 houses: 1 for 2, 1 for 4, 1 for 4-6. Single room in main house.
price	€38-€73; €343-€1,015 per week. .
meals	Good restaurants nearby.
closed	Rarely.
directions	Follow m'way to Marvão. After Portagem, pass Jardim; 1st left; 1st right; 1st left. Follow small road to house (1.2km).

	Michiel Ibelings
tel	+351 245 993970
fax	+351 245 909060
email	saimeira@saimeira.com
web	www.saimeira.com

Self-catering

Map 4 Entry 119

Pousada de Marvão/Santa Maria

R. 24 de Janeiro, 7, 7330-122 Marvão, Alentejo

Exit the narrow, cobbled street, enter the simple wooden door and hold your breath – the view will knock your socks off. The rocky landscape surrounding hilltop Marvão is savage in its beauty. This pousada, created out of two old village houses, takes full advantage of its lofty position; the restaurant, sitting room and bar have floor to ceiling windows and you feel as though you're sitting on a cloud. Low, beamed ceilings, simple decoration and friendly staff help create a cosy feel and a relaxed family atmosphere. Bedrooms are modestly comfortable and are gradually being rejuvenated, dark woods and chintzy curtains replaced with rattan furniture and apricot shades. Light, sunny, restful. Some have mountain views, others give glimpses into the winding alleyways of the medieval town. Room 312 is small but has a private terrace; suite 210 has the best views. Marvão is a gorgeous muddle of cobbled streets and dazzlingly white buildings, crowned by its castle – gaze into Spain from its rooftop. Then back for dinner, innovative and regional (goat with thyme cabbage, perhaps?) and those mesmerising views.

rooms	31: 9 doubles, 19 twins, 3 suites.
price	€100-€130. Special offers available - see web site.
meals	Dinner, 3 courses, from €25.
closed	Rarely.
directions	In Marvão follow signs for Pousada Santa Maria.

	Senhor João Amaral
tel	+351 255 460030
fax	+351 255 461353
email	recepcao.sgoncalo@pousadas.pt
web	www.pousadas.pt

Hotel

Map 4 Entry 120

Albergaria el Rei Dom Manuel

Largo de Olivença, 7330-104 Marvão, Alentejo

You are just inside Marvão's castle walls - step from the patio onto the ramparts and gaze across to Spain. This small hotel is run by Manuel and Celeste, a warm and smiley couple who go the extra mile to make your stay memorable. Inside, good colours, shining terracotta, polished wood - it all feels well cared for. Bedrooms are freshly functional with white walls, green doors and shutters, bold patterned curtains, dried flowers and swish crested towels. Book ahead and ask for a room with a castle view; no. 202 is a favourite with its terrace and vistas. Downstairs, with windows at street level, is a very good restaurant. The *entradinhas*, or starters, are a treat: little dishes with chickpea and bacalhão salad, salamis, olives and cheese; main dishes may include such delights as turkey breast with chestnuts, and the vegetables are excellent. Just off the restaurant is a small courtyard patio – a good spot for morning coffee. A stupendous setting, here in Portugal's highest village, and a World Heritage site to boot. This is great value for money.

rooms	15: 8 doubles, 6 twins, 1 single.
price	€60. Singles from €53.
meals	Dinner, 3 courses, from €15.
closed	Rarely.
directions	At entrance to Marvão, Albergaria in Square in front of you. You reach it by the road to the left & can park just in front.

	Manuel & Celeste Gaio
tel	+351 245 909150
fax	+351 245 909159
email	alberg.d.manuel@mail.telepac.pt
web	www.turismarvao.pt

B&B

Map 4 Entry 121

Pomar Velho

Galegos, 7330-072 Marvão, Alentejo

A rural paradise on the Spanish frontier… the tinkling of bells as the shepherd drives his flock home, the rumble of the mule cart further down the valley. A sense of timelessness pervades the 18th-century farmhouse in its five terraced acres of fruit, olive and cork oak trees – an ancient mulberry shading the slate terrace, perfect for an aperitif. From the pool, gaze at the spectacular São Mamede range; if the weather's not too warm, head off for the hills – the walking is great. There's a chestnut-beamed lounge with blue sofas and board games, and a spiral wrought-iron stair down to a dining room whose stone bread oven makes a fine open fireplace. And the granite grape press is as old as the house. Bedrooms are fresh with a French feel: blue limed furniture, big square pillows, crisp white beds. Bathrooms are spotless. Marvão Castle dominates this mountain village where many festivals take place; come in November for the Chestnut Festival when the council subsidises the wine! Carole and Ken have been here for years, have a rather fine wine cellar and love to cook. Breakfasts, too, are feasts.

rooms	4 twins/doubles.
price	€60-€80.
meals	Dinner with wine, €35.
closed	22 December–2 January.
directions	From main road to Spain, left at sign to Galegos. Through village, then, as road starts to descend, 1st track on right for 200m. Park at end of track & ring bell at gate.

	Ken Parr & Carole Young
tel	+351 245 964465
fax	+351 245 964465
email	parryoung@pomarv.jazznet.pt
web	www.pomarv.jazznet.pt

B&B

Map 4 Entry 122

Tapada do Barreiro

Carreiras, Castelo de Vide, 7300 Portalegre, Alentejo

The charming farmhouse sits 500m above the village of Carreiras, in the heart of the São Mamede Natural Park. The whole area is beautiful with wooded hills, rocky crests and fertile valleys running along the Spanish frontier. Sensitively modernized, this is an excellent holiday home: fresh white walls, modern terracotta floors, wonderfully rustic wooden ceilings. The ground floor is given over almost entirely to the kitchen/dining room; French windows open onto a terrace. The bathroom, with washing machine, is also on this floor. Upstairs are three good-sized, wooden-floored bedrooms, two with great views, and a sitting room with log-burner. The garden — with a tiny plunge pool — leads into open hillside studded with olive groves and cork trees. Everything you could wish for is here: a shop, bar and restaurant in the village below, the hilltop village of Marvão for good eating out, the Apartadura lake for swimming and fishing and a fine golf course. Peter, the English owner who lives nearby, can take you on birdwatching and walking trips.

rooms	1 farmhouse for 6 (2 doubles, 1 twin).
price	€400-€500 for 2 per week; extra adult €100; extra child (2-12) €50.
meals	Good restaurants nearby.
closed	Rarely.
directions	8km from Portalegre & 6km from Castelo de Vide. Detailed directions on booking.

Peter & Rosemary Eden

tel	+351 268 629899
fax	+351 268 629899
email	peter_eden@hotmail.com

Self-catering

Map 4 Entry 123

Pousada do Crato

Flor da Rosa, Mosteiro Sta. Maria Flor da Rosa, 7430-999 Crato, Alentejo

You're in the middle of nowhere. This small, bright village on the northern edge of the Alentejan plain has been lived in since Carthaginian times and was given to the Knights Templar (their distinctive cross appears as a motif all over the pousada – even on the delicious convent puddings). The monastery and castle were built in 1356 and the pousada incorporates part of the old building, with the addition of a superb modern wing in warm pink granite. To enter, you must run the gauntlet of a dark, guano-spattered outside cloister (pigeons everywhere) but don't be daunted – once inside, you'll be impressed by the imaginative blend of old and new. A tower has been converted into a sitting area and the bar is in a vaulted refectory with barley sugar-twist pillars, while the vast new bedrooms are given a northern, contemporary flavour by stylish use of wood, creamy fabrics and lots of glass. The restaurant, in an upper cloister, overlooks lawns and fruit trees. There's a cobbled shaded patio in the garden, too, and a big pool. This is a hot part of the Alentejo, so you'll need frequent dips.

rooms	24 twins/doubles.
price	€125-€190. Special offers available - see web site.
meals	Dinner, 3 courses, from €25.
closed	Rarely.
directions	From Portalegre, N119 north towards Crato. There, pousada is signed in village of Flor de Rosa.

	Senhor Domingo Lameiras
tel	+351 245 997210
fax	+351 245 997210
email	recepcao.frosa@pousadas.pt
web	www.pousadas.pt

Hotel

Map 4 Entry 124

Hotel Rural de Lameira
Rua João A azevedo Coutinho no 14, 7440-154 Alter de Chão, Alentejo

Five years ago this 1,000-hectare farm had neither running water nor electricity – they've come some way! The conversion has been an extended Abreu family project and the results are impressive. There's also a surprising harmony for a place where loads of activities – hunting (quail, partridge), fishing, quad bikes, horse riding, windsurfing etc are on the agenda. (Use of pedalos, canoes, bicycles and gym are included in the price.) So, it's terrific if you want sports *and* comfort. Of the two bedroom wings the newer has huge designer rooms, and some suites have mezzanine sitting areas and private terraces with lake views. The other wing has smaller but equally luxurious rooms. All have sound systems, good bathrooms (handmade soaps), and warm, earthy and neutral colours. The bar and restaurant are attractively done, too; beef, lamb and pork come from the farm and the staff are super-helpful. This part of the Alentejo – two hours from Lisbon and with important megalithic sites – has a flattish landscape with echoes of the plains of Africa. Come for a total change of scene.

rooms	30: 5 doubles, 8 twins, 5 suites, 12 mezzanine suites.
price	€80-€175. Singles €60.
meals	Lunch/dinner, à la carte, €15-€18.
closed	Never.
directions	From Coudelaria de Alter do Chão, towards Mata; before Mata left towards Coudelaria. Hotel between Mata & Coudelaria.

	Senhora Annabela Abréu
tel	+351 245 697495
fax	+351 245 697330
email	hrlameira@netc.pt
web	www.hotelruraldalameira.com

Hotel

Map 4 Entry 125

Herdade da Sanguinheira

Longomel, 7400-452 Ponte de Sôr, Alentejo

Well away from the rest of the world, deep in the Alentejo, you're immersed in sunshine, silence and trees. What nicer way to explore the countryside than on horseback – on thoroughbred Lusitanians, too? Annette's husband used to breed them and she runs a professional riding set-up, with two schooling rings and 22 boxes. But you could happily stay here without being horsey at all for Annette is delightful company – German, relaxed and friendly – and this is the pleasantest place to be. The herdade has been attractively restored and adapted and there are two quite separate cottages above the house. Retreat to your roomy, pristine apartment or cottage and be as private as you like, or enjoy the cheerful, convivial atmosphere of the communal areas with their woodburning stoves. Meals are eaten sociably at a long table in the bright dining room and, if you're feeling saddle-sore or idle, you can veg out in front of the television in the little sitting room, well stocked with books, videos, comics and games. There's a big games room, too, and a swimming pool. *Montes Alentejanos member.*

rooms	4 apartments: 1 for 2, 2 for 4, 1 for 6.
price	€72–€190.
meals	Breakfast €5. Dinner from €15.
closed	Rarely.
directions	From Ponte do Sôr towards Gavião. After 6km, pass sign to Longomel. Pass sign at entrance to village of Escusa. 50m on, left onto track (for Centro Equestre); follow for 4km to farm.

	Anette Zurhausen Vaz Pinto
tel	+351 242 283379
fax	+351 242 283410
email	info@sanguinheira.com
web	www.sanguinheira.com

Self-catering

Map 4 Entry 126

Monte da Varzea d'Água de Salteiros

Salteiros, 7400 Ponte de Sôr, Alentejo

The *monte* has been in the family for six generations. It's in a wooded valley close to the river, with the 'big house' down near the gates. Above, like a little village with two rows of houses facing each other, are the farmworkers' cottages and barns – a typical Alentejan set-up. Ducks pad around under the trees and you'll glimpse sheep and lambs through an archway between two of the cottages. There's a dovecote, too. Three of the casas, Ganhão, Pastor and Adega, are in one row with the caretaker's cottage, and have big, plain, well-equipped kitchens. Casa de Eira, at the end (with the advantage for families of being next to the vast new games room) has a kitchenette. The bedrooms are traditional: plain white walls, simple furnishings and *alcobaça* bedspreads on chunky wooden beds. Sunbathe on the lawn, swim in the pool down near the road – or go for a ride in a horse-drawn carriage. Staying here for a day or two will give you a real insight into local agricultural history and you'll have a very friendly greeting on arrival from Senhor Bucho. *Montes Alentejanos member.*

rooms	4 apartments: 1 for 2, 3 for 4.
price	€65-€95.
meals	DIY breakfast included. Good restaurants nearby.
closed	Rarely.
directions	From Lisbon IP6 to Abrantes. Turn off to Ponte de Sor. N244 towards Gaviao. Signposted on left.

	Senhor Luís da Várzea d'Agua de Salteiros
tel	+351 242 283112
fax	+351 242 206235
web	www.montesalentejanos.com.pt

Self-catering

Map 4 Entry 127

Herdade de Chamusquinho
7425 Montargil, Alentejo

This is a relaxing, undemanding place for families to stay – pleasant, functional and miles from anywhere in 150 hectares of cork forest. The four houses are grouped round two sides of a swimming pool, their wide, tiled verandas giving extra space and generous shade. Big, light and airy rooms have crisp clean lines, cool terracotta floors and simple furnishing. Some of the houses have spiral staircases leading to long attic rooms – heaven for children. The kitchens are plain and well equipped, with marble slabs and painted cupboard doors adding a cheerfully rustic note. António's family have owned the herdade for five generations; he used to work on oil rigs off Africa but is now devoting his time to the estate and running the Montes Alentejanos Association. Friendly and easygoing, he's keen to organise trips to watch the cork-cutting, May to July – and to visit local cork factories. There's plenty to do if you're sporty and the great lake at Montargil is not far away, its still blue waters, wooded shores and sandy beaches still relatively undiscovered. *Montes Alentejanos member.*

rooms	4 houses: 3 for 4, 1 for 6.
price	€90-€120.
meals	Good restaurants 5km.
closed	Rarely.
directions	From Montargil, towards Mora. Left towards Foros do Mocho; right at sign to house. Down dirt track for 4km.

	Senhor António Azevedo
tel	+351 242 904567
email	chamusquinho@iol.pt
web	www.montesalentejanos.com.pt

Self-catering

Map 3 Entry 128

Monte da Fraga
Herdade de Paço de Baixo, 7490 Mora, Alentejo

The farm, set in a huge landscape of cork oaks, pines and olive trees, is run by Senhor Almeida, a doctor at the local hospital, and his brothers. Follow a long sandy track past peach orchards and farm buildings to reach the former watermill. It's an attractive building, beautifully positioned above the river, with tantalising views down between the rocks and trees to the water. The accommodation is simple, comfortable and flexible, and works well when a group takes over the whole place. Apart from Casa 1, which is in the old mill, the rooms are close together, their stable doors opening straight off a covered veranda. Beams, terracotta floors and painted iron bedsteads give a traditional, rustic feel; each room has a woodburner, as does (beneath the old bread oven) the communal sitting/dining room. There's a big barbecue outside, plenty of shady places to sit and a small childrens' play area. Or you can go out for a jaunt in a traditional horse-drawn carriage. It all feels peaceful and isolated yet only a few minutes from Mora – and Alfonsos, an exceptionally good restaurant. *Montes Alentejanos member.*

rooms	4 + 2: 4 twins. 2 apartments for 2.
price	Ask for details on booking.
meals	Excellent restaurants nearby.
closed	Rarely.
directions	Just before Mora, opposite petrol station, right & follow road down over river, then follow signs along dirt road through farm.

	Senhor Manuel Caldas Almeida
tel	+351 266 439125
fax	+351 266 403243
email	manuel.caldas.almeida@net.pt
web	www.montesalentejanos.com.pt

B&B & Self-catering

Map 3 Entry 129

Monte do Padrão

Figueira e Barros, 7840 Avis, Alentejo

Olive groves and cork trees as far as the eye can see. This really is the back of beyond, but delightfully so. Leave the main road and a lengthy avenue of olive trees brings you at last to a long, low farmhouse. It's rather grand, with creamy walls, lush creepers, pot-bellied Spanish-style railings at the windows, great green pots and a swimming pool. But it's a real family house on a real working farm; you pass a weighbridge and tractors on the way in. Senhor de Carvalho, the jolly owner, is a retired vet with five daughters and 12 grandchildren and cares very much about preserving the countryside for them. The farm is organic, producing olive oil, sunflowers and cereal crops, as well as raising cows, pigs and sheep. Inside, the house is very comfortable and traditional. Cast-iron beds are painted dark green, the heavy wooden furniture is draped with embroidered linen cloths, the washstands are marble and the bathrooms are big, white and slightly old-fashioned. It could hardly be more Portuguese. This is hunting territory and there's a large annexe to house visiting sportsmen. *Montes Alentejanos member.*

rooms	7: 6 twins/doubles, 1 suite.
price	From €95. Suite €120.
meals	Lunch & dinner from €20, by arrangement.
closed	Rarely.
directions	Exit Figueria e Barros towards Alter do Chão, left at sign for Monte do Padrão & Turismo Rural.

Senhor Jose Godinho de Carvalho

tel	+351 242 465153
fax	+351 242 465327
email	jose-trancas@netc.com
web	www.montesalentejanos.com.pt

B&B

Map 4 Entry 130

Monte dos Aroeirais

Trav. Paiva Lobato, 8, 7460 Fronteira, Alentejo

From the moment you go through the front door, straight into the big sitting/dining room, you feel well looked after. Helena has achieved a happy blend of the traditionally Alentejan and the modern stylish. Low beams criss-cross the ceiling, antlers hang above the big fireplace (this is hunting country), chairs and lamps are invitingly placed, pictures and hangings add interest to bright white walls. It's all very cosily and attractively done. The six suites are in the main house, which adds a pleasant feeling of intimacy, and are delightful, with masses of space, pretty fabrics and some inspired, luxurious touches (one has a fairytale white four-poster bed). Each has its own sitting area and charming bathroom; two have private terraces. There's a swimming pool and a pleasant shady courtyard to take a book and a drink. If you enjoy riding, you'll be in your element: take lessons in the covered school or go out in the gentle hills among the olive trees and sheep. Helena and her daughter Maria José are immensely friendly and warm. The *Monte* has just won a sustainable tourism award. *Montes Alentejanos member.*

rooms	6 + 1: 6 suites for 2. 1 apartment for 4.
price	€76. Apartment €380 for 2; €550 for 4, per week.
meals	Dinner by arrangement.
closed	Apartments closed October-May. B&B open all year.
directions	From Lisbon head to Estremoz & then Fronteira. Follow signs to house from Fronteira.

	Senhora Maria Helena Carvalho
tel	+351 245 604250
fax	+351 245 609049
email	jose-trancas@netc.pt
web	www.montedosaroeirais.com

B&B & Self-catering

Map 4 Entry 131

Pousada de Sousel

São Miguel, Serra de S. Miguel, 7470 – 999 Sousel, Alentejo

Gaze to the ends of the earth, and then a bit further. The views from the dazzlingly white hilltop pousada, just north of the marble towns, spill over the Alentejo plains, a carpet of olive groves receding to a blue horizon. Sunrise, moonrise, sunset… they take your breath away. Wisely, the hotel doesn't try to compete. Airy, bright and modern, it has wide marble corridors leading to rooms unfussily furnished – tiled floors, creamy walls and light, wooden beds. A simple rug, elegant chairs and floor length curtains add softness. You'll probably sleep with the curtains open – let the sunrise steal in over the balcony and wake you. Bathrooms are elegant and cool in pinky-white marble. Hunting is a passion here; hunting scenes and trophy heads decorate the walls while game features on the dinner menu. A wide terrace means every mealtime allows you to savour the views. The large, circular swimming pools – a separate one for children – are spectacularly set on the lowest terrace with plenty of room for loungers. Comfortable, unpretentious, friendly – and thrilling at full moon.

rooms	32: 28 twins/doubles, 4 suites.
price	€100-€145. Special offers available - see web site.
meals	Dinner, 3 courses, from €25.
closed	Rarely.
directions	From Estremoz, N245 towards Alter do Chão. When you approach Sousel, Pousada is signposted. It is outside the town on top of a hill.

	Senhora Maria Amalia Vaz de Silva
tel	+351 268 550050
fax	+351 268 551155
email	recepcao.smiguel@pousadas.pt
web	www.pousadas.pt

Hotel

Map 4 Entry 132

Pousada de Estremoz
Rainha Santa Isabel, Lg. D. Dinis, 7100-509 Estremoz, Alentejo

Since this is a real palace, built for the sainted Queen Isabel of Aragon, you'll want to approach it in a regal way. So... don't go into town, but follow signs to the *centro historico*, arrive at the castle walls and enter over the magnificent drawbridge. The pousada is in the former armoury and has a right royal grandeur: high vaulted ceilings, elaborate arches, acres of red velvet and carpet, gilt, tassels and swags galore. The bedrooms, especially those on the first floor, are similarly magnificent, stuffed with oil paintings and dark massive antique furniture. It's one of the most splendid of the pousadas, impeccably run by a glossy, attentive staff. The striking central courtyard is dominated by the castle keep; a small garden full of semi-tropical trees and shrubs leads to a swimming pool by the castle ramparts and views over the town to the plain. The restaurant is said to be good and you can actually get a reasonable cup of tea here – they even have teapots! On the walls of the chapel are *azulejos* depicting the life of Queen Isabel and the nearby museum has a fine collection of folk art.

rooms	33: 30 twins/doubles, 2 singles, 1 suite.
price	€165-€210. Special offers available - see Pousadas web site.
meals	Dinner, 3 courses, from €25.
closed	Rarely.
directions	In the centre of Estremoz, follow sign for Centro histórico. Pousada signed inside the Castelo of Rainha Santa Isabel.

	Senhor Anibal Coxexo
tel	+351 268 332075
fax	+351 268 332079
email	recepcao.staisabel@pousadas.pt
web	www.pousadas.pt

Hotel

Map 4 Entry 133

Casa de Borba

Rua da Cruz 5, 7150-125 Borba, Alentejo

A gem of a house in the centre of lovely Borba, built by Senhora's family in the 18th century, surrounded by its estate (olives, livestock, vines). An extraordinary neo-classical staircase leads you to the first-floor quarters (ask for help with heavy bags: there is no lift) where fine bedrooms have high, delicately moulded ceilings and parquet floors softened by Arraiolos rugs. And there is no shortage of family antiques! The Bishop's Room (where the Archbishop of Évora stayed) has an 18th-century canopied bed, Grandmother's Room an unusual lift-up sink. There are claw-footed baths, elegant curtains framing windows that overlook a delectable garden, and jewel-like colours in furnishings and flowers. The lounge and breakfast room are similarly elegant; breakfast arrives via the dumb waiter. Your hostess is quietly charming and skimps on nothing to please you; at night, hot water to drink is delivered to your room, together with cake and a selection of teas. There's a long covered gallery, and a billiard room too. This is *turismo de habitacão* at its best.

rooms	5: 4 twins, 1 four-poster.
price	€80. Singles €70.
meals	Restaurants nearby.
closed	20-28 December.
directions	From Estremoz, N4 to Borba. House in town centre, close to post office (Correios).

	Senhora Maria José Tavares Lobo de Vasconcellos
tel	+351 268 894528
fax	+351 268 841448

B&B

Map 4 Entry 134

Aldeia de São Gregório

Rio de Moinhos, 7150-390 Villa Borba, Alentejo

São Gregório is a sweet hamlet set in beautiful countryside, saved from dereliction by the conversion of its old houses into delightful bed and breakfast accommodation. The renovation exudes simplicity and good taste, from the bright and cheerful hues of the Alentejan furniture and textiles to the whitewashed walls, terracotta floors, rustic fireplaces and low beams. There are nine dwelling houses in all, with varying mixes of gaily painted woodwork, cast-iron beds, verandas and vineyard views – they are roomy, cosy, comfortable. Outside: a sociable, village-like atmosphere, plenty of shady spots in which to sit and chat, and flowers and shrubs that look good to the end of summer. Although all houses bar one have kitchenettes, they're not really equipped for serious catering. Carla happily looks after guests serving local honey, jams and bread are served at breakfast, and there are good restaurants in Rio de Moinhos. If you fancy a picnic but don't feel like leaving, wander 200m down the hill to the dreamy pool with its lawn and shaded sitting area.

rooms	9 houses: 6 for 2, 1 for 3, 1 for 4, 1 for 5.
price	€70-€160; €490-€1,120 per week. Breakfast included.
meals	Good restaurant in village.
closed	Christmas & rarely.
directions	A6, exit for Borba on to Barro Branco & towards S. Tiago de Rio de Moihos. At entrance to village, left; where road forks right until sign for Aldeia.

	Senhora Ana Guimarães
tel	+351 268 802140
fax	+351 268 802140
email	saogregorio@iol.pt
web	www.sgregorio.com

B&B

Map 4 Entry 135

Monte da Fornalha
7100 Arcos-Estremoz, Alentejo

Arriving here is a delight – tall trees and greenery, an oasis in a scorching part of the Alentejo. Once a row of workers cottages housing 10 families, it has been successfully converted to B&B rooms with private terraces. Orlanda is friendly and informal. Originally from Madeira, she has travelled a lot, and her love of Morocco is reflected in the colourful, eclectic style. The interiors are beautiful, the décor making good use of terracotta and blue; there are lots of white sofas and armchairs, and everything has a feel of good quality and taste. The gorgeous, light bedrooms, full of space, have pristine white bedding and prettily edged pillows. Two of them have *pias* – little stone sinks with rose petals floating on the water. There is a wonderful living room too. Outside, trees and shrubs lead to olive groves, and some big shaded terraces next to a smallish pool. If you manage to tear yourself away and explore, you're conveniently near the main road that brings you to the wine-growing estates – and Évora, Estremoz and the marble towns. *Minimum stay two nights.*

rooms	5: 2 twins/doubles, 3 family rooms.
price	€95–€120. Singles €75.
meals	Dinner €25, for 6 or more only.
closed	Rarely.
directions	From Lisbon, A6 to Spain, exit at Borba onto A4 for Estremoz. After 900m right on to country road. Follow signs for 1km.

	Senhora Orlanda Alves
tel	+351 268 840314
fax	351 268 891885
email	monte.da.fornalha@oninet.pt
web	www.montedafornalha.com

B&B

Map 4 Entry 136

Pousada de Vila Viçosa

D. João IV, Convento das Chagas, 7160 Vila Viçosa, Alentejo

A monastic calm combines with gentle luxury in this restored former convent. Fragments of frescos, richly tiled dados and vaulted ceilings give a sense of history, in spite of modern enhancements, while piped Gregorian chanting adds to the mood. Built round a secluded cloister garden, some bedrooms overlook the cloisters while others overlook the town's patchwork of red roofs. All are a good size and have a fresh, understatedly modern style; white walls, rugs on polished floors, soft lights and brightly coloured fabrics. The suites are more elaborate, one with hand-painted bedheads, another with a cream-draped four-poster. Ask for a room with a pretty trellised balcony. The vaulted dining room is grander than the other main rooms and has a Last Supper fresco, baroque style chairs, gold colours and glowing terracotta. Good, traditional Alentejan fare is well served by bright young staff. In warm weather, eat outside in the atmospherically lit cloisters. With a herb garden and swimming pool, this is a blissfully peaceful place – despite being in the heart of 'museum town' Vila Viçosa.

rooms	32: 10 doubles, 20 twins, 2 suites.
price	€125–€180. Special offers available – see web site.
meals	Dinner, 3 courses, from €25.
closed	Rarely.
directions	In Vila Viçosa follow signs for Pousada.

	Senhor Anibal Coxexo
tel	+351 268 980742
fax	+351 268 980747
email	recepcao.djoao@pousadas.pt
web	www.pousadas.pt

Hotel

Map 4 Entry 137

Casa de Peixinhos

7160 Vila Viçosa, Alentejo

Like vintage port, a rich, mellow experience. Down the avenue of orange trees, pass beneath the portal into the cobbled courtyard and there is the castellated façade, its exotic arches and triple turrets softened by whitewashed walls and broad bands of ochre. Inside, the mood is classical and aristocratic; much of the décor is period, and formal, but everything sparkles. The sitting room is a handsome introduction to the house, with its mouldings, leather three-piece and coat of arms above the hearth. Leading off it is the dining room: more mouldings, gold drapes, chandeliers, grand flowers. You wouldn't feel out of place dressing up for dinner; food is traditional Alentejan. Bedrooms are comfortable and old-fashioned, among the best we've seen, with wrought-iron beds and thick fabrics, some in blues, others in deep red; all have gorgeous bathrooms of local marble. In contrast to the grandiosity of the house is a new complex of big, swish, terraced apartments, nicely secluded on the far side of the olive groves and the pool. Vila Viçosa is walking distance – a modest delight.

rooms	8 + 26 apartments: 7 twins/doubles, 1 suite. 26 self-catering apts for 2-6.
price	€105-€140. Singles €86. Suite €130. Extra bed €22.50. Apts €90-€150; €540-€900 p.w..
meals	Lunch/dinner €30, on request.
closed	Rarely.
directions	From Évora to Vila Viçosa. There, follow signs for Borba into Vila V. town centre. Just past Mercado Municipal, left & follow signs.

	Senhor José Passanha
tel	+351 268 980472
fax	+351 268 881348

B&B & Self-catering

Map 4 Entry 138

Herdade do Monte Branco

Rio de Moinhos, 7150 BRB Borba, Alentejo

Few places can be more tranquil than this estate, on the sunny flanks of a hillside near Borba. Well off the beaten track, the farmhouse and outbuildings have been converted into apartments by their architect owner. (Your Lisbon-based hosts may be around at weekends.) They are well furnished in Alentejan style with an arty feel: whitewashed walls, antique or repro beds, hand-painted tiles. Bedrooms are countrified, simple and spotless, with painted beams, stone floors and comfortable beds. Bathrooms are good, kitchens have microwaves only (except in the casa for eight), and breakfast is included in the price. Wake to birdsong and rustling trees. There's a pool, a large, rustic games room/bar and a dining room where you may eat by arrangement. The Herdade is near cork trees and forest and there's a lovely short walk to a freshwater lake hidden in the trees. On the edge of the Sierra you are spoiled for walks. Or visit the production centres of cork, wine and cheese, explore the prehistoric sites, go clay-pigeon shooting. A good spot for nature lovers and for families.

rooms	4 self-catering apartments for 2-8.
price	€55-€90. Weekly rates available.
meals	Dinner €18, by arrangment.
closed	Rarely.
directions	On A2 from Lisbon, southbound, A6 eastbound; exit at Estremoz & join N4. Follow signs to Gloria & then to Rio de Moinhos. Monte Branco signed to right.

The Medeiros family

tel	+351 214 830834
mobile	+351 962 988099
email	montebranco@netcabo.pt
web	www.herdadedomontebranco.com

Self-catering

Map 4 Entry 139

Hotel Convento de São Paulo

Aldeia da Serra, 7170-120 Redondo, Alentejo

Superb in all respects, this massive monastery was built by Paulist monks who came to these mountain slopes in the 12th century. It is still imbued with an atmosphere of spirituality and calm, and the 54,000 hand-painted tiles that decorate chapel and corridors comprise the largest collection in Europe. A red carpet softens terracotta floors and sweeps you along to the rooms, each occupying two cells: luxurious yet uncluttered, in keeping with São Paulo's past. Bathrooms have brass taps and white marble; little cakes are put out for you when staff turn back the sheets before bed. The living rooms are no less interesting, filled with modern art and family heirlooms, atmospherically lit by oil lamps and candles, and there's a bar with billiards and cards. In spite of vaulted chapel ceilings, the dining room is an intimate setting for authentic regional dishes; staff are young and charming, breakfasts are lavish. Outside, a beautiful tiled patio depicting the four seasons, a shaded pool with a view, and walks through the wooded slopes of the 600-hectare estate. The setting is exquisite and the spirit soars.

rooms	33 twins/doubles.
price	€130-€195. Singles €115-€167.
meals	Lunch/dinner €60.
closed	Rarely.
directions	From Lisbon on m'way A6 for Madrid. Exit for Estremoz, then towards Elvas for approx. 5km, then for Redondo. Hotel 15km further.

	Senhora Maria Helena Passão
tel	+351 266 989160
fax	+351 266 989167
email	hotelconvspaulo@mail.telepac.pt
web	www.hotelconventospaulo.com

Hotel

Map 4 Entry 140

Água d'Alte

Aldeia da Serra Dossa nº 14, 7170-120 Redondo, Alentejo

This amalgamation of a number of workers' cottages on an old farm is in a class of its own. And the peace is a balm. The overall style is striking and classy: beautiful colours, a grand living room, a gorgeous pool. En route to the dining room is an interior courtyard – and there's a second tiny one for Maria's herb garden, tucked behind the breakfast buffet. The quest for quality is evident from the soothing fabrics in the bedrooms to the bathrooms that combine lavishness with originality. Every day something different is served for breakfast; during quiet periods Maria, your warm and friendly hostess, is happy to rustle up a good lunch or dinner, too. The serene saltwater pool overlooks an olive grove, home to seven breeding horses, and there are bikes and games. Itineraries and maps are available, showing places of interest and good restaurants too, and there are walks from the door. Maria and Victor are naturally keen to keep the place in perfect condition, so bear this in mind if travelling with hordes of little ones!

rooms	7 + 2: 2 doubles, 5 suites. 1 house for 2, 1 house for 4.
price	€75-€80. Singles from €70. Suites €80-€95. Apartments €110-€170; €700-€1,190 per week.
meals	Lunch & dinner occasionally available, from €25.
closed	Rarely.
directions	Between Rédondo & Estremoz; just outside Aldeia da Serra.

	Victor & Maria Alexandra Fernandes
tel	+351 266 989170
fax	+351 266 989179
email	herdade@aguadalte.com
web	www.aguadalte.com

B&B

Map 4 Entry 141

Casa de Terena

Rua Direita, 45, 7250-065 Terena-Alandroal, Alentejo

A seductive blend of eclectic pieces and natural colours and textures: African wall hangings, unusual pottery, simple, stylish chic. Bedrooms are fresh and comfortable in terracottas, olive greens, golds and creams – and blissfully cool for this sun-baked part of the Alentejo. Stella and Jeremy have brought new life to the relaxed manor house; they lived in South Africa and their creativity has transformed the old place. They are natural hosts, love having people to stay and give you delicious food – go first for a sundowner and canapés at the Castelo de Terena and watch the 1,000-year old castle's walls turn orange with the setting sun. Uplighters in the downstairs sitting room have a similar effect on the wafer-bricked vaulting; wallow in sumptuous sofas before a monumental fire. Some bedrooms have views to countryside and lake, others have balconies and look onto cobbled village life. Spin off on a cycling safari picnic, try your hand at archery or visit the historical masterpieces of the area – your hosts will show you it all. Deep peace in a remarkably authentic part of the country.

rooms	6: 3 doubles, 2 twins, 1 family room.
price	€80-€90. Singles €65-€75. Extra bed €25.
meals	Dinner €20, on request. Good restaurants nearby.
closed	15 December-15 January.
directions	From Lisbon A6/IP7 for Évora, exit junc. 8 (Estremoz & Borba). From Borba, N255 to Alandroal & Terena. House in upper village, near to castle.

	Jeremy & Stella Doveton-Helps
tel	+351 268 459132
fax	+351 268 459155
email	casadeterena@mail.telepac.pt
web	www.casadeterena.com

B&B

Map 4 Entry 142

Monte Branco
Motrinos, 7200 Monsaraz, Alentejo

Olive groves, cornfields and the spectacular medieval village of Monsaraz peering down from its battlemented walls… views from the farmstead have changed little in the last few hundred years. Its clutch of converted farmworkers' cottages, set amongst lawns and palm trees, has a sleepy timelessness. Rooms are cosy with beamed ceilings, exposed brick walls, wooden shutters and polished floors. Authentic features have been kept – some rooms have inglenook fireplaces, others domed ceilings or slate kitchen countertops. The style is intimate with every inch of space put to good use. Two cottages squeeze a bunk bed above a double bed while others slip beds into alcoves. Furniture is colourful-rustic with a comfy, lived-in feel – rush-seated chairs, throws on sofas, scrubbed tables. The simple bathrooms are prettily tiled. Kitchens, although small, have an Alentejan charm to their quirkiness. Most cottages have a private terrace while the shared pool is surrounded by a covered barbecue area. Motrinos village, a short walk, has a handful of good local shops. A genuine homely feel. *Minimum stay two nights.*

rooms	4 cottages: 1 for 2-3, 1 for 4-5, 2 for 6-8.
price	€65-€140; €450-€980 per week.
meals	Several restaurants nearby.
closed	Rarely.
directions	From Évora towards Monsaraz; before Monsaraz (historico) left for Motrinos (Alandroal). Just before Motrinos right for Monte Branco. At farm, right & house just there.

	Jane Doody
tel	+351 219291304
email	janedoody@hotmail.com
web	www.janedoody.com

Map 6 Entry 143

Monte Saraz

Horta dos Révoredos, Barrada, 7200-172 Monsaraz, Alentejo

Marc, the new Dutch owner, had the good taste to choose and buy this stylish property. When we visited not all the bedrooms were ready, and the cottages were awaiting finishing touches, but, with Mark's background in sustainable development, all bodes well. Monte Saraz is a lovely place, set below medieval Monsaraz in a very quiet area of goat herds and olive trees – you approach through some very gnarled, twisted and old ones. The main house is a delightful building with vaulted brick ceilings and ancient wooden doors; push open a pair at the top of the steps to enter. Inside, a cool and calming atmosphere: carved wooden furniture, flagstone floors, Persian rugs. The cottages have been repainted white, and show great promise. The bedrooms in the house are in Alentejan style, some with views of Monsaraz. Outside are lovely gardens, trees and nice shady corners to sit in, and the pool is gorgeous, framed by the arches of an old olive press. Proper Dutch breakfasts are served, and the view of Monsaraz, perched on a hilltop, is wonderful – particularly poignant when floodlit at night.

rooms	2 + 3: 2 doubles. 3 self-catering cottages for up to 4.
price	€85. Cottage €505 per week.
meals	Good restaurants nearby.
closed	Rarely.
directions	From Évora, N258 to Reguengos de Monsaraz; then Monsaraz via São Pedro de Corval. 4km before Monsaraz, left at sign for Anta, along track. At T-junc., right; 1st house.

	Marc P. Lammerink
tel	+351 266 557385
fax	+351 266 557485
email	info@montesaraz.com
web	www.montesaraz.com

B&B & Self-catering

Map 6 Entry 144

Hotel Rural Horta da Moura

Apartado 64, Monsaraz, 7200-999 Monsaraz, Alentejo

Monsaraz! It's one of the treasures of the Alentejo, an ancient hilltop fortress village of cobbled streets and whitewashed walls, visible for miles. On the slopes below lies this estate, its name recalling the Moorish invaders. The hotel's purpose-built extension to the old house has been beautifully done and has plenty of regional character: exposed stone and local slate, arched wafer-brick Moorish ceilings and rustic chunky beams. Both suites and rooms are a good size, comfortable and attractive with traditional dark wood beds, monogrammed pillowcases and beautiful, locally woven rugs. The whole place feels reassuringly solid, and the thick walls keep you cool in the hottest weather. Try the regional restaurant's meat and fish, the superb local wines and the good vegetarian dishes; take a drink to the circular bar with its rooftop terrace for fresh air with views. Further pleasures include a games room with billiards, tennis, a pool and, a mile or so down the road, Portugal's newest man-made lake – sail off from the hotel's jetty. There's also an elegant horse-drawn carriage to ride, and horses and bikes.

rooms	26: 6 twins/doubles, 20 suites.
price	€85-€100. Suites €100-€125. Full-board option €30 p.p. extra.
meals	Lunch/dinner €17.50.
closed	Rarely.
directions	To Monsaraz; just below fortress walls, do not turn right, follow road to Mourão. Signed.

Senhora Sara Zambujinho

tel	+351 266 550100
fax	+351 266 550108
email	hortadamoura@hotmail.com
web	www.hortadamoura.pt

Hotel

Map 6 Entry 145

Refúgio da Vila Hotel & Cooking School
Largo Dr Miguel Bombarda 8, 7220-369 Portel, Alentejo

Don't be fooled by the hotel's name: it is in the busy Alentejan town of Portel.
Under the castle walls, in fact. The Vieira family have done a great job here and
the once-abandoned building is now grand and infused with light. The designers
have combined vaulted ceilings and character with a refreshingly modern feel,
there's much exposed brickwork, and trompe l'oeil paintings on the first floor.
The luxurious bedrooms have wooden floors, lush harmonious fabrics, generous
beds and a cool, airy feel. And space. Bathrooms are woody, and decked with
fluffy white towels and robes. Five rooms have terraces with views of the castle;
the four 'garden' rooms are also terraced. Sitting rooms, too, are comfortable and
cool, and the very pretty restaurant is in the old coach house with stone pillars
and a vaulted ceiling. Outside is equally appealing – plenty of shady places on the
large lawn, several terraces smartly furnished, play equipment for children and a
big pool. Sofia has always dreamed of owning a place such as this and now she has
her own cookery school; the gardens supply the vegetables and herbs.

rooms	30: 18 twins/doubles in annexe, 12 twins/doubles in house.
price	€80-€118.
meals	Lunch/dinner €25-€30.
closed	Christmas.
directions	From Lisbon A6 to Évora; IP2 towards Béja. Turn off for Portel & follow signs to Hotel Rural.

	Senhora Sofia Vieira
tel	+351 266 619010
fax	+351 266 619011
email	info@refugiovila.com
web	www.refugiodavila.com

Hotel

Map 6 Entry 146

Herdade da Samarra

7090 Viana do Alentejo, Alentejo

José has thought of everything – even kennels for your dogs! This is a new enterprise for the organic farmer and affable host; an enthusiast about all things Alentejan he is a director of an organisation promoting local produce. His is a new house, approached by an avenue of young trees, a typical herdade with a cool veranda looking onto a pool with palm trees and lawns. It may lack the mellow patina of age but it is an attractive building and inside is as comfortable as can be. The large sitting/dining room with bar has tiled columns and gleaming red-tiled floor. Bedrooms (air-conditioned) are elegant, neat and new – a touch of toile de Jouy here, a polished antique there. The rooms have bird names: the area is an ornithologist's dream. Food is regional, and home-grown lamb roasted in home-pressed olive oil could be on the menu. There's lot to see and do beside lolling by the pool: watersports on the nearby lake, castles at Alvito, Portel and Viana, Roman remains at Cucufate. As for Évora, it is so teeming with medieval monuments it has been classed a World Heritage site. *Horses available in summer.*

rooms	5 twins/doubles.
price	€63.
meals	Dinner €20, on request.
closed	Rarely.
directions	From Évora for Viana do Alentejo (about 2km). Large white & yellow entrance, just off to right.

Senhor José Manuel
Pertana de Vasconcelos
tel   +351 266 953670
fax   +351 266 705045
email herdsamarra@yahoo.com

B&B

Map 6 Entry 147

Pousada do Alvito

Castelo de Alvito, Apartado 9 Alvito, 7920-999 Alvito, Alentejo

From the arched window of your bedroom, you look onto an unexpectedly green and park-like garden. Peacocks strut and call between the palms and there's an inviting swimming pool. The pousada is at the top of an attractive little town surrounded by olives, vines and cork trees. It's a 15th-century fortified palace, an intriguing mix of Moorish and Manueline architecture with a quiet cool interior. Only the restaurant is new and it fits in well – a low vaulted gallery with glassed-in arches overlooking the cobbled courtyard. The whole place has a pleasantly intimate atmosphere and the staff are young and eager. Attractive bedrooms are enhanced by clever use of fabrics; the Queen's Room has a beautiful lacy stucco ceiling and a four-poster bed. Don't be put off by the unprepossessing approach, up a grimy flight of steps; everything else is immaculate. From the tower and the battlements you can gaze on the town and the rolling countyside. This is an olive-oil producing area and in the summer it's hot, hot, hot. But, not far away, is a *barragem* (resevoir) where you can fish, boat and swim.

rooms	20: 7 doubles, 12 twins, 1 suite.
price	€125–€200. Special offers available - see web site.
meals	Dinner, 3 courses, from €25.
closed	Rarely.
directions	From Évora IP2 south towards Beja. Rght to Vidigueira & on to Alvito. Pousada in middle of town.

	Senhor Bruno Henrique
tel	+351 284 480700
fax	+351 284 485383
email	recepcao.alvito@pousadas.pt
web	www.pousadas.pt

Hotel

Map 5 Entry 148

Casa Santos Murteira

Rua de S. Pedro 68/70/72, 7090-041 Alcáçovas, Alentejo

The façade captures the eye with its exquisite wrought-iron balconies and baroque flourishes above the cornicing but in spite of the seigneurial air, there's an easy, unpretentious elegance within. The lounge is a gem with its polished parquet floor, comfy chairs, chandelier, fine paintings and books. The cream and mustard dining/breakfast room, too, is special: light floods in from shuttered windows on two sides and there is a beautiful Arraiolos rug beneath a Queen Anne-style dining table. Just outside is a terrace for meals when the weather is warm. The back of the house has more of an Alentejan feel with its terracotta tiles, wafer bricking and bands of blue highlighting windows and doors. A spring-fed swimming pool sits prettily in an orange-treed garden, romantic with crocheted hammock; no wonder the Casa is popular for weddings. The bedrooms are among the nicest anywhere: fine old beds, marble-topped bedside tables, planked and rugged floors, splendid moulded ceilings. Your hostess is proud of her family home and works hard to make your stay memorable.

rooms	6 twins/doubles.
price	€80. Singles €70. Family room from €75.
meals	Dinner occasionally available, on request.
closed	Rarely.
directions	From Évora, ring road round town until Alcáçovas signed. There, Rua de S. Pedro runs parallel to main street; house halfway up on left.

	Senhora Maria da Encarnação Fernandes
tel	+351 266 948220
fax	+351 266 948229
email	casasantosmurteira@iol.pt
web	www.montedosobral.pt

B&B

Map 5 Entry 149

Pousada de Évora/Lóios

Lg. Conde Vila Flor, 7000-804 Évora, Alentejo

An intriguing juxtaposition – a 16th-century monastery rubbing shoulders with a temple of Diana. Inside the monastery, secularised into a private house at the time of the Dissolution, there's another strange union – monastic architecture and baroque comfort. The bedrooms are small, with vaulted ceilings and religious pictures recalling their early life as cells, but there the austerity ends. They are lavishly furnished with antique mahogany beds and brocade and lace aplenty. This gorgeousness pervades the rest of the pousada: 18th-century frescos (especially fine in the imperial *sala*) provide a backdrop for velvet plush sofas, brocade curtains, gilt mirrors, Arraiolos rugs, vases of intoxicating lilies... The arches on the ground floor are gothic, those on the floor above romanesque, with remnants of the Manueline scattered about. Part of the cloister, now glassed in, is a restaurant serving excellent food. The staff are good, too – well-trained and friendly young men. Outside is a vine-covered cobbled terrace with a bar, rattan chairs and Moroccan lamps.

rooms	32: 30 twins/doubles, 2 suites.
price	€165-€210. Special offers available - see web site.
meals	Dinner, 3 courses, from €25.
closed	Rarely.
directions	Follow signs to the centre of Évora. Pousada is signposted, next to temple of Diana.

	Senhor Paolo Silva
tel	+351 266 730070
fax	+351 266 707248
email	recepcao.loios@pousadas.pt
web	www.pousadas.pt

Hotel

Map 4 Entry 150

Casa de Sam Pedro
Quinta de Sam Pedro, 7000-173 Évora, Alentejo

A delectable address, close to wonderful Évora and utterly bucolic. A sense of well-being takes hold as soon as you turn off the narrow country road and follow a winding track through old olive groves. The grand house offers a benevolent greeting; acacias throw shade across its uncluttered façade and the air is filled with birdsong. Inside, the decoration is gentle, unshowy: a grandfather clock, coats of arms, parquet floors set against old *azulejos* (tiles), gilt mirrors and the family china. The dining room is elegant but cosy, the kitchen as a great kitchen should be, the real heart of the house. Snuggle down with a good book on one of the sofas in front of the white-tiled hearth, beneath the collection of old plates and copper saucepans. (You may breakfast here, too.) The peace of the place makes you more aware of those gently creaking floorboards as you climb to your room. Here the decoration is again subdued and utterly 'family'; perhaps a Mater Dolorosa above a bed, a lovely old antique wardrobe, or a fine old dressing table. Wholly authentic and admirable.

rooms	4 twins/doubles.
price	€50-€70.
meals	Available locally.
closed	15-30 August; 15-30 December.
directions	From Évora follow sign to Arraiolos; right at sign for Quinta da Espada. Stay on dirt track until you reach house.

	Senhor António Pestana de Vasconcellos
tel	+351 266 707731
fax	+351 266 752034
email	casa-spedro@ciberguia.pt

B&B

Map 4 Entry 151

Pensão Policarpo

Rua da Freiria de Baixo 16, 7000-898 Évora, Alentejo

This grand town mansion was built by the Counts of Lousã in the 16th century, only to be lost to the State during the purges of Pombal. It was later rescued by the Policarpo family. They have created the most unpretentious of B&Bs, fronted by Michèlle, who is French, and who still enjoys her guests. It's a simple city guesthouse, popular and busy, and the breakfast room is delightful, with its lofty, vaulted brick ceiling and huge windows capturing the morning sunlight. The sweet sound of fado takes your first meal of the day into a lyrical dimension. There's a terrace where you can eat out on warm days, and a cosy sitting room in the former kitchen – hence the hand-painted tiles. No bar here but plenty in town. Bedrooms are reached via the original granite staircase; some have vaulted ceilings, others pretty hand-painted Alentejan furniture, and most have their own small shower rooms. Ask for the room with the Azulego frieze – it's the nicest – and expect some noise: this is a university city! The private car park, unsecured but safe, is a big plus.

rooms	20: 6 doubles, 2 triples, 1 quadruple; 3 twins with shower & separate wc; 4 doubles, 2 twins, 1 triple, 1 single sharing bath.
price	€55-€65. Singles €50-€60. Family room €75-€85.
meals	Restaurants nearby.
closed	Christmas Day.
directions	In Évora ring road round city until Policarpo signs (close to university). Free car park under archway (R. Conde da Serra da Tourega).

	Michèle Policarpo
tel	+351 266 702424
fax	+351 266 702424
email	mail@pensaopolicarpo.com
web	www.pensaopolicarpo.com

B&B

Map 4 Entry 152

Albergaria Solar de Monfalim
Largo da Misericórdia 1, 7000-646 Évora, Alentejo

A treat to stay in the middle of beautiful old Évora, on a cobbled square where huge jacaranda trees soften the urban contours – and the old inn has an attractive façade, with its first-floor arcade over the old stables. Pass beneath the coat of arms, ascend the heavy granite staircase and emerge to meet uniformed reception staff to the strains of piped opera... it may be hotelly, but there is a rambling charm. More inviting than the dark lounge/TV room is the little bar, warmed by a wood-burning stove, where old photos reveal aspects of the Alentejo's rural life. The pretty dining room is large and light and leads to an arcaded terrace where you can linger in the sunshine over your (buffet) breakfast. This is a labyrinthine place with many stairs to negotiate before bed. But what bedrooms! The best are high-ceilinged with antique iron and brass bedsteads, lovely bedlinen and bedspreads, old lamps and Arraiolos rugs. Others, however, are small and dingy, so ask for the best when you book. And try to visit in May or June, when those jacarandas burst into glorious purple.

rooms	26 twins/doubles.
price	From €85. Singles €70.
meals	Restaurants nearby.
closed	Rarely.
directions	In Évora follow green tourist hotel signs. Exit ring road on Rua de Machede, via Portas de Moura, into Rua Misericórdia; then right into Largo da Misericórdia.

	Senhora Ana Ramalho Serrabulho
tel	+351 266 750000
fax	+351 266 742367
email	reservas@monfalimtur.pt
web	www.monfalimtur.pt

B&B

Map 4 Entry 153

Quinta da Espada

Apartado 68, Estrada de Arraiolos km4, 7002-501 Évora, Alentejo

Quinta da Espada: Quinta of the Sword. The sword in question was hidden on this farm by Geraldo Geraldes, who snatched Évora back from the Moors. With views down to that lovely city, surrounded by cork oaks and olive groves, is this peaceful, whitewashed, mimosa-graced farmhouse. Bedrooms vary in size and colour, and are simply furnished with delicately hand-painted Alentejan beds; terracotta tiles, *estera* matting and dark beams create a traditional country mood. Slate is an unusual and attractive alternative in the bathrooms, which are spotless. The Green Room occupies what was once the tiny family chapel, and the smaller sitting room, where you breakfast – or dine – before a lit hearth in winter, is particularly charming, its shelves crammed with Alentejan artefacts. You may be tempted by your friendly hostess's country cooking, but there is also a well-equipped kitchen for you to share with other guests. Leave the car behind and follow the tracks that lead to Évora from the estate – than back to the pool, bliss in summer.

rooms	7: 6 twins/doubles, 1 suite.
price	€71. Singles €47.50. Suite €92.
meals	Lunch/dinner €22, by arrangement.
closed	Christmas.
directions	From Évora towards Arraiolos. After 4km, Quinta signed to right.

	Senhora Maria Isabel Sousa Cabral
tel	+351 266 734549
fax	+351 266 736464
email	quintadaespada@clix.pt
web	www.softline.pt/quintadaespada

B&B

Map 4 Entry 154

Monte da Serralheira

Estrada de Bairro de Almeirim, 7000-788 Évora, Alentejo

Dutch George and Lucia discovered the wide, open spaces of the Alentejo long ago and here they are now, farming the land just outside historic Évora and well integrated into the local community. They are still as enthralled by this wonderful country as they were in their pioneering days, and their generosity is reflected in the size and design of these lofty apartments in the old workers' quarters. They're not stylish but are comfortable and well-equipped, and spotless (they're cleaned daily). Some have woodburning stoves, all have private terraces. Space too, inside and out – a great place for a family stay. Put the guidebooks aside and let Lucia steer you in various directions: she is a qualified guide and will suggest a number of well-documented circuits for you to follow. If birdwatching is your thing, George is the expert; on spring evenings you'll hear the nightingale sing. Horses and bikes are available, and there are a swimming pool and a games room, too. The old blue and white farmhouse, with its large garden and bougainvillea-draped terraces, is a happy homestead.

rooms	5 apartments for 2-4, for self-catering or B&B.
price	€50-€88. Extra bed €12.
meals	Breakfast €6. Dinner available locally.
closed	Rarely.
directions	From Lisbon to Évora. Right onto ring road; right at r'bout next to Opel garage for Almeirim (sul). Follow road to end, to farm.

	George & Lucia van der Feltz
tel	+351 266 741286
fax	+351 266 741286
email	monteserralheira@mail.telepac.pt
web	www.monteserralheira.com

B&B & Self-catering

Map 4 Entry 155

Pousada de Arraiolos

Nossa Senhora da Assunção, Apartado 61, 7044-909 Arraiolos, Alentejo

What strikes you at once is the extraordinary feeling of space – acres of it. It's a remarkable achievement. The original 16th-century convent has been converted and a new wing added but there are no jarring notes; everything has been beautifully designed and integrated. Huge, restful *salas* are linked by long corridors floored in matt grey granite. No fuss, no clutter, and everywhere so quiet – a blissful place! Superb bedrooms, glowing with cherrywood, have glass walls opening on to private verandas that overlook lawns and an irresistible pool. Beyond is the hillside, dotted with olive trees and grazing sheep. A magnificent patio has been built between the old part and the new wing, just outside the dining room, and, everywhere, a lovely light is reflected off the white walls of the terrace and the cloister. Staff are young, pleasant and attentive. Above the convent loom the castle walls. Arraiolos, a pretty, cobbled hilltop town, is the home of the ubiquitous carpets – precious fragments of old ones, survivors from the days when they were still made from natural undyed wools, are on display.

rooms	32: 30 twins/doubles, 2 suites.
price	€125-€190. Special offers available - see web site.
meals	Dinner, 3 courses, from €25.
closed	Rarely.
directions	Just outside Arraiolos, off road to Paria, signposted down very steep hill.

	Senhor Paolo Garcia
tel	+351 266 419340
fax	+351 266 419280
email	recepcao.assuncao@pousadas.pt
web	www.pousadas.pt

Hotel

Map 4 Entry 156

Monte do Chora Cascas

Turismo Rural, Apartado 296, Montemor-o-Novo, 7050 Évora, Alentejo

Irresistible: elegant without being stuffy, lavish without being flouncy. Sónia is welcoming and friendly – she's an architect and has designed and decorated the house with flair and imagination. She was keen to strike the right balance between hotel standards and the feel of staying in a private home – and it's worked. The bedrooms have inviting wrought-iron beds and four-posters, the very best linen, wooden ceilings and original paintings. All have lavish bathrooms. Breakfasts are generous and delicious: fresh ham, locally-produced jams, cheeses, yogurts, breads and over 20 types of tea, all served in the formal dining room. The vast sitting room has four plump blue sofas with cashmere and silk throws, an array of shapely pottery, gorgeous candles, a baby grand, an open fire and ambient music, and there's a games room with a snooker table. Outside: a courtyard with designer sunshades and loungers by the paddling pool, a shaded terrace, a tennis court and a tree house. Palm trees, fat terracotta plant pots, a ruined castle on the doorstep and great walking and mountain biking nearby.

rooms	7: 2 doubles, 5 twins.
price	€115-€130. Singles €95.
meals	Restaurants nearby.
closed	Rarely.
directions	From Montemor-o-Novo N235 for Alcácer do Sal & follow Turismo Rural signs. After 3km, right at r'bout. 3rd house on right after 800m, through security gate.

	Senhora Sónia Estima Marques
tel	+351 266 899690
fax	+351 266 899699
email	info@montechoracascas.com
web	www.montechoracascas.com

B&B & Self-catering

Map 3 Entry 157

Parque Markádia

Apartado 17, Barragem de Odivelas, 7920-999 Alvito, Alentejo

Here, in the flat, open, tree-dotted Alentejan countryside, is the Parque Markádia: its potential as a recreational oasis was spotted by this dedicated Dutch couple many years ago. They fell in love with the area, the climate and the lakeside shores, resplendent with holm oaks and corks. There's a campsite and 50 acres to explore. Six self-catering apartments and a swimming pool are surrounded by chickens, sheep, horses and donkeys and the owners are on-hand should you need anything. Décor is basic and cheerful: bright prints, mottled yellow-tiled floors, functional modern furniture, checked tablecloths. You will be spending every daylight hour outdoors, where staff are friendly and facilities all you'd expect. There's masses to do, from watersports on the freshwater lake (windsurfers, pedaloes, kayaks and row boats for hire) to tennis to swimming in the lake or two pools. Tuck into proper Portuguese food in the restaurant where a reasonable range of dishes is served, vegetarian included. A great place for an outdoor holiday that won't break the bank, and wonderful news for families.

rooms	6 self-catering apartments for 2-6.
price	€267-€482 for 2; €533-€666 for 4; €738-€922 for 6; prices per week.
meals	Lunch/dinner from €13.50.
closed	Never
directions	Signed from N2 between Torrão & Ferreira do Alentejo. 7km from Odivelas.

	Eduardo & Sofia van der Mark
tel	+351 284 763141
fax	+351 284 763102

Self-catering

Map 5 Entry 158

Pousada de Beja

São Francisco, Lg. D. Nuno Álvares Pereira, 7801-901 Beja, Alentejo

Lazing in the big, quiet garden, surrounded by lawns, shady pergolas and palm trees, it's hard to believe you're in the middle of a city. The feeling of gentle calm continues inside the pousada. Despite expert modernisation, this lovely former monastery still has a peaceful, unhurried air. The austerity of the massive white walls, vaulted ceilings and wide passageways is softened by serene colours and terracotta or dove-grey marble floors. Even in summer in Portugal's hottest city, sizzling in a vast, flat plain, you should be able to keep cool here. There are several sitting areas – one *sala* is in the chapter house – and the bedrooms are arranged on two floors around three sides of a cloister. Though not large (they were once monks' cells) they have comfortable beds, the finest linen, and marble bathrooms. The restaurant, in the huge refectory, serves traditional, rather heavy Alentejan fare. Nearby is the convent where the famous *Cartas Portuguesas* are said to have been written by Mariana Alcoforado, a nun smitten with love for a French knight she glimpsed from her window.

rooms	35: 34 twins/doubles, 1 suite.
price	€125-€180. Special offers available - see web site.
meals	Dinner, 3 courses, from €25.
closed	Never.
directions	In Beja, follow signs for Centro Histórico/PSP & pousada.

	Senhor Paulo J.R. Silva
tel	+351 284 313580
fax	+351 284 329143
email	recepcao.sfrancisco@pousadas.pt
web	www.pousadas.pt

Hotel

Map 6 Entry 159

Pousada de Santiago de Cacém

Quinta da Ortiga, Estrada IP8, 7540–909 Santiago do Cacém, Alentejo

There's a good, old-fashioned Portuguese mood to your arrival at this rural quinta for it is surrounded by mature trees and approached through cork forests and eucalyptus plantations. Delightful staff live on site and, with only 20-odd rooms, the atmosphere is more home than hotel. A log fire blazes a welcome on cool days and the décor is suburban-stylish. In the main house, eight traditionally comfortable bedrooms have fitted carpets and wooden ceilings; the newer bedrooms are more 'Alentejan-rustic', though still with carpeted comfort. The apartments, in the chapel and garden, have two bedrooms each, a sitting room and a kitchen for making snacks. Four forested hectares are yours to explore and there's a handsome swimming pool in which to contemplate and cool off. A 15-minute drive brings you to some of the finest (and almost empty) beaches of the west coast; nearby Melides and Santo André have important saltwater lagoons popular with migrating birds. And do go to Santiago with its Roman ruins and cobbled streets leading down from the castle walls (but give industrialised Sines a wide berth).

rooms	21 + 2: 21 twins/doubles. 2 apartments for 4.
price	€100–€155. Special offers available - see web site.
meals	Dinner, 3 courses, from €25.
closed	Never.
directions	From Lisbon, exit A2 at junction 9 onto IP8. Pousada is signposted off this road, 10km before Sines, though woods.

	Senhor Augusto Rosa
tel	+351 269 822871
fax	+351 269 822073
email	recepcao.ortiga@pousadas.pt
web	www.pousadas.pt

Hotel

Map 5 Entry 160

Herdade da Matinha

7555-231 Cercal do Alentejo, Alentejo

Encircled by the russet trunks of the cork oak, this classic, long, low Alentejan farmhouse glows with contemporary colours and beautiful things. Monica works part of the year as a tourist guide and will help plan your trips; Alfredo is an artist and looks after the cooking. He loves to chat with guests in the kitchen while preparing meals – usually to classical or baroque music. His paintings add life and colour to the large, light, delightful living room; this leads to a terrace where camellias give way to groves of citrus, a heavenly spot for meals. Centre stage at Matinha is the kitchen with its big wooden table where you eat breakfast en famille and where dinner promises the best of modern Portuguese: baked codfish with cream, red bean ragout with seafood, grouse casserole. Bedrooms are large, uncluttered, stylish, slate-floored and bright with Alfredo's paintings. Come for the peace, the beauty and your civilised, artistic hosts. Though the setting is deeply rural you are close to the wonders of the protected Costa Vicentina – and to the historic towns of Cercal and Vila Nova de Milfontes.

rooms	8 twins.
price	€70-€90. Singles €60-€80 (low season only) .
meals	Dinner €25.
closed	Rarely.
directions	From Lisbon A2, exit Beja-Ferreira, then for Algarve-Ourique. At Mimosa, right to Alvalade-Cercal. At Cercal to Vila Nova de Milfontes. House signed, right. Follow track for 3km.

	Senhor Alfredo Moreira da Silva
tel	+351 269 949247
fax	+351 269 949247
email	info@herdadedamatinha.com
web	www.herdadedamatinha.com

B&B

Map 5 Entry 161

Castelo de Milfontes
7645-234 Vila Nova de Milfontes, Alentejo

Carthaginians, Romans, Moors and Algerian pirates have coveted the remarkable site now held by the Castelo de Milfontes. The fort dates from the 16th century and was rescued from ruin by the family years ago. This is no ordinary 'hotel' and the spirit of welcome is conveyed in the plaque above the hearth: *viver sem amigos não é viver* ('living without friends is not living'). Half-board is the thing and dinner the occasion to meet your fellow guests – and Ema, who graciously presides. An occasion to dress up for: sparkling young staff usher you into the dining room at 8pm, where silver service and traditional Portuguese food await. Beautiful bedrooms have views that challenge descriptive powers; the tower rooms have their own terraces. The furniture, poised between vaulted ceilings and parquet floors, is as atmospheric as the castle – antique writing desks, baldequin beds, original oils. There is a disco across the bay in summer, but a night spent in this stunning small hotel is worth small sacrifices. *Supplement for extra beds for children aged 2-15.*

rooms	7 + 1: 2 tower rooms, 5 twins. 1 self-catering apartment for 2.
price	Half-board only: €155-€166. Singles €110-€116. Annexe €71. Singles €55.
meals	Breakfast €5. Dinner €27.
closed	Rarely.
directions	From Lisbon, A2 for Grãndola. Before Grãndola IP8, for Sines. On to Cercal; N390 to V.N. de Milfontes. At edge of estuary.

	Senhora Ema M. da Câmara Machado
tel	+351 283 998231
fax	+351 283 997122

B&B & Self-catering

Map 5 Entry 162

Cortinhas

Vale Bejinha, 2581 Cx. S. Luis, 7630 Odemira/Milfontes, Alentejo

You arrive at the back... to what seems like a tiny house limewashed in ochre. Inside, what space! More than enough for four, and outside, a lush garden and a veranda with views. All is light and sunny inside, with soothing colours and unglazed terracotta floors. Your lofty, white-raftered living space is rustic and charming, with sofa and sofabed, woodburner, pictures and books; the kitchen is lovely. The powder-blue bedroom opens to a corner of the terrace, the twin room is white and cool. It is all very appealing, and homely. The owners live next door and Sophie's green fingers have nurtured the wisteria and plumbago that romps all over the house, herbs and flowers peeping in through every window. The garden leads to a meadow, a picture in spring, and a small lake two minutes away; all you hear are the tinkling of sheep bells and the occasional dog bark. Behind, on the edge of hills, are a eucalyptus plantation, olives and oaks, good walks (which Tuke will guide or provide maps for) and plentiful birdlife. And the coast is 12km away. *Second house available in village.*

rooms	House for 4-6: 1 double, 1 twin, 1 large sofa-bed in living room. Extra single also available.
price	€60-€72; €416-€550 per week.
meals	Restaurants 10-15km.
closed	Rarely.
directions	From Cercal, south for Odemira. After S. Luis, right at cemetery for Val Bejinha; 2km on, right at mail boxes, left at top.

	Sophie & Tuke Taylor
tel	+351 283 976076
email	walkdontwalk80@hotmail.com

Map 5 Entry 163

Monte da Moita Nova

Apt. 4424, 7630-055 Cavaleiro, Alentejo

If horse riding and unspoilt beaches are your pleasure, stay a week with Ute and Walter at their Alentejo farm. This exceptionally beautiful and unspoilt part of Portugal's Atlantic coastline has recently been designated a Natural Park; the eco-system of the dunes nurtures a huge variety of plant and animal life. You can reach them, and hidden coves beyond, by walking 300m across Cavaleiro's pastures. The original farmhouse has two apartments and a large guest lounge; the other two have been newly built and horseshoe around a central swathe of green. South-facing to catch the sun, each has its own terrace and woodburner and they have a fresh and uncluttered feel: you benefit from architect Walter's clever use of space. Floors are of terracotta, sheets of good linen, beds of pine, and the kitchens have full self-catering kit. The buildings are softened by a riot of climbers: a wonderful spot to watch the sun dipping into the sea. Nice to come across a place which is so friendly to children; there are a paddling pool, beach toys and games, and you ride out on well-mannered thoroughbreds.

rooms	4 apartments for 4.
price	€55-€80; €280-€485 per week.
meals	Self-catering. Good restaurant 1km.
closed	Rarely.
directions	From Faro A22 to Besafrim. Then N120 to S. Teotónio via Aljezur, left here via Zambujeira to Cavaleiro. Here towards beach (not Cabo Sardão), & right after bridge to Moita Nova.

	Ute Gerhardt
tel	+351 283 647357
fax	+351 283 647167
email	moitanova@mail.telepac.pt
web	www.moitanova.com

Self-catering

Map 5 Entry 164

Casa do Adro

Rua Diario de Noticias 10, 7645-257 Vila Nova de Milfontes, Alentejo

Come in June and the Festa do St Antonio is on your doorstep: watch the folk-dancing from the privacy of your street-side terrace. The Casa is in the middle of town, with a castle up the road and good (fish) restaurants round the corner. Friendly and kind Doña Idalia fills the house with flowers – paper ones, silk ones and fresh blooms too; bedrooms have flower names. She has a fondness for big checks – most of the beds are covered boldly. Hers is a charmingly spruce little place, where paintwork is as fresh as a daisy and tiled floors gleam. Décor is traditionally feminine with modern touches; the dining room is Portuguese-pretty. Beds are antique or have painted headboards; one room has a terrace where pets are allowed. There's also a small kitchen for guests. Breakfasts are quite a spread, served on the terrace in summer; evening meals are typically Alentejan. Your hostess is a good cook and owns the café next door, known for its excellent cakes. And the beaches are superb, both the sheltered-estuary kind and the wild ones with waves. A great little spot all year round. *Casas Brancas member.*

rooms	6 twins/doubles.
price	€50-€75.
meals	Dinner on request.
closed	Rarely.
directions	From centre of Vila Nova de Milfontes, follow one-way system to beach, back up past castle to church, then left. House on right.

Dona Idalia Maria Costa José

tel	+351 283 997102
fax	+351 283 997102

Map 5 Entry 165

Verdemar

Casas Novas, Caixa Postal 1223, 7555-026 Cercal do Alentejo, Alentejo

Holiday heaven in a bucolic setting, near the beaches, hidden among ancient cork oaks. Guest rooms are spread around the outbuildings but the hub of the place is the farmhouse and its dining room. The atmosphere is easy – and cosy: a beamed ceiling, an open kitchen/bar, a comfy chair. You'll share fun and good food around one big table. Dutch Christine and Nuno – a chef from Amsterdam – are utterly hands-on, happily swapping recipes with you as they prepare scrumptious dinners. Leading off the kitchen is the lounge, equally cosy with guitar, paintings, books – a cool retreat from summer's heat. Bedrooms are simple, light, colorful and enlivened by Nuno's paintings; the cottages have chunky beams and open hearths. It is heartening to find somewhere so ready to welcome families: not only is there a rustic playground, high tea and masses of space but ducks, cats, chickens, sheep and a donkey to ride. It's peaceful, friendly and refreshingly free of hotelly extras. The swimming pool is wisely fenced for safety, and the whole place is especially lovely in spring. *Casas Brancas member.*

rooms	7 + 3: 2 doubles, 5 twins. 3 self-catering cottages.
price	From €50-€80. Cottages from €40-€120 (min. 2 nights).
meals	Dinner €23, on request (not Sun).
closed	Rarely.
directions	From Lisbon A2, exit Beja Ferreira; N262 for Ourique. 500m after Mimosa, right for Cercal. 7km before Cercal, house signed up track on left.

	Nuno Vilas-Boas & Christine Nijhoff
tel	+351 269 904544
fax	+351 269 904544
email	verdemar.cercal@mail.telepac.pt
web	www.verdemar.net

B&B & Self-catering

Map 5 Entry 166

Monte do Papa Léguas

Alpenduradas, 7630-732 Zambujeira do Mar, Alentejo

Zambujeira do Mar is a small, fun place, popular with the Portuguese, drawn to its beaches like bees to a honey-pot. Stay awhile in this privileged spot: you are a mile from the bars, restaurants, shops and beach life yet may beat an easy retreat to your quiet corner for a dip in the saltwater pool. Teresa, who once ran activity holidays, provides mountain bikes, helmets, water-bottles and trail maps free of charge. She can also tell you about canoeing, horse riding or Atlantic cliff-top walks. The bedrooms in this rebuilt *monte* are attractive and typically Portuguese, with wooden floors, cane ceilings and calico covers on traditional iron bedsteads; fridges and TVs are neatly concealed behind doors, and there's central heating for winter stays (much recommended). Breakfast is to be lingered over under parasols in the palm-fringed courtyard: a feast of ham, cheese, eggs and homemade jams, two types of bread, fresh juice. For those who have been up half the night acquainting themselves with the local bars, breakfast is served until 1pm. *Casas Brancas member.*

rooms	8: 5 twins, 3 studios.
price	€55-€75.
meals	Restaurants nearby.
closed	Rarely.
directions	From São Teotónio, follow signs to Zambujeira 2km before village, on right shortly after a road junction.

Senhora Teresa Albarran

tel	+351 283 961470
fax	+351 283 961470
email	montedopapa@sapo.pt
web	www.montedopapaleguas.com

B&B & Self-catering

Map 5 Entry 167

Cerro da Fontinha

Turismo da Natuereza Lda, Brejão, 7630-575 São Teótonio, Alentejo

Miguel has used locally sourced, natural materials in these unique self-catering cottages. The simple character of the simple dwellings has been kept, while funky, chunky touches have been added. And to reveal the different building methods Miguel has left visible areas of *taipa* so you can see the mix of soil and stones between lath and plaster. Everything is as natural as can be: showers have stone bases and terracotta surrounds, a bunk bed has a carved ladder and fat wooden legs. Hooks for coats, towels and lavatory rolls have been created by embedding pebbles in the walls. Thick chunks of wood become mantelpieces, sofas have stone bases (cosily cushioned!). Work surfaces curve, there are alcoves for oil and vinegar, and cheerful stripes and gingham. You have countryside on the doorstep, a eucalyptus wood for shade, good restaurants and Carcalhal beach nearby – hire mountain bikes to get there. There's also a little lake for swimming and fishing, and a communal seating area as well as private seating for each house. Astonishing and inspiring. *Minimum stay two nights. Casas Brancas member.*

rooms	6 cottages: 2 for 2, 4 for 4.
price	€60–€90 for 2; €80–€110 for 4.
meals	Restaurants nearby.
closed	Rarely.
directions	From Faro A22 (IPI) to Lagos, then N120 for São Teotónio. 5km after crossing into Alentejo, left to Brejão, then 1st left. House on right just after lake.

	Senhor Miguel Godinho
tel	+351 282 949083
fax	+351 282 949083
email	info@cerrodafontinha.com
web	www.cerrodafontinha.com

Self-catering

Map 5 Entry 168

Monte da Choça
Apartada 57, São Teotónio, 7630 Odemira, Alentejo

Set in 20 acres of private land, the pretty low-slung *monte* has superb views over the wide valley to the Monchique hills and the sea. Five white-walled apartments have been beautifully converted; simply and attractively furnished, with striped rugs and cotton bedcovers. Bedrooms are fresh, light and comfortable. In the lounges find soft, neutral colours, open fires and comfy sofas. Kitchens hold all you need. There's masses of space in which to spread your wings outdoors, good wooden seating under feathery acacia, two barbecues with big tables – and a very fine pool, with ping-pong and play areas. Rodolfo, the smiling, extrovert Swiss owner, has lots of ideas on where to go and what to do; ask about local walks (laminated maps provided), birdwatching routes and the coolest, secret surf beaches. Or, just bask in the peace and catch some rays on a lounger with a good book. A five-mile drive west brings you to the rugged Atlantic coastline with its amazing white sandy beaches and, north, to the shops and restaurants of São Teotónio with its windy, cobbled streets. Great value. *Casas Brancas member.*

rooms	5 apartments for 2-4.
price	€40-€65 for 2; €50-€100 for 4.
meals	Self-catering.
closed	Rarely.
directions	From Lisbon to São Teotónio, then to Odeceixe & Lagos. After 4km, left to Vale Juncal & through village. 800m on dirt track. House ahead, through gap in high hedge.

	Rudolfo Muller do Carmo
tel	+351 283 962 608325
fax	+351 283 959135
email	contacto@montevivo.com
web	www.montevivo.com

Self-catering

Map 5 Entry 169

Quinta do Barranco da Estrada
7665-880 Santa Clara a Velha, Alentejo

Hugging the shore of one of the Alentejo's largest freshwater lakes, the Quinta is ideal if you love wild beauty and are looking for a hideaway. The whole area has a micro-climate that keeps the water warm enough for a long swimming season and nurtures an amazing range of plant and animal life; visit in spring and the wild flowers will have you in raptures. The renovation of the original low house took a decade and then a row of guest rooms was added. They are light, cool and minimalist and their terraces look towards the lake. Lounge, dining room and bar share one large room and happily embrace Portuguese and English styles of décor. Beyond huge windows there is a vine-festooned terrace where you spend most of your time when it's warm. A further series of terraces have been planted with hibiscus, oleander, palm, jasmine, plumbago and cactus. Follow the path to the jetty where you can canoe, fish for crayfish, sail, water-ski or walk the shoreline, perhaps in the company of one of the six dogs. Frank will help with the naming of all those birds. *Casas Brancas member*.

rooms	11: 10 twins/doubles, 1 family room.
price	€70–€150. Singles €60–€135. Family €175–€300. Extra bed €25.
meals	Cooked breakfast €10. Lunch €15. Dinner €25.
closed	Rarely.
directions	From S. Martinho das Amoreiras for Portimão. At T-junc., left to Monchique; 8km, left to Cortes Pereiras; 8.5km, right to Quinta.

	Frank McClintock
tel	+351 283 933065
fax	+351 283 933066
email	paradiseinportugal@mail.telepac.pt
web	www.paradise-in-portugal.com

B&B

Map 5 Entry 170

Pousada de Santa Clara-a-Velha

Santa Clara, Barragem de Sta. Clara, 7665-879 Sta. Clara-a-Velha, Algarve

In the Sierra, on the lake – what a setting! The terrace next to the bar has the dreamiest views. The building – not the prettiest in this book – was originally the house of the engineer who built the dam; in the 90s it was extended, and became this fabulous hotel. Enter to a sea of cool white marble; beyond, the warm restaurant; above, the bedrooms-with-views. Those at the back look over the Monchique hills but the best look over the lake and have a tiny private terrace. The apricot theme runs throughout, the bedcovers and curtains match, the mood is harmonious, the bathrooms are plush. Outside, pleasant gardens lead down to a curved pool – and then to the lake, a delight in summer. There are two well-priced restaurants in the village, but do eat in at least once: the food is as delicious as it looks (seafood salad, grilled bass, honey pudding...). Staff are pousada-professional, friendly too, ready with info on walks and bike rides, shooting and fishing. They even give you a brief guide to local flora and fauna. A tranquil, relaxing, comforting place.

rooms	19: 18 twins/doubles, 1 suite.
price	€100–€155. Special offers available - see Pousadas web site.
meals	Dinner, 3 courses, from €25.
closed	Never.
directions	From Faro or Lisbon IC1; exit at São Marcos da Serra. Cross railway line; right for Benafátima. At T-junction right for Odemira; Pousada signed to right.

Senhora Isabel Guerreiro

tel	+351 283 882 250
fax	+351 283 882 402
email	recepcao.staclara@pousadas.pt
web	www.pousadas.pt

Hotel

Map 5 Entry 171

Photo Julia Richardson

algarve

algarve

The name Algarve comes from Moorish 'al-gharb', meaning the west country. The Algarve has been inhabited by Phoenicians, Carthaginians, Romans, Visigoths and Moors

• Wild surfing beaches and coastline on the westerly tip of the Algarve between **Sagres** and **Odeceixe**; try **Carrapateira** for a relaxed pace

• **Faro** – stroll around the old town; **Tavira** – an elegant fishing town with beautiful architecture; nearly 40 churches; **Lagos** – cosmopolitan beach parade, shops and restaurants

• **Monchique** – the forested hills with great walking, cycling and horse-riding. Drink the local firewater – **medronho** – made from the strawberry tree

• **Parque Natural de Ria Formosa** – lagoon system with saltpans, creeks and unspoilt sand-dune islands. Spectacular beaches and rock formations

• Fabulous fish restaurants, especially in **Olhão**

Inn Albergeria Bica-Boa
Estrada de Lisboa 266, 8550 Monchique, Algarve

A great place to unwind with massage, reiki, meditation… and delicious food, much of it vegetarian. All thanks to Susan, who has run this restaurant with rooms for years. Bica-Boa is the only inn in Monchique, its name inspired by the springs that well up on this wooded mountainside. As you wind your way up from the western Algarve, the exuberant vegetation will surprise you – and there are walks galore. Though the building stands just to the side of the road there is very little traffic, and the bedrooms are tucked away to the rear. Fresh, light and simple, with dark wooden floors and ceilings, they have super-comfortable mattresses and views across the valley. There is a quiet little guest lounge with the same view and a homely feel: corner chimney, *azulejo*-clad walls and a table set for chess. The restaurant is popular with locals and ex-pats up from the coast. You get terraces for outdoor dining when the weather is right, a terraced garden with shady corners and a tiny pool. Staff are delightful. *Alternative health courses available.*

rooms	4 twins.
price	€53-€63.
meals	Lunch/dinner €15-€20.
closed	Rarely.
directions	From Faro, N125 west for Lagos. Exit for Monchique. Follow signs for Lisboa through town. Inn approx. 300m after town on right, signed.

	Susan Clare Cassidy
tel	+351 282 912271
fax	+351 282 912360
email	enigma@mail.telepac.pt

Restaurant with rooms

Map 5 Entry 172

Cabana dos Rouxinois

Apt. 33, 8550 Monchique, Algarve

Great swathes of the Algarve coast have been consumed by developers and concrete-pourers; up in these hills, a half hour from the coast, it doesn't seem to matter. The house and pool have some of the best views in the Algarve – its splendid gardens are a haven of peace. It's on several levels: enter at the back, step down to the living room and thence to the terrace. You will be immediately captivated by the light, the space and the comfort. Everywhere are soft colours, good furniture, watercolours and colourful ceramics. Bedrooms, too, are gorgeous. One has blue toile de Jouy fabric, blue and white painted furniture and a matching bathroom that opens onto the main terrace, another a pretty pink and white theme, its own entrance and Alentejan painted furniture and bed. In the cottage are three bedrooms and a sitting room, perfect for children and a nanny. Maria and António will look after you very well – you buy the food and they will do the cooking, the laundry, the cleaning and the pool every day; they can babysit too. It's lavish yet elegant – the house belongs to an 'old' English family and little expense has been spared.

rooms	2: 1 house for 8-10; 1 cottage for 5.
price	£1,000-£3,000 per week.
meals	Cooking by housekeeper as required; you buy food. Good restaurants nearby.
closed	Rarely.
directions	From Faro A22 for Portimão & Lagos to Monchique. From centre of Monchique towards Foia. Left opposite A Rampa restaurant & on down to house.

	Pippa Dennis
tel	+44 (0)207 603 9739
email	pippa_dennis@yahoo.com
web	www.cabanadosrouxinois.com

Casa Vicentina
Monte Novo, 8670-312 Odeceixe, Algarve

This west coast deserves visitors, not developers, and *turísmo rural* is the answer. Spanking new, rebuilt with sensitivity and imagination, the Casa is a restructed Taipa farmhouse. It has been extended and transformed, repainted with ecological paint, and has a very fine roof. Even the swimming pool is 'eco', the water lilies, rushes and papyrus guaranteeing a thoroughly natural swim. Bamboo and plentiful trees have been planted by the thoughtful and charming owners; José is a retired civil servant and his English is excellent. Huge bedrooms have a touch of Morocco, with their lamps, wall hangings and colourful rugs. Each has big French windows that open to the lawn or the olive trees; you may be able to glimpse the distant sea over the tops of the eucalyptus trees. Bathrooms are functional rather than stylish. The house is more summer retreat than cosy winter bolthole, its little outdoor sitting areas shielded by whitewashed buttresses. There's masses to do – you can be at the beach within 20 minutes (borrow a bike), and the walking is wonderful. *Casa Brancas member.*

rooms	6 doubles.
price	€60-€85.
meals	Dinner, 3 courses, from €15.
closed	January.
directions	From Lisbon A2 towards Algarve. Exit for Sines, Odemira & Lagos; follow signs for Lagos & Aljezur, exit before Maria Vinape; head towards Monte Novo.

	José & Fatima Gomes de Almeida
tel	+351 282 947447
fax	+351 282 947448
email	geral@casavicentina.pt
web	www.casavicentina.pt

B&B

Map 5 Entry 174

Monte Velho Nature Resort

Bordeira, 8670-230 Carrapateira, Algarve

Near to one of best surfing beaches in Portugal is this stylish, ecological nature resort – the rolling breakers can be seen from the house. Henrique, his partner and their young family are warm and friendly and know all the surfing spots. Splashes of orange, blue, violet, ochre and red – not forgetting some lovely hand-painted fish – fill this simple place with fun and good humour. Polished floors, Indian beds, floaty fabrics, bold art, sofas with plump cushions, warm lighting, music, books and magazines add to the sense of ease. A Moroccan mood hangs in the air. Bedrooms face south and have their own private terraces with hammocks, lanterns and rattan chairs, and each is different; some have mezzanines, others woodburning stoves. The large windows in the living room pull in the views and the peace is total – you are in a wild, empty, birdsonged natural park. Come evening, the west coast sunsets are inspiring, the stars dazzling. Get to the beach by donkey, take a surfing lesson or a boat trip, return for massage, yoga or tai chi. A sybarite's paradise. *Minimum stay 7 nights July/August.*

rooms	9: 2 doubles, 7 suites (twin/double, single & lounge).
price	€90-€100.
meals	Good restaurants 3km.
closed	Rarely.
directions	From Lagos, N125 to Vila do Bispo; N268 for Aljezur & Sines. Right at sign to Vilarinha; after 800m left to Monte Velho.

	Senhor Henrique Balsemão
tel	+351 282 973 207
fax	+351 282 973 208
email	montevelho.carrapateira@sapo.pt
web	www.wonderfulland.com/montevelho

B&B

Map 5 Entry 175

Monte Rosa

Lagoa da Rosa, 8600-016 Barão de S. João, Algarve

In four hectares of unspoilt Algarve hinterland, Dutch Sandra has converted the old farmstead into a well-organised but charmingly laid back, sociable and 'green' place to stay. Go B&B, opt for the independence of self-catering, or bring your tent/camper van and pitch up under the almond, olive and fig trees. Décor is modest but attractive, some rooms have their own kitchens, others share. And you get acres of lovely untamed space. Make friends over dinner – the dining room, open during summer, serves tasty dishes from organic home produce, with plenty for vegetarians – or around the saltwater pool. Cafés, grocery stores and restaurants are just walkable (one mile), there's a daily bus to Lagos and wonderful clifftop walks on the south and west coasts; delightful Sandra and her relaxed staff know all the best spots and beaches. Massage and meditation, babysitting, riding and boat trips are bookable, there are bikes, billiards, books and games, hammocks and hens, pathways, terraces, barbecue areas and playground… families will be in heaven. *Shared washing machine. Minimum stay three nights.*

rooms	7 + 3: 5 twins/doubles, 1 single, 1 family. 3 houses for 4-8.
price	€45-€60. Singles €23-€40. Family room €55-€65. Apartment €90-€120.
meals	Dinner with wine €15, April-November, Mon-Thurs.
closed	Rarely.
directions	From Lagos for Aljezur; after 2km through Portelas; at end of village left to Barão. 6km on left.

	Sandra Falkena
tel	+351 282 687002
fax	+351 282 687015
email	info@monterosaportugal.com
web	www.monterosaportugal.com

B&B & Self-catering

Map 5 Entry 176

Pousada de Sagres
Infante, 8650–385 Sagres, Algarve

In the fifth century BC Sagres was "a meeting place for the gods, and forbidden to mankind". Well, mankind came and Sagres has a great history; in the 15th century, Henry the Navigator established the Escola Nautica here, and Portugal began its rule of the world. The pousada, whose 1960s origins set alarm bells ringing, is remarkably sympathetic to its environment, and lies low on the cliff top, above a sea that clashes audibly on a wild day; the storms are thrilling. It has had a brilliant facelift under the new Pestana influence: fresh colours, white walls, crisp linen, warm wooden floors. The shared spaces are beautifully done, too: choice antiques and comfortable armchairs, and a sensational tapestry. There is a games room for children, with huge white bean bags – great to sink into but impossible to get out of. The dining room is as stylish as the hotel, and the fish, meat and vegetables are locally sourced. Everyone loves Sagres, with its attractive working harbour full of fishing boats and not a yacht in sight. Fish, surf, windsurf, watch migrating birds – or just loaf about.

rooms	51: 50 doubles; 1 suite.
price	€110–€190. Special offers available - see web site.
meals	Dinner, 3 courses, from €25.
closed	Never.
directions	From Faro IC4 for Lagos. There, N125 to Vila do Bispo. There, N268 towards Sagres; follow signs for pousada.

	Senhor João Portugal
tel	+351 282 620240
fax	+351 282 624225
email	recepcao.infante@pousadas.pt
web	www.pousadas.pt

Hotel

Map 5 Entry 177

Salsalito

Estrada da Luz, Burgau, 8600-146 Lagos, Algarve

A dream home that Ralph and Sally have spent some years creating. It's top-drawer 'Santa Fe' – all chunky beams, tree trunk shelves and curious 'junk' collections. The guest book tells it like it is: "perfect", "wonderful" and "award yourself 20 stars". Sally will read your cards at the drop of a hat and Ralph is a master of all trades, including carpentry; his are the wardrobes, tables and door lintels. The lounge has a huge log fire for cool nights and the bars – one on the top terrace – are brilliantly stocked. Sociable folk will love it. Relax in summer in the horseshoe cloister with bamboo seats and wooden ceiling festooned with bougainvillea... then pad across to the lush pool, set among mixed trees with a 'tropical' waterfall. The bedrooms have a touch of British B&B, with kettles and teabags; the newest, nicely private in a converted building with its own terrace, is semi-Mexican in style. You'll find plenty to do here: Burgau, with its bars and restaurants, two minutes by car, has kept something of its old fishing village character. *Minimum stay three nights. Children over 13 welcome.*

rooms	4 twins/doubles.
price	€55-€90; £280 per week.
meals	Good restaurants nearby.
closed	November–March.
directions	A22 exit Lagos, to Vila do Bispo onto N125. Left at traffic lights for Almadena, then towards Burgau. At T-junc. by mustard balustrade, immed. right. If you reach the Pig's Head, you've gone too far.

	Ralph & Sally Eveleigh
tel	+351 282 697628
fax	+351 282 788272
email	salsalito@clix.pt
web	www.algarve-salsalito.com

B&B

Map 5 Entry 178

Casa Tardis

Estrada da Praia, 0101-101, Algarve

Can this possibly be? We all know that architects can send long arms of steel soaring over deep valleys, thrust gigantic metallic creations to the Heavens and cover them in concrete. But this?! Three tiny beach-huts enclosing a gargantuan, and vastly ugly, shopping mall? The secret, of course, is the brilliant use of underground building. This is a new fad in Portugal, brought on by tough new planning laws and high land prices. This unusual little hotel is cunningly disguised within these three beach-huts: just three luxurious rooms. But you can slip effortlessly downstairs on those escalators to pillage the cornucopia of good things to eat in the supermarket. Yet when all is done we must take heed of Shakespeare's words in the Tempest:

Our revels now are ended. These our actors / As I foretold you, were all spirits and / Are melted into air, into thin air: / And like the baseless fabric, the gorgeous palaces, / The solemn temples, the great globe itself, / Yea, all which it inherit, shall dissolve / And, like this insubstantial pageant faded / Leave not a rack behind.

rooms	3: all with sea views.
price	Bring your credit card.
meals	Several soulless cafés available in the food hall.
closed	Never.
directions	Just keep going down the escalators.

	Senhor Subterraneo
tel	+351 010 101010
email	smallmall@thebeach.com
web	www.tardis.com

Tardis

Map 222 Entry 179

Casa Colina
Mont Fonseca, Burgau, Algarve

A simple, fig-shaded, single-story former farmhouse set back from the village of Burgau – now more tourist than fishing – up a steep and winding drive. Inside is evidence of Roger's artistic flair. He is a painter and journalist and unusual in being so easy about sharing his peaceful space. If you want to paint, feel free to borrow an easel and head for the studio. There's a stack of art books, some beautiful plates collected at gypsy markets and a fascinating collection of old bottles (Roger has written a book about them). The studio overflows with abstract and colourful paintings – this obviously encourages creativity. There are two self-catering studios: the cosy Picasso, perfect for a couple, has an open-plan bedroom/lounge with a beamed ceiling, red tiled floors, a woodburning stove, antique furniture, red throws and rugs and several arches. Matisse is larger, with two bedrooms and the same rustic, functional feel; both share a pretty terrace and tropical garden with climbers, cacti and ferns. Unpretentious, inexpensive and close to good walking, cycling, birdwatching and watersports.

rooms	2 self-catering apartments: 1 for 2; 1 for 4.
price	€234–€593 per week.
meals	Restaurants nearby.
closed	Rarely.
directions	From Faro, A22/IPI to Lagos & Sagres; after Almadena left to Burgau. Look for sports centre on right & shortly after, right (on a bad bend) onto dirt track. Continue until sign; furthest half of house.

	Roger Green
tel	+351 282 697518
fax	+351 282 697518
email	rogerwords@sapo.pt

Self-catering

Map 5 Entry 180

Quinta das Achadas

Estrada da Barragem, Odiáxere, 8600-251 Lagos, Algarve

Hats off to attentive owners Júlio and Jill: their Quinta is one of the most idyllic B&Bs of the Algarve. The approach is a delight, through groves of olive, almond and orange trees which give way to a wonderful subtropical garden where maguey and palm, geranium and bourgainvillea, pine and jasmine jostle for position; there's a heated, saltwater pool too, a *cabana* with 'honesty' bar, a hydro-massage jacuzzi and a small children's playground. The bedrooms, each with its own small terrace, look out across the gardens and are in a converted barn and stables. They are Algarve-rustic, with wooden ceilings, white walls, modern art and beautiful country antiques. Gorgeous bathrooms come with Santa Katerina tiles and swish showers. In colder weather you breakfast in a cosy dining room but most of the year it's mild enough to sit out on the rooftop terrace with views. You can self-cater in the apartments. Dinners are three-course, eclectic and very good; your hosts, who used to work in the restaurant trade, combine professionalism with a warm, human touch. *Minimum three nights in apartments.*

rooms	3 + 3: 3 twins/doubles. 3 apartments, for 2-4.
price	€70-€90. Apartments €95-€160.
meals	Dinner with wine €25 (2-3 times a week).
closed	Rarely.
directions	From airport IP22 for Vilamoura & Portimao; exit 3. Straight at 1st r'bout; right for Odiaxere at 2nd r'bout. There, right at lights. Past windmill, bear left for Barragem. 1.3km on, house signed.

	Jill, Júlio & Isabella Pires
tel	+351 282 798425
fax	+351 282 799162
email	info@algarveholiday.net
web	www.algarveholiday.net

B&B & Self-catering

Map 5 Entry 181

Alto da Lua

Corte Pero Jacques - Serra do Espinhaço de Cão, 8670-120 Aljezur, Algarve

Up here, on the Espinhaco de Cão mountain ridge, there's nothing but the wind in the trees, the scent of pine and eucalyptus and uninterrupted, 360° views. Scarcely a house or road disturbs the vista down to the sea, glinting in the distance. Unexpectedly modern – sharply defined shapes, plate glass windows, uncluttered spaces – the hotel has been designed to capitalise on its 'away from everything' position. Bedrooms are elegantly simple with tiled floors, stark walls, fuss-free wooden furniture and sliding doors to balconies. Families might prefer the two apartments in a nearby converted schoolhouse. The cottagey dining room is pretty in blue and white while two lounges have books, games and fires in winter. There's also a terrace bar and a large garden with barbecue area. The peace is beguiling; indeed, young Senhor Lino eschewed the Lisbon life to run this family hotel with his father. Swimming, surfing and watersports are a 20-minute drive. But why stir from this peaceful spot? In the evening, rest by the pool – or on your balcony, as you watch the sun dip behind the hills and into the sea.

rooms	9 + 2: 9 twins/doubles. 2 apartments for 2 + 2 children.
price	€70-€100. Apartments €595-€840 per week.
meals	Dinner, 3 courses, €25.
closed	November.
directions	From Via do Infante exit for Lagos & Aljezur. On for 8km; left down dirt track. Past watch tower, through eucalyptus plantation, to house signed, above on right.

	Miguel Schmidt Lino
tel	Mobile: +351 968 135788
fax	+351 282 688332
email	info@altodalua.com
web	www.altodalua.com

B&B & Self-catering

Map 5 Entry 182

Quinta da Alfarrobeira

Estrada do Palmares, Odiáxere, 8600-252 Lagos, Algarve

For the young family from Holland, now embellishing their dream home, it was love at first sight. The 1730 farmhouse stands on a hill just inland from the Algarve coast and is surrounded by six hectares of old fruit groves. You might be fired by similar dreams as you sit beneath the enormous *alfarrobeira* (carob) and gaze out across the old olive and almond trees, or watch the family's three sons playing happily with their pets on a sunny flower-filled patio. Choose between the room in the main house, with own bathroom, and one of two guest houses renovated in traditional Algarve style where terracotta, beam and bamboo are the essential ingredients. We were impressed with their beautiful, light and airy feel and the antique furnishings that have been collected piecemeal from all over Europe. There are biggish bathrooms, private terraces and views – and little kitchens if you plan to cook. Add to this a hammock in the garden, a stylish pool, good walks from the door (less than a mile to the sea), exceptionally kind hosts and you may never want to leave. *Minimum stay three nights.*

rooms	1 + 2: 1 double.
	2 houses: 1 for 2-4, 1 for 4-6.
price	€50-€70. Houses €62-€145;
	€430-€1,010 per week.
meals	Excellent choice of restaurants
	nearby.
closed	Rarely.
directions	From Faro A22, then N125 towards Portimão & Lagos exit Odiáxere. Left at square for Palmares. After 1.3km (cow sign on right), left. 1st house on right.

	Theo Bakker & Inge Keizer
tel	+351 282 798424
fax	+351 282 799630
email	bakker@mail.telepac.pt

B&B & Self-catering

Map 5 Entry 183

Mad Manor

Vale das Amoreiras, Lote 7 Alcalar, 8500-120 Mexilhoeira Grande, Algarve

A great alternative to renting your own villa – and you don't even have to make breakfast. Your delightful hosts will book things up for you, too: golf, riding, surfing, tennis. The large and stately white villa is one of a development of eight, each in an oleander- and hibiscus-filled garden. You have your own marble-floored suite of rooms. The main bedroom, with blue carpeting and white walls, satin bedcovers, soft lighting and swagged curtain has lovely views of the Monchique hills. The two twins are pretty with pine furniture and rugs; the bathroom, with 'his' and 'hers' basins, is big and shared. In the kitchen are fridge, kettle, toaster and microwave to prepare your own snacks and drinks, and there's an 'honesty' table of drinks. The lounge/dining room leads onto a terrace with lovely views. Angela and David, who live downstairs, are happy for you to join them for barbecues in the evenings; if you prefer to eat out, the village is a walk away. The large and lovely pool – yours to share – is the colour of the Algarve sky. And glorious white sand beaches are a short drive away.

rooms	1 apartment for 2-6.
price	€80 double; €40 extra room.
meals	Breakfast included. Restaurants nearby.
closed	Rarely.
directions	From Alvor, EN125 to Lagos. 1st right after BP petrol station to Alcalar. Under railway, over m'way, past Alcalar until Monumentos Megalithicos sign. Right, then 1st left. 2nd house on left.

	David & Angela Broad
tel	+351 282 471530
fax	+351 282 470359
email	madmanor@mail.telepac.pt

B&B & Self-catering

Map 5 Entry 184

Casa da Palmeirinha

Rua da Igreja, 1, Mexilhoeira Grande, 8500-132 Portimão, Algarve

This graceful old house, centred on its lush inner courtyard and garden, may remind you of houses of Seville or Morocco; it is also bigger than it seems. José, a local journalist who speaks very good English, was born here. The bedrooms have varied views of the church and village; our favourites open to a terrace and roof garden with views of the Alvor bird sanctuary. The Spanish-influenced sitting room has walls decorated with flamboyant tiles, a beautiful terracotta floor and a stylish rustic feel. Then there's that huge courtyard with its ornamental pool, swimming pool and lawn, shaded by arching palms – a cool and lovely place to relax. This is an unusual opportunity to stay in a truly Portuguese townhouse that is attractive inside and out, where you are very much left to your own devices and free to make tea and coffee in the kitchen. The village is genuine, full of locals with the bonus of the famous Vila Lisa restaurant. There's the bird sanctuary nearby, and good walks – you may meet the owner's elderly Algarve water dogs and labrador. *Minimum stay two nights.*

rooms	5: 3 doubles, 2 family rooms.
price	€60-€80. Singles €50-€60. Family rooms €77-€97.
meals	Restaurants nearby.
closed	December.
directions	From Portimão or Lagos on N125; into Mexilhoeira Grande to church. House on left, turn left.

	Senhor José Manuel Júdice Glória
tel	+351 282 969277
fax	+351 282 969277
email	josejudice@mail.telepac.pt

B&B

Map 5 Entry 185

Quinta das Flores

Vale de Dega, Mexilhoeira Grande, Figueira, 8500 Portimão, Algarve

There is art in the very fabric of the colourful House of Flowers: hospitable Gaelle and David, who farmed in Africa, are landscape gardener and painter. The gracious gardens lead from the house: lovely lawns and rampant climbers, palms and pergolas, figs and bougainvillea, shady spots. And there are a cane-canopied terrace, a barbecue, an honesty bar, tennis and a pool. The house interior has a colonial feel, thanks partly to Gaelle's vibrant paintings of zebras and her landscapes of Africa and the Alentejo. The galleried sitting room is warm with terracotta floors strewn with rugs, cream walls, large inviting sofas and chairs, and open fires for cooler seasons. On the terrace, big, beautiful wicker armchairs for dreaming in. Down two steps from the pool is a cool, subterranean double room with a lovely comfy bed. And you can self-cater: in the 'cottage' (a wing of the house), with its two bedrooms and super kitchen, or in the airy studio. The décor is fresh and sunny, beds are large and the atmosphere homely. Breakfasts can be full English or continental. *Minimum stay three nights.*

rooms	1 + 2: 1 double. 1 studio for 2; 1 cottage for 4.
price	€85. Studio €85. Cottage €800 p.w.
meals	Dinner, 3 courses, €25.
closed	Rarely.
directions	From Portimão, to Lagos, past Penina, right into Figueira. Past church & just before pink Café Célia, right.

	Gaelle & David Hamp-Adams
tel	+351 282 968649
fax	+351 282 969293
email	ghampadams@hotmail.com

B&B & Self-catering

Map 5 Entry 186

Casa Três Palmeiras
Apartado 84, 8501-909 Portimão, Algarve

What a setting! From the Casa's perch by the cliff edge the view is a symphony of rock, sea and sky – ever-changing according to the day's mood, ever beautiful. The villa was built in the Sixties when the Algarve was discovered, and the mood is luxurious Zen... all you hear are seagulls and waves. Simple white arches and three tall palms (*três palmeiras*) soften the façade and give welcome shade once the temperature rises. Bedrooms have everything you might expect for the price – polished floors, walk-in wardrobes, generous beds and bathrooms lavishly tiled; all is beautifully uncluttered. Four lead directly onto a parasoled terrace with heavenly views and saltwater pool. It is a supremely comfortable house full of fruit and flowers, and a woodburner for winter cosiness. The service is warm yet professional: kind Dolly, from Brazil, makes everything perfect, from massage to pedicure. A path leads from the house down to the beach; breakfast early and you may find you have it all to yourself, even in midsummer. Book ahead for July/August. *Reduced green fees and car hire rates available for guests.*

rooms	5 twins/doubles.
price	€205–€211. Singles €184.50–€190.
meals	Snacks available.
closed	December–January.
directions	From Portimão, dual carriageway for Praia da Rocha. Right at last r'bout for Praia do Vau; at next r'bout double back & turn up track on right after 100m. Right along track at 1st villa.

	Dolly Schlingensiepen
tel	+351 282 401275
fax	+351 282 401029
email	dolly@casatrespalmeiras.com
web	www.casatrespalmeiras.com

B&B

Map 5 Entry 187

Casa O Palmeiral

Montes de Cima, 8500-142 Mexilhoiera, Algarve

Pines, palms and cacti give a semi-tropical feel to this sprawling farmhouse hidden in the dusty foothills of Monchique. A former artist's studio, it's splashed with vibrant colours, local artists' work, walls of glass and open terraces that invite you to linger over breakfast coffee or a glass of Medronho. Rooms are sultry with a Moroccan flavour – striped fabrics, richly tiled bathrooms – and share a wide, plant-decked terrace. For privacy choose the apartment: big rooms and terrace, rustic-style kitchen. English owners Patricia and Will have backgrounds in landscape design and running a tea room… plants and foliage are exotic and bold while Patricia's breakfasts make the best of local produce: grapefruits and figs from the garden, homemade coconut bread. In the evening, dine alfresco on salt cod fishcakes or goat with almonds. Life revolves around the large, sunshiney yellow terrace bar and lazy pool – well beyond sunset. A blissfully sleepy rural spot only half an hour from beaches, walking and cycling country. *Children over 10 welcome.*

rooms	5 + 1: 2 doubles, 3 twins. 1 self-catering apartment for 2.
price	€60-€90.
meals	Dinner with wine, €20-€30.
closed	Rarely.
directions	From Faro A2 for Lagos; exit for Alvor. At r'bout N125 for Figueira. After BP petrol station, right for Alcalar. Left at T-junction at Montes de Cima, then immed right; house 50m on right.

	Patricia & Will Davey
tel	+351 282 471145
email	relaxwithpatricia@hotmail.com
web	www.algarverelax.co.uk

B&B & Self-catering

Map 5 Entry 188

Rio Arade

Rua D.Joáo II 33, Mexilhoeira da Carregacáo, 8400-092 Estombar, Algarve

Wrought-iron balconies, colourful window mouldings and gleaming beamed ceilings – this is every inch the handsome Portuguese townhouse. To find it amongst the hurly-burly of the Algarve coast is a treat. The 18th-century house in this former fishing village has been smartly modernised: step in to a cool, light space and a honey-coloured floor studded with creamy sofas. Behind is the dining area, traditional with rush-seated ladderback chairs and bright yellow china; beyond, the courtyard with its brilliant blue pool, terraces and shady corners. Very peaceful, very Portuguese – bougainvillea, palms, fountains and sufficient space to tuck yourself away from other guests. Sunny bedrooms are comfortable and uncluttered with breezy colour themes. Some rooms have rugs on polished wooden floors, others have creamy ceramic tiles, the best have private terraces overlooking the pool. Free use of the swish leisure spa nearby is a big plus. John, affable Irishman and retired marathon runner, might join you. He'll also point you in the direction of the village's best restaurants. *Minimum stay three nights.*

rooms	8: 3 doubles, 5 twins.
price	€49-€110.
meals	Breakfast included. Good restaurants nearby.
closed	Rarely.
directions	From Faro or Lisbon A22; at r'bout in Lagos, right & on for 1km. In Semaforós, right, then left; 200m to house.

	John O'Neill
tel	+351 282 423202
fax	+351 282 483870
email	info@rioarade-accommodation.com
web	www.rioarade-accommodation.com

B&B

Map 5 Entry 189

Casa Domilu

Estrada de Benagil, Alfanzina, 8400 Carvoeiro, Algarve

This small resort-hotel under new ownership flaunts its frills at every turn. If neo-Doric columns and musak are not your thing, stay away... But if you secretly hanker after a glitzy place to stay on the Algarve, then you will love it! The décor of lounge and dining room is pick-and-mix: repro antiques, art-deco-ish chairs, glass-topped tables, dragon-tooth floors. Bedrooms are big, light, cheerful and marble-floored and have all the extras: book the honeymoon suite and you get a sunken whirlpool bath surrounded by potted palms. Outside, sweeping colonnaded steps lead to a fabulous new palm-studded terrace with curvaceous pool and children's pool; new bedrooms too. The saltwater indoor pool, with jacuzzi, is equally gorgeous. Breakfast is buffet, big and designed to please a northern European palate, while dinner (candlelit) is resolutely Portuguese. There is tennis – floodlit at night – a gymnasium, sauna and beauty spa, and mountain bikes; beaches and golf courses are a saunter away. Guests, many of whom are German, return year after year.

rooms	30: 24 twins/doubles, 6 suites.
price	€62–€145. Singles €51–€116. Suites €127–€303.
meals	Dinner, 3 courses, €25.
closed	Rarely.
directions	From N125, exit for Carvoeiro. 200m after Intermarché supermarket, left at signs for house.

	Senhor Miguel Estêvão
tel	+351 282 350610
fax	+351 282 358410
email	casa.domilu@mail.telepac.pt
web	www.casa-domilu.com

Hotel

Map 5 Entry 190

Casa Bela Moura

Estrada de Porches 530, Alporchinhos, 8400-450 Porches, Algarve

The welcome is exceptional. Christophe and Sofie are Belgian, fired up with enthusiasm for their new venture, and plan to marry in the little chapel on the beach. This is a small, charming villa-hotel, set well back from the road, three minutes from the pretty beach of Senhora da Rocha. Breakfasts are lavish and change every day: ham, cereal, yogurt, fresh pineapple, just-squeezed orange juice, four different types of bread, scrambled eggs, French toast... and there are coffee and cakes in the afternoon. After a lazy day by the pool, retire to the cosy lounge for a summery aperitif – or a nightcap before the fire; this is where plans are made, often with the help of fellow guests, for tomorrow's excursions. Visit Lagos, Silves, the Serra de Monchique, the old centre of Faro – you are perfectly sited for all. Cheery bedrooms are divided between the main villa and a villa set aside for families. Five rooms have terraces, three have baths (some modern and snazzy), the rest showers, and the suite, with its 'rain' shower, is an absolute treat. *Minimum stay two nights.*

rooms	14: 5 doubles, 8 twins, 1 suite.
price	€70–€150. Singles €40–€90.
meals	Light lunches €2–€5. Half-board deal with good local restaurant.
closed	January.
directions	From Faro A22, exit 7 Alcantarilha. At r'bout right on N125 to Portimao. After 3km left in Porches for Armaçao de Pera. House on right after 3km, before Cespa petrol station.

	Christophe Rijnders & Sofie Blyaert
tel	+351 282 313422
fax	+351 282 313025
email	casabelamoura@sapo.pt
web	www.casabelamoura.com

Hotel

Map 5 Entry 191

Cerro da Horta

Vale Fuzeiros, Messines, 8375-082 Silves, Algarve

From the first glimpse of a red roof, tucked below on the hillside, the views get better and better. Hidden on the far side of the sprawling farmhouse is a terrace overlooking orange groves, hills and valleys all the way down to the sea. Below is a terraced garden with pool, badminton lawn, swings and trapeze – super child-friendly. Owners Janet and Martin, a gracious and friendly retired couple with a passion for Portugal – Martin's side of the family has connections going back four generations – love sharing their knowledge of the country. The guest rooms in a self-contained wing, one en suite, are simple, light and sunny with white-painted furniture from Martin's family's Portuguese estate. Colourful bedspreads or painted headboards add a warm, country feel. Bathrooms are generous, with the shared 'family-friendly' bathroom decked out with a tiled border of animals. There's breakfast only, but it is possible to make snacks in the living room and it's an easy stroll to the village restaurants. You are also close to the Moorish town of Silves, and the beaches.

rooms	4: 1 double, 2 twins, 1 room with bunks. Extra folding beds available.
price	€55-€65. Bunk room €35. Singles from €45.
meals	Good restaurants nearby.
closed	Rarely.
directions	A22, exit Messines, to Silves. Right for Vale Fuzeiros. There, right up hill before O Gralha restaurant; right again at top.

	Janet & Martin Reynolds
tel	+351 282 332842
fax	+351 282 332843
email	casarey@mail.telepac.pt

B&B

Map 5 Entry 192

Quintinha de Nova
Barrocal, Messines, Algarve

Countryside enfolds you, yet you are close to Faro. The gallery library in this rambling Algarve farmhouse has a bamboo ceiling, curved windows, comfortable armchairs, paintings, CDs and a wall of books – you'll feel at home. And there's a garden, a flower-filled patio, a swimming pool and lots of shady spots – perfect for a family. The vast dining room with wooden table, carved chairs and quirky chandelier made from a mule cartwheel was once the cow barn; now the old mangers hold Portuguese and English pottery. Prepare all you need in the well-furnished kitchen. Nova, who lives in Scotland, exports Portuguese ceramics, along with local honey and lavender, to her farm shop. Four double bedrooms, one with its own bath, and two shared showers; one room is particularly lovely, a good size and prettily tiled, with lacy and hand-embroidered little cushions on the bed. Maria lives next door and looks after the place – she is delightful and pops in to feed the two cats and to have a chat. The large walled garden has a barbecue, lots of trees, fragrant herbs and a hammock.

rooms	House for 8.
price	£525–£1,596 per week.
meals	Restaurants nearby.
closed	Rarely.
directions	From Faro, A22 to Boliqueime. Through Paderne for Messines, turn off for Barrocal. Follow signs to Mouricão; quintinha is on the road.

	Nova Gourlay
tel	+44 (0)1273 747811
fax	+44 (0)1273 329344
email	rentals@thevillaagency.co.uk

Self-catering

Map 5 Entry 193

Casa Belaventura

Campina de Boliqueime, 8100-073 Loulé, Algarve

For a big family party looking for independence, this is a good bet. Belaventura lies deep in the Algarve hinterland, in such a pastoral setting you will soon forget that the highway and coastal towns of Vilamoura and Albufeira are close by. Carlos converted the old farmhouse with self-catering, not just B&B, in mind; as well as a well-proportioned sitting room with fine open fire, there's a dining room with a view of the pool and a largish, darkish kitchen. Generally the house is light and airy from the open arches that link the spaces; deeply traditional are the terracotta floor, wafer brickwork and weathered roof tiles. By the pool in the garden – a riot of colour in July – are two long dining tables and a hammock in the shade of an olive tree; beyond, through the almond groves, glimpses of the glittering sea. Traditional bedrooms have modern paintings (some by Carlos's wife), durries, perhaps a view across the garden and the suite comes with an inglenook. Carlos has a boat and can take you for a day's sailing along the coast. *20% supplement during public holidays.*

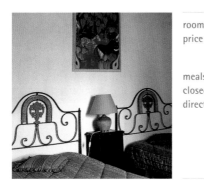

rooms	4: 3 twins/doubles, 1 suite.
price	€75-€100. Singles €65-€90. Whole house, self-catering, €1,750-€2,750 per week.
meals	Restaurants nearby.
closed	November–February.
directions	From Faro, IP1 for Spain. Exit for Boliqueime, after 250m, right. House signed on right after approx. 750m.

	Senhor Carlos Jorge Dias
tel	+351 289 360633
fax	+351 289 366053
email	belaventura@mail.telepac.pt

B&B & Self-catering

Map 5 Entry 194

Quinta da Cebola Vermelha

Campina, PO Box 141, 8100-908 Boliqueime, Algarve

So pristine one wonders how the old farmhouse can have so much personality – but it has. The owners are special too: cultured, stylish and friendly, adept at combining ancient and modern yet quite capable of witty and imaginative flourishes. (Paintings by 'new' Portuguese artists are high on their list for the future.) Much of the mood is Moroccan – but not at the hippy end of the spectrum! Bedrooms sparkle with colour, generosity and space, there are big quarry tiles and pale, plain walls. The taste is refreshing, and impeccable. The roomy beds are singles side by side, the bathrooms are vast and gorgeous. The swimming pool, too, is huge, set about with straw parasols and smart recliners, and a tabled lawn fragrant with orange trees to one side – bliss for a lunchtime snack. There are also some very gnarled and magnificent old olive trees. The food is the best of home cooking, the sea is 15 minutes by car, and the Algarve's hustle is safely out of reach. Let our inspector have the last word: "I defy anyone not to like it here: it is utterly gorgeous."

rooms	6 doubles/twins.
price	€95. Singles €85.
meals	Dinner, 3 courses €25, 3 times a week. Good local restaurants 1-3km.
closed	January.
directions	From Faro A22 for Albufeira, exit to Boliqueme. At r'bout into village; straight on then right for Picota & S. Fonntino. Right & at sign to Campina, right again. Continue to house.

	Ard & Noor Yssel de Schepper
tel	+351 289 363680
fax	+351 289 363688
email	info@quintadacebolavermelha.com
web	www.quintadacebolavermelha.com

B&B

Map 5 Entry 195

The Garden Cottages

North of Vilamoura, 8100-292 Loulé, Algarve

In a lush valley a couple of miles back from the coast, long hours of sunshine and rich soil allow nearly everything to grow in profusion. The English owner found this old wine farm in ruins in the early 70s and has put in years of patient restoration and planting. This is a place of peace and privacy; behind the whitewashed outer wall the cottages stand apart from one another facing the gardens and, tucked away beyond, is an enormous round swimming pool known as 'the library'… such is the peace. Each cottage has a sun and a shade terrace, a tiled kitchen, a sitting room and double bedroom – perfect for two. Dried flowers, eucalyptus beams and terracotta give a 'country' feel, while mementos from Africa and Turkey add an exotic note. This year, the Almond House, a tranquil wooden chalet (pictured) with pretty veranda and cool, cream interior has been added. But what we remember most are the gardens: olive, pomegranate, almonds and lemon and, beneath them, a profusion of flowers. The benign climate means that visiting out of season is just as special.

rooms	6 cottages for 2.
price	£200-£400 (sterling) per week.
meals	Good restaurants & snack bars nearby.
closed	Rarely.
directions	Information will be given at time of booking.

	Margot Firkin
tel	+44 (0)1295 760826
fax	+44 (0)1295 760826
email	m.firkin@btinternet.com
web	www.algarvegardencottage.co.uk

Self-catering

Map 5 Entry 196

Quintassential

Caixa Postal 101Z, Cruz Da Assumada, 8100-296 Loulé, Algarve

The road is steep, but the views spilling over the Atlantic will take your breath away – blue, sparkling, unbroken. This old Portuguese farmhouse and its outbuildings have been sensitively converted and extended. Rooms have a rustic, modern simplicity: solid wood furniture, pretty tiles, embroidered cushions, colourful pottery. There are woodburning stoves and microwaves, shelves of books, private terraces and barbecues – sophisticated yet cosy. For complete privacy, choose Casa do Forno, the converted bread oven; tiny, gorgeous, intimate, it is the ultimate in ergonomic design. Although temptingly near lively beaches and Loulé town, it's hard to drag yourself away from those views: the roof terrace has a horizon-wide panorama from the foothills of Monchique all the way to the Algarve coast. A terraced garden, swimming pool and shady patio bar – you dine on well-priced, traditional dishes during the summer – add to the choice of places to linger. Rosa (Portuguese) and Mike (English) are friendly without being intrusive. Great for a couple – or a big party. *Minimum stay three nights.*

rooms	5 cottages for 2-4. (Max. 14 people.)
price	£270-£595 (sterling) per week.
meals	Dinner, 3 courses, €15-€17.50 (May-Oct). Good restaurants nearby.
closed	Rarely.
directions	From airport to Loulé. From Loulé towards Salir to Cruz de Assumada. On sharp left bend, take track up to right. Take first left steeply up to house.

	Rosa Gulliver
tel	+351 289 463867
email	info@quintassential.com
web	www.quintassential.com

Casa Charneca

Sítio da Charneca 502A, 8005-440 Santa Barbara de Nexe, Algarve

A sanctuary above the Algarve, yet only 15 minutes from the dazzling white beaches. This stylish villa, in the hills of Santa Barbara, combines privacy with idiosyncratic touches. Modern lighting, French antiques, contemporary sofas and 19th and 20th century art sit delightfully together. White bedrooms are understatedly comfortable with large beds, clubby armchairs and rich fabrics; a Casablanca fan, Art Nouveau lampshade or splash of art add an exotic feel. The separate bedroom by the fish-shaped, dolphin-mosaic pool, although smaller, is a favourite with couples. Views stretch for miles, the peace is total. Breakfasts and dinners have a French flavour and are dictated by the day's markets and guests' requests. After a mouthwatering mousse au chocolat (a speciality), work off the calories in the small gym, sauna and jacuzzi. Owners Thierry and Ronny, an engaging and gentle pair, know how to spoil – there's breakfast in bed if you prefer, and free refreshments by the pool. Children would be bored but for grown-ups it's refreshing and fun. *Minimum stay three nights.*

rooms	4 doubles.
price	€70–€110. Singles from €55.
meals	Dinner, 3 courses, €20.
closed	Rarely.
directions	At S. Barbara Church head towards S. Bras for 2km; right at Casa Crow. House at very end of track.

	Ronny & Thierry Soenen
tel	+351 289 992842
email	casacharneca@hotmail.com
web	www.casacharneca.com

B&B

Map 6 Entry 198

Monte do Casal

Estoi, 8005-436 Faro, Algarve

Breakfast on your terrace, take afternoon tea round the pool, dine above a magically lit garden. It has taken Bill Hawkins 20 years to get this 18th-century manor house, high above the Algarve, to his liking. It is luxurious but not grand, smart but easy. The colonial-style drawing room has padded sofas, piles of books, beautiful flowers. Bedrooms – some in a separate villa a short walk away – are large but homely in understated country-house style: polished mahogany, pastel walls, watercolours, books and a choice of pillows! Some overlook the gardens, others have views to the sea. There are special touches everywhere: flowers, CD players, books, internet access and sunloungers on each private terrace. The Waterfall Villa spoils with a garden *and* a waterfall. When you tire of the swimming pools and whirlpools (two of each), explore the gardens, fountains and rockpools, rich with scent and colour. Dine – gourmand? Thai? classic Algarve? you choose – accompanied by candles and open fires; in summer under the pergola. A relaxing place for grown-ups, with a real welcome.

rooms	19: 12 twins/doubles. Villa: 7 twins/doubles.
price	€130–€400.
meals	Lunch €15. Dinner €29. Menu 'gourmand', 5 courses, €50.
closed	2-16 December; 6-20 January.
directions	In Estoi, at square, turn towards Moncarapacho; hotel approx. 2.5km along road, signed to left.

	Bill Hawkins
tel	+351 289 991503
fax	+351 289 991341
email	montecasal@mail.telepac.pt
web	www.montedocasal.pt

Hotel

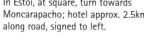 

Map 6 Entry 199

Pedras Verdes Guesthouse

Sítio da Boavista, CP 658 T Quelfes, 8700 Olhão, Algarve

The house is low and north-African style, surrounded by carob and olive trees. The bedrooms are all different, all sensational. Each has a theme: baroque, African, Asiatic, Zen, Arabic. Funky walk-in showers with pebbled or wooden flooring, plain walls, minimalist décor, Portuguese antiques and some modern pieces. The Asiatic room has fresh palms, lime green bedcovers and ceiling nets over the bed. Little touches make a real impact and each key has a symbol – a cowrie shell for the Asiatic room, an ebony sculpted head for the African room. Artistically placed fruit in the bedrooms, sweets, fresh flowers and postcards. The humour in the décor reflects the character of the lovely owners – Muriel and André are genuinely welcoming and enthusiastic about creating beautiful spaces. The same minimalist and stylish feel extends to the garden where stone sculptures are filled with exotic shells and crystals. Relax by the divine pool or under the canvas canopy; there is an overriding sense of calm. Dinner is served on a beautiful wooden table, is French and delicious; the cocktails are sublime.

rooms	6 twins/doubles.
price	€89-€99.
meals	Dinner €18-€22, Fridays.
closed	15 November-15 February.
directions	From Faro airport EN125-10 to Sâo Brás; on to N2 A22 to Spain; exit 15 Olhão "Quelfes". Entering village, sharp left-hand bend at white building with red base; sharp right, follow green stones (or phone & André will meet you.)

	Muriel & André Mandi
tel	+351 289 721343
fax	+351 289 721343
email	info@pedrasverdes.com
web	www.pedrasverdes.com

B&B

Map 6 Entry 200

Quinta da Belgica
Sítio da Fornalha, 8700 Moncarapacho, Algarve

On the road, but half-hidden by trees and climbers, this two-storey, purpose-built holiday complex is perfect for families with young children. The atmosphere created by Belgians Mieke and Jef is casual and relaxed, and they delight in sharing it all. Bedrooms are basic rather than luxurious, with glazed floors, cheery striped curtains, framed photos by Mieke on pale walls, and aluminium doors that double as windows. Some are air-conditioned. But you probably won't spend much time indoors when life revolves around the pool and easy gardens. There is almost a hectare of grounds here with plenty of shady spots beneath palm, orange, almond and pepper trees. Outdoor tables shaded by a bamboo roof and, near the pool, the combined bar, dining room and lounge, with black squashy sofa and armchairs – and a woodburning stove for cool evenings. Mieke cooks both Portuguese and northern European dishes. For children: ping-pong and table football, an old fishing boat in the garden, and dressing-up clothes. From the first-floor rooms you can see the sea – just! Bring the buckets and spades.

rooms	12: 3 doubles, 3 twins, 6 family rooms.
price	€65. Half-board €120.
meals	Dinner €25.
closed	January–mid-February.
directions	From A22 exit for Moncarapacho then head to Olhão. After 1km sharp bend, entrance on right, marked with flags.

	Mieke Everaert & Jef Cloots
tel	+351 289 791193
fax	+351 289 791192
email	info@quinta-da-belgica.com
web	www.quinta-da-belgica.com

B&B

Map 6 Entry 201

Solar da Fornalha

Largo do Poço no. 3, Sítio de Fornalha, 8700-091 Moncarapacho, Algarve

The lofty entrance hall and sitting area – a gracious space of Moorish arches, richly coloured sofas and luxurious plants – was the old olive press. Tucked among orange groves, the 19th-century farmhouse has kept its rustic good looks. And it's classy and hugely comfortable – polished floors, gleaming dark furniture, embroidered cushions, brightly dressed tables. The bedrooms vary in size and price, from airy suites with carved wooden beds to cosier rooms with pretty wrought-iron bedheads. Some are in a separate building on the hillside with sea views. Furniture is polished and solid – with the occasional antique – giving these newer rooms a simple, uncluttered feel. Rugs and rich fabrics add softness while the bathrooms, some with free-standing tubs, others with hydromassage baths, are lavishly tiled. The dining room, where *cataplana* (seafood stew) is a speciality, has a smartly rustic feel, and the detail extends to the gardens and shady patios. Linger at night with a glass of wine in the glow of a dozen garden flares. This atmosphere is that of a hotel, yet Renato and his family are charmingly hands-on.

rooms	30: 23 twins/doubles in main hotel; 7 twins/doubles in annexe.
price	€55-€155. Singles €45.
meals	Lunch/dinner €15-€25.
closed	Rarely.
directions	On A22, take Olhão junction. At r'bout follow signs for Moncarapacho. Take Estoi road, signposted Sítio de Fornalja. After 500m Solar is on left.

	Senhor Renato Gabriel
tel	+351 289 790270
email	solardafornalha@portugalmail.pt
web	www.solardafornalha.com

Hotel

Map 6 Entry 202

Vila Monte Resort

Sitio dos Caliços, 8700-069 Moncarapacho, Algarve

Just outside sleepy little Moncarapacho are the green and rolling acres of Vila Monte. Formerly the home of German artist 'Adolfo', this resort hotel is now owned by the Judice family, owners of the much loved Quinta das Lágrimas (see entry 55). Several newish buildings are dotted around the lush grounds, each with a distinct style. Standard rooms are in the Ermitage, a modern take on the Portuguese manor house, while deluxe rooms and suites are in the Orangerie, an Alhambra-inspired place of long pools, shady cloisters and tinkling fountains. The formal dining room has a soaring ceiling and Italian chandeliers. Vila d'Este is set slightly apart with five bedrooms with their own private pool – ideal for a group of friends or a family gathering. Bedrooms are simple and modern, given individuality by the many examples of Adolfo's artwork. There's golf, a fitness centre and salon and two swimming pools to choose from. In summertime: live music and special activities for children. Not for those in search of 'real' Portugal, but fun for lotus eaters of any age.

rooms	Ermitage: 20; Orangerie: 24 suites; Vila d'Este: 5 rooms with private pool; Quinta: 6 self-catering rooms.
price	From €129. Half-board €219.
meals	Dinner, 5 courses, €45.
closed	Rarely.
directions	From Faro airport A22 towards Spain. Exit for Olhão & Montcarapacho. At first r'bout head to Moncarapacho. Signed from there.

	Senhora Michaela Frick
tel	+351 289 790 790
fax	+351 289 790 799
email	info@adolfodaquinta.com
web	www.aldolfodaquinta.com

Hotel

Map 6 Entry 203

Quinta da Fonte Bispo

Estrada National 270, Cx Postal 797-A, Fonte do Bispo, 8800-161 Tavira, Algarve

Enjoy the benign climate, exceptional vegetation, closeness to the sea and interesting folk architecture in the gentle hills of the Algarve hinterland. This old farmstead will inspire affection for the region; we can see why painting courses are held here. It is a long, low, white building with pretty chimney stacks and broad bands of blue around doors and windows – typical of the area. Parts of the farm are 200 years old but it has been completely renovated. The six apartments in the converted outbuildings of the farm, fronting a cobbled central patio, were designed with families in mind: open-plan sitting rooms have beds which double up as sofas, a kitchenette and open fires for cosy winter days. The style is local and 'country': herringbone terracotta floors, beamed and bamboo roofs, simple yet adequate shower rooms. There is a large communal sitting room in similar style but most of the year you will be out by the pool; find a shady spot beneath the orange, almond or olive trees. The restaurant serves Mediterranean and Portuguese food, and there are a sauna, table-tennis, pool and mini-gym.

rooms	6 apartments for 4.
price	€60–€90. Call for further details of prices.
meals	Lunch €15. Dinner €20.
closed	Rarely.
directions	From Faro, A22 for Spain. Pass Loulé then exit for Santa Catarina. There, right for Tavira. Quinta signed on left after 1km.

	Senhora Helena Brito Neto
tel	+351 281 971484
fax	+351 281 971714
email	info@qtfontebispo.com
web	www.qtfontebispo.com

B&B

Map 6 Entry 204

Casa da Calma

Sitio do Pereiro, Cx Postal 327x, Moncarapacho/Olhão, 8700-123 Moncarapacho, Algarve

Pick your own oranges for breakfast! Nicole's small hotel in the unspoiled Algarve hills, is surrounded by amazingly verdant gardens and lawns. Hospitality runs in the family: German-born Nicole worked in the tourist industry for several years and her mother, House Cook, once ran a guesthouse in California. Décor at the renovated farm is hotel-comfortable but not hotel-anonymous and each bedroom is different: matching paisley bedcovers and curtains in one, wooden Portuguese beds in another. All have air-con, their own generous terraces and pleasing extras like fluffy white bathrobes and poolside towels. Breakfasts – brunches too – are a spread; the fish dinners are delicious. The heated pool is decked with yellow-cushioned loungers and jolly parasols, and there's a sauna. Further afield lie the fantastic island beaches of Armona and Tavira. Your hostess is an expert when it comes to organizing trips – horse riding, sailing, fishing, waterskiing and jeep safaris are all within your grasp. She also organises shopping trips to charming Lisbon – or over the border to Seville.

rooms	8: 7 twins/doubles (2 can be linked to make a family room), 1 family suite.
price	€92–€138. Singles €58–€68. Suite €160–€240.
meals	Dinner €15–€20, by arrangement.
closed	Rarely.
directions	Faro IP1 for Spain. Exit Olhâo & Moncarapacho. Then towards Sta Catarina. House on left after 2km.

	Nicole Effenberg
tel	+351 289 791098
fax	+351 289 791599
email	nicole.effenberg@clix.pt
web	www.casadacalma.com

Hotel

Map 6 Entry 205

Quinta da Lua

Bernardinheiro 1622-X, S. Estevão, 8800-513 Tavira, Algarve

Staying at the 'Farm of the Moon' is delightful on many levels. Miguel and Vimal have stacks of enthusiasm, love looking after people and the food is especially good; don't miss Vimal's once-weekly dinners. Breakfast, served under the green parasol, is different every day, and guests are asked their preferences. The house, surrounded by orange trees and vineyards, carob, oleander, bougainvillea and palms, is a two-storey addition to an old Algarve farmhouse, and there's a lovely saltwater pool in the well-groomed gardens – with shaded verandas to the side, and an 'honesty' fridge/bar for drinks. Inside: a stylish blend of modern and traditional, with rustic terracotta tiles and beamed ceilings throughout. Bedrooms are perfect: simple but luxurious; beds are generous, the soundproofing is good and the suites are huge. The moon logo is duplicated in two colours in the bath and shower rooms – you won't borrow your room mate's towel by mistake! Not one for families, but a surprise to find such a special place so close to the island beaches and the restaurants of Tavira, run by such nice people.

rooms	8: 6 twins/doubles, 2 suites.
price	€65–€120. Suites €100–€150.
meals	Lunch, €17. Dinner €25 (once a week).
closed	Never.
directions	From Faro, A22 to Spain, exit Tavira. At 2nd r'bout, N125 for Olhão. Right to S. Estevão. 1st left & next right, & look for arch over Quinta gateway.

	Miguel Martins & Vimal Willems
tel	+351 281 961070
fax	+351 281 961070
email	quintadalua@iol.pt
web	www.quintadalua.com.pt

B&B

Map 6 Entry 206

Casa Vale del Rei
Almargem, 8800-053 Tavira, Algarve

Robin and Geraldine fell in love with their holiday guesthouse and came back to buy it. You can see why. Perched on a hilltop close – but not too close – to the cobbled fishing town of Tavira, this handsome, whitewashed villa is surrounded by orange and olive groves and sweeping views of the coastline. Cabanas beach is a five-minute drive, three golf courses lie not much further. Not that you will want to leave in a hurry; Casa Vale del Rei is heaven in summer with its waterlily ponds, fountains and shady corners, its oleander, lavender, palms, pines and lazy pool. Your genial, friendly hosts have created a stylish and contemporary interior without spoiling the authentic Algarve feel. Bathrooms are glistening white, bedrooms cool and lofty with natural materials: muslin curtains, white-painted furniture, pretty cotton fabrics. Breakfast and sitting rooms are similarly spare, in cool creams and taupes, with stylish splashes from chandeliers, antiqued mirrors and vibrant fabric pictures. If it's warm, breakfast under the old alfarabos tree. After dinner, return to the peace of your hideaway.

rooms	7: 2 doubles, 3 twins, 2 family rooms.
price	€45–€60; children €20.
meals	Good local restaurant nearby; Tavira a short drive.
closed	Rarely.
directions	From Faro A22 E for Spain, exit junc. 16 Tavira. At 2nd r'bout N125 for Vila Real. Pass Eurotel on left, left at sign to Almargem. Left up track after white bridge on right.

	Robin Ford-Jones
tel	+351 281 323099
fax	+351 281 323099
email	casavaledelrei@hotmail.com
web	www.casavaledelrei.co.uk

B&B

Map 6 Entry 207

The Tavira Inn

Rua Chefe António Afonso, 39, 8800-251 Tavira, Algarve

Warm and witty, fun and funky; if a guesthouse can reflect its owner, the Tavira Inn surely does. Sebastião Bastos, a man of middle years and relaxed good humour, has combined his love of travel, music and art with his background in hotel management to create an off-beat but deliciously relaxing Special Place. Close to the centre of Tavira and overlooking the river, the townhouse combines old with new: tiled floors and Portuguese fireplaces with bold art and bright chairs. The seawater pool and terrace hide beneath a railway bridge – which strangely adds to the fun. The five guest rooms, double-glazed and very quiet, are colourfully and eclectically furnished – perhaps an antique wardrobe, a quilted bedspread, an exotically patterned rug, a Moroccan ceramic. Bathrooms are cool and modern with prettily tiled mirrors. The bar is the centre of activity, full of huge umbrellas and good humour. Laze by the pool, stroll into Tavira (three minutes), catch the boat to the beach. Come evening, relax to soul, jazz or gentle music around the bar. You'll probably decide to stay another day.

rooms	5 doubles.
price	€65-€130.
meals	Good restaurants nearby.
closed	November-January.
directions	From motorway follow signs for Tavira. House below bridge on N125 next to river. Follow signs for Tavira & follow junction for Ponte Ferroviária.

Senhor Sebastião Bastos

tel	+351 281 326578
fax	+351 281 326578
email	booking@tavira-inn.com
web	www.tavira-inn.com

B&B

Map 6 Entry 208

Convento de Santo António

Rua de Santo António 56, 8800-705 Tavira, Algarve

What a surprise! An inauspicious area, but seek out a tiny door in the ancient wooden gate by the chapel… it leads, incredibly, to this dazzling white convent surrounded by lush vegetation and circular pool. Isabel is almost apologetic that "the home has only been in the family for five generations". A portrait of great-grandmother gazes down one of the vaulted corridors that runs the length of the 17th-century cloister while Santo António looks on benignly from his chapel. The whole place is a Lusitanian feast of hand-crafted terracotta, flowered and striped *alcobaça* fabrics and carefully chosen, often naïve, paintings. The bedrooms vary in size and have a convent-like charm: here a vaulted ceiling, there a fine dresser. We loved the lofty Chapel Room for honeymooners, its bathroom sitting snugly inside what was a chimney breast. Lounge and bar are just as special and entirely candlelit at night – as peaceful as when the Capuchin monks dwelt here. You are near the historic centre of Tavira, yet a short walk from the beach. Gracious and special. *Minimum stay 3-5 nights depending on season.*

rooms	4: 2 twins/doubles, 1 suite, 1 suite for 4.
price	€120-€180. Suites €200-€350.
meals	Restaurants within walking distance.
closed	Never.
directions	From Faro east on N125; IP1 exit 16 to Tavira; under archway, over r'bout & T-junc., right after church, following signs 'Centro Saude'. Right past army barracks, 1st left; 200m, fork right.

	Senhora Isabel Maria Castanho Paes
tel	+351 281 321573
fax	+351 281 325632

B&B

Map 6 Entry 209

Photo Casa Velha do Palheiro, entry 210

madeira

madeira

Madeira means wood, and the island was thickly forested and known for its fortified wine – vines were planted not long after the Portuguese discovered the island in 1419

• A rugged volcanic Atlantic island with sub-tropical vegetation – 400 miles west of Casablanca off the coast of North Africa

• Also includes the islands of **Porto Santo, Desertas** and **Selvagens** – the latter two are uninhabited

• Madeira's capital **Funchal**, 1.5 hours flight from Lisbon. Admire the forts of San Tiago & São Lourenço, the 15th-century Cathedral & exquisite botanical gardens. Crazy toboggan run from hill-side Terreiro da Luta to Funchal

• Carnival – go wild the weekend before Ash Wednesday in February

• Visit the pretty village of **Santana** near Pico de Ruivo, Madeira's highest peak (1862m). There are many great walking paths around the island, many following the **levadas** or irrigation channels

• For white sands and water sports take a boat to the island of Porto Santo, 40km west of Madeira

• World championship surfing and excellent scuba diving

• Seek out the **laurissilva**, the remaining ancient trees, which, due to Madeira's position, survived the last glaciation

Casa Velha do Palheiro

Rua da Etalagem 24, Sao Gonçaio, 9060-415 Madeira

The elegant house was originally designed for the first Count of Carvalhal as a hunting lodge and was frequented by the royal family and the nobility. It has a distinctly English country manor feel. Trees from the southern hemisphere – some were a gift from King Dom João VI of Portugal – were planted and deer grazed the land. These days the place is still grand: 30 acres of gardens with formal plantings and mature woodland, a chapel, a smart lounge for afternoon tea and an ecological golf course. Luxurious country-style bedrooms, all individual, have floral bedcovers and curtains, long windows and some antiques. An intimate, friendly atmosphere prevails. Trace the history throught the rooms – studying the paintings, prints and maps – a short guide has been thoughtfully provided. The birdsong is vibrant and the friendly staff can arrange for you to go fishing on their yacht. They can also arrange transport to and from Funchal. Unwind with an aromatherapy treatment after a blast in the steam room – and there's tennis, badminton, croquet, billiards and cards.

rooms	37: 31 twins/ doubles; 6 suites split between main building, garden wing and new wing.
price	€180–€245.
meals	Dinner, 3 courses, €40.
closed	Never.
directions	15 mins from airport. Exit for Camacha & Palheiro Golf. Right, then left at next sign for Palheiro Golf. Up hill; right at sign for Casa Velha. Left after entering Palheiro Estate.

	James Scott
tel	+351 291 790350
fax	+351 291 794925
email	info@casa-velha.com
web	www.casa-velha.com

Hotel

Map 6 Entry 210

Choupana Hills Resort

Travessa do Largo da Choupana, 9060-348 Funchal, Madeira

Be spoiled by this designer hotel with its sumptuous Portuguese-Asian twist. A gold embossed wall-hanging above an open fire, a water bowl flickering with tiny candles, vibrant armchairs – orange, lime, mulberry in the bar, plum and red in the dining room – and vast, glass candle-holders. This new hotel is filled with gorgeous antiques and modern things, its large lagoon-like pool is surrounded by young gardens of cacti and palms, and you'll skip with pleasure when you discover your luxurious bungalow on stilts… its exotic canopied wooden bed, its crisper-than-crisp bedlinen, its rich polished floors, its private terrace with views of Funchal bay. All the rooms feel private and peaceful, sparkling bathrooms have lush goodies and fat bathrobes to lounge in, and the suites get outdoor jacuzzis. Pad down to the spa where a medley of blissful treatments can be arranged, have a steamy Turkish bath or take a dip in the serene indoor pool. Then afternoon tea in the lounge, or a cocktail at the bar. Charming staff, fusion cuisine, tranquillity – a hedonists' retreat.

rooms	63: 59 twins/doubles, 4 suites.
price	From €313.
meals	Lunch €30. Dinner, 3 courses, €40.
closed	Never.
directions	Follow the main road towards the Botanical Gardens. Follow signs to Choupana Hills.

	Senhor Philippe Moreau
tel	+351 291 206020
fax	+351 291 206021
email	info@choupanahills.com
web	www.choupanahills.com

Hotel

Map 6 Entry 211

Quinta da Bela Vista

Caminho do Avista Navios, 4, 9000 Funchal, Madeira

Simply stunning – a manor house with exquisite formal walled gardens and sweeping views of Funchal bay. The quinta is not short of antiques, and bedrooms in the main house are classical with warm colours and traditional prints. Bathrooms are marble. Bedrooms in the new annexe are equally good, but with a modern feel; choose those in the main house for old-fashioned ambience. For privacy, ask for breakfast to be served on your own terrace. The cheerful restaurant – yellow walls, black and white tiled floors – serves mouthwatering dishes at one big old table; there's also à la carte. Elegant lounges have open fires in winter, there are a billiard room, card room, library and small fitness room with jacuzzi and sauna, and outside a tennis court and a pool – relax with a drink or a snack from the bar and soak up those glorious views. If you prefer to go snorkelling or scuba diving, the friendly and courteous staff will suggest local trips and even lay on a minibus service to and from Funchal. Or make the most of the hotel's yacht and drop in on the local islands – bliss!

rooms	89: 82 twins/doubles, 7 suites.
price	€176–€248.
meals	Dinner, 3 courses, €37.50.
closed	Never.
directions	From Airport follow signs for Funchal; exit for S. Martinho. In village, left at next roundabout. 3rd road left, 'Caminho do Avista Navios'. Signed.

	Senhor Goncalo Monteiro
tel	+351 291 706400
fax	+351 291 706401
email	info@belavistamadeira.com
web	www.belavistamadeira.com

Hotel

Map 6 Entry 212

Quinta das Vinhas

Lombo dos Serrões - Est° Calheta, 9370-221 Calheta, Madeira

Stay at one of the oldest manor houses on the island. It is flanked by the mountains and has views that sweep over its vineyards to the blue sea. The 17th-century homestead – all flagstone floors, wooden ceilings and handpainted tiles – exudes tradition. The owner's family, of English origin, once ran the biggest sugar cane mill in Madeira. Now the dining room – where food and wines are delicious – is in the old kitchen, and the old prayer room is a reading room; both are adorned with elegant antiques. This peaceful and gracious atmosphere extends to the lush grounds, where you may stroll among the tulip trees and the angel's trumpets, and perhaps pluck a passion fruit or two. Then back for a glass of the Quinta's very fine Madeira. Bedrooms in the main house have traditional furnishings and are flooded with light; the apartments, built of Madeiran stone, with minimalist interiors and bold colours, are set apart. Fish from the village pier, take a dip in the sea, surf the winter swell, visit the Chapel of the Three Kings. A fabulous place.

rooms	6 + 14: 6 doubles. 14 self-catering cottages for 2-3. Extra beds poss.
price	€80-€100. Cottages from €560 p.w.
meals	Dinner €15. Pool snacks available.
closed	Rarely.
directions	In Ribeira Brava 1st right, through tunnel. On to Calheta. Pass C. Beach Hotel; right for Est da Calheta. Through 2 tunnels; right. Pass chemist on left. Large pine tree on right before entrance; bright pink walls.

	Senhor Henrique Jamie Welsh
tel	+351 291 824086
fax	+351 291 822187
email	info@qdvmadeira.com
web	www.qdvmadeira.com

B&B & Self-catering

Map 6 Entry 213

Solar da Bica

Sítio dos Lameiros, São Vicente, 9240-211 Funchal, Madeira

The house is enveloped by emerald mountains and the views are breathtaking. 'Bica' means brook and the villagers used to come here to collect their water. Joel and Ferdinanda adore their house and delight in helping guests explore this unspoilt part of northern Madeira (walks from the door, and volcanic caves to discover). The breakfast room combines the simplicity of rough wooden beams and old agricultural equipment with sleek cream chairs, funky lights and white linen cloths, while bedrooms are simple and cosy – pine beds, floral bedcovers, patterned rugs. You share a beautiful, glass-sided indoor heated pool with wooden loungers, and a garden full of fruit, flowers and vegetables. Relax on the terrace on a summer's evening, or in the living room with a drink from the honesty bar. You can eat in if you book in advance – or use the barbecue area, complete with open-plan outdoor kitchen and bread oven. Children will love the play area – and the nearby beaches. It's homely, friendly, tranquil and excellent value.

rooms	14 doubles.
price	€50-€60.
meals	Dinner, 3 courses, €15-€20.
closed	Never.
directions	Leave tunnel at exit to S. Vicente; follow towards sea; at 2nd r'bout 1st road, follow sign to Solar do Bica; 1.2km to house.

	Senhor Joel Freitas
tel	+351 291 842018
fax	+351 291 842023
email	reservas@solarbica.com
web	www.solarbica.com

B&B

Map 6 Entry 214

Quinta do Arco

9230-018 Arco de S. Jorge, Madeira

Madeira is known for its subtropical landscape and stunning flowers; these pretty yellow cottages, carefully designed to mirror the style of the main house, are surrounded by both. Although this is a fair-sized complex, the cottages surface on many levels and the gorgeous, lush gardens soften — and add privacy. Fragrances drift on the breeze, from roses to fruit trees: oranges, avocados, figs, loquats, bananas... a little piece of heaven. Vegetables are also grown, and grapes: this is a wine estate. The houses are rustic in style, with their wooden floors, beamed ceilings, open-stone walls, mezzanines and woodburning stoves. Add striped rugs, crisp linen, soft lighting and the odd dazzle of colour and you have 18 deeply relaxing places to stay. Kitchens are beautifully equipped, fresh bread is delivered to your door for breakfast. And if you feel like being sociable, there are a communal honesty bar, pool table, restaurant and pool. The old wine press and workers' quarters are worth a visit, and your friendly and helpful hosts and their children are there at weekends should you need them.

rooms	18 villas for 2.
price	€80 per night. Singles €70.
meals	Breakfast items in the fridge. Good restaurants nearby.
closed	Rarely.
directions	From Funchal airport, north towards Santana. Continue, past São Jorge until Arco de S. Jorge. Signed.

	Senhora Elizabete Albuquerque
tel	+351 291 570 270
fax	+351 291 570 276
email	info@quintadoarco.com
web	www.quintadoarco.com

Self-catering

Map 6 Entry 215

Useful vocabulary

Making the booking
Do you speak English? *Fala inglês?*
Do you have a single / double / twin / triple room available?
Tem um quarto para uma pessoa /quarto de casal/um triplo disponível
For this evening/tomorrow
Para este noite/amanhã
With private bathroom
Com casa de banho privada
Shower/bath *O chuveiro/ a banheira*
With a balcony *Com uma veranda*
Is breakfast included?
O pequêno almoço é incluído no preço?
Half-board *Meia-pensão*
Full-board *Pensão completa*
How much does it cost? *Quanto custa?*
We will arrive at 6pm
Chegaremos por volta das seis da tarde
We would like to have dinner
Gostariamos de jantar
Left/right *Esquerda/direita*
Excuse me *Com licença*

Getting There
We're lost *Estamos perdidos*
Where is...? *Onde é/onde fica...?*
Could you show me on the map?
O Senhor/a Senhora pode mostrar-me no mapa?
Where are we? *Aonde estamos?*
We are in Lisbon *Estamos em Lisboa*
We will be late *Vamos chegar tarde*

On Arrival
Hi *Olá*
Good morning *Bom dia*
Good afternoon *Boa tarde*
Good evening *Bom noite*

I am Mr/Mrs Kinch-Ross
Eu sou o Senhor/a Senhora Kinch-Ross
Can I see a room?
Posso ver um quarto?
I would like to reserve a room
Eu gostaria reservar um quarto
We will stay three nights
Vamos ficar três noites

While you are there
A light bulb needs changing
Uma lâmpada necessita de ser mudada
The room is too cold/hot
O quarto é muito frio/quente
Do you have a fan?
Têm um ventoinha?
We don't have any hot water
Não temos água quente
What time is... *A que hora é...*
Breakfast/lunch/dinner
O pequeno-almoço/ o almoço/ o jantar
What time is it? *Que horas são?*

On Leaving
We would like to pay the bill
Queremos a conta, se faz favor
Do you take credit cards?
Aceita cartões de crédito?
Goodbye! *Adeus*
This is a beautiful spot
Este é um lugar muito bonito
We've had a very pleasant stay
Tivemos uma estadia muito agradável
Thank you so much
Muito obrigado/a

Flying to Portugal
Flybe www.flybe.com
0871 700 0535 Exeter-Faro
Easyjet www.easyjet.com
0871 750 0100 Bristol, E. Midlands,
Luton, Stanstead & Gatwick-Faro
Bmi Baby www.bmibaby.com
0870 264 2229 E. Midlands-Faro
Ryanair www.ryanair.com
0871 246 0000 Dublin-Faro;
Stanstead-Porto
Air Luxor www.airluxor.com
+351 210 062 450 Gatwick-Lisbon;
Lisbon-Madeira
British Airways www.ba.com
0870 850 9 850 Heathrow-Lisbon;
Gatwick-Faro, Funchal, Porto;
London-Vigo
Globespanwww.flyglobespan.com
0870 556 1522
Edinburgh, Glasgow -Faro
Jet2 www.jet2.com 0870 040 6300
Leeds/Bradford & Manchester - Faro
Monarch Schedules
www.flymonarch.com
0870 040 6300 Gatwick, Luton,
Manchester-Faro
Palmair www.bathtravel.com
01202 200700 Bournemouth-Faro
PGA Portugalia Airlines www.pga.pt
0870 755 0025
Manchester-Lisbon, Porto
TAP Air Portugal
www.tap-airportugal.com
0845 601 0932 Heathrow-Faro,
Funchal, Lisbon & Porto
Gatwick-Funchal & Lisbon

Photo Casa d'Alem, entry 32

Travel By Train
Rail Europe
http://www.raileurope.com
Portuguese railways: Caminhos de
Ferro Portugueses (CP) +351 808
208208 www.cp.pt. You will need to
load the page in English.

Travel by Coach/bus
www.rede-expressos.pt gives
timetable information.

Travel by Ferry
You can travel to Northern Spain by
ferry (Plymouth-Santander) and it
takes approximately 24 hours. It is a
further 6 hours driving to northern
Portugal.
P&O Portsmouth 0870 242 4999
www.poportsmouth.com
Brittany Ferries 0870 366 5333
www.brittany-ferries.com
The alternative is to cross the
Channel (ferry or Eurotunnel) to
France and travel the rest of the way
by car or train. It is approximately
1900km to Lisbon, 1800km to Porto
or 2200km to Faro.

Shopping in Lisbon

Ken Parr, owner of Mouraria in Lisbon (entry 98) and Pomar Velho near Marvão (entry 122) gives an insider view of the best places to shop in Lisbon.

Since I first came to Lisbon, 25 years ago, there has been a notable change in the shopping practices of 'Lisboetas'. The shopping centres that are to be found in and around the city now dominate the scene - but they do still rub shoulders with the little family-run shops that specialize in such delights as church candles made of pure beeswax and perfectly-crafted leather gloves.

Should you visit the Columbo Shopping Centre, next to the new Stadium of Light (metro Colégio Militar), seek out the Oil and Vinegar Shop and sample the many delicious ingredients used in mediterranean cuisine. The second big shopping centre, Vasco da Gama, Parc das Nacões, has a cheery, nautical theme.

The Spanish department store chain, El Corte Inglés, has opened a huge store by São Sebastião Station, complete with Multiplex cinema. Nearby is the Gulbenkian Museum shop, full of beautiful replicas of museum artifacts. Also worth a visit is the museum shop in the Praça das Restauradores - come for superb reproductions of ancient tiles,

pottery, Roman jewellery, Art Deco packed soap and silk scarves patterned with the pavement mosaics of Lisbon.

The most interesting shopping centre in Lisbon is Mouraria in the Largo de Martim Moniz. Packed with Indian, Asian and African shops, it is also the place to have your hair braided and beaded. Just up the road, in Rua da Palma, is the pottery factory/shop of Viuva Lamego. Note its fabulous tiled façade. The goods are pricey but the vases, pots and tiles are beautiful, authentic Portuguese.

Fortunately the old flea markets of Lisbon still exist. The best known is the Feira da Ladra, behind the church of São Vicente, just down from Graça, open Tuesdays and Saturdays; hop on tram 28. The most outrageous market is the Sunday morning Feira do

Relógio near the airport, where gypsies trade clothes, household goods, fruit, veg and trinkets. Many Portuguese would not be seen dead here - which makes it all the more appealing! There's also a Thursday morning market in Carcavelos, half-way between Lisbon and Cascais; take the train and make a day of it - Estoril and Cascais are nearby.

Small, century-old, family-run shops abound. Halfway up Rua do Carmo, on the right, at the point where the Rossio links to Rua Garret, is a tiny place that stocks the most exquisite gloves in Lisbon. The Chiado area, principally Rua Garret, is the most exclusive shopping area of the city, full of designer clothes shops. Downtown in Baixa are many shops selling gold jewellery - a testament to Portugal's trading past. Peering into these exquisite shops, with their stained glass and their chandeliers, is a treat in itself. And the quality of the gold is unbeatable for the price (note that the minimum legal requirement for gold is 18 carats).

In a small street behind the Praça da Figueira is Braz & Braz, a seven-floor department store specializing in glassware, pottery, china and kitchenware. Your purchases may involve three assistants: one to help you, one to wrap (ask for gift wrapping - it's free), and one to write out the bill. This is a wonderful

shop for gifts and souvenirs - and cheaper than the tourist-targeted artesenato shops. Pollux, Rua das Fanqueiras in the Baixa, is similar.

Finally, should you wish to take home a bottle of vintage port or well-priced wine, then head for Napoleão, at the bottom of Rua dos Fanqueiros. Senhor Napoleão reminds me of Sidney Greenstreet, the actor who starred alongside Bogart in The Maltese Falcon. His assistants speak English and will offer you some ports to try - and you will almost certainly end up buying at least one bottle!

Photos Convento de São Paulo, entry 140

Wine production in northern Portugal

Piers Gallie at Quinta do Convento da Franqueira (entry 13) produces his own wine & gives his expert opinion on wine production in the north.

A young generation of Portuguese wine-makers, a careful selection of grape varieties in newly planted vineyards and modern wineries with state-of-the-art equipment - these three elements have combined to give the wine industry in the north a new lease of life.

Photo Casa d'Alem, entry 32

Douro
One of the oldest wine regions in the world follows the great river and its tributaries, from the west-coast town of Régua to the Spanish border in the east. Spectacular scenery and beautiful vineyards are best seen by boat. Famous for its port, the area is increasingly being recognised as the source of some great red wines based on local grape varieties such as *Tinta Roriz, Tinta Barroca, Touriga Nacional* and *Touriga Francesa.* For an audio tour that explains it all - from the history of the region to the final bottling process - visit the Quinta do Panascal, owned by the Fonseca Guimaraens Company. Tel: 351 254 732321. panascal@fonsecaport.com

After the harvest, the wines are taken for storage and bottling to lodges in Vila Nova de Gaia on the south bank of the river, facing Porto. All the main shippers are open to visitors; Grahams have a well-organised tour and Taylors an excellent dining room. Wine route: www.ivp.pt

Vinho Verde
This large wine region runs north from Porto to the Spanish border, and inland to the National Parks and mountain ranges to the east. It is a densely populated and cultivated area with many historic towns surrounded by year-round lush green vegetation

– hence the name 'green wine'. The light, white, slightly sparkling wines are made from local grapes such as Lourairo, Trajadura, Azal, Avesso and Alvarinho. Many small producers hand their grapes over to cooperatives, a small group of large companies handles the production of the commercial brands, and there are a number of 'château'-style quintas that produce own label wines.

The wine routes cover the various rivers of the region and allow you to visit large cooperatives, such as that at Ponte de Lima, as well as small producers like the Quinta da Franqueira near the market town of Barcelos.
Wine route: rota@vinhoverde.pt
www.vinhoverde.pt

Dão

This wine region follows the rivers Mondêgo and Dão that run through some rough and heavily wooded countryside in the centre of Portugal, with Viseu the capital town. The demise of the cooperative monopoly that followed joining the EU has resulted in many independents, and several large wine companies, investing in the area. Now the Dão produces some excellent and long-lasting red and white wines. Grape varieties include *Touriga Nacional*, *Jaen*, *Alfrocheiro Preto*, *Bastardo* and *Tinta Pinheira*. Wine route: 232 410060.

Photo Laura Kinch

cvrdao@mail.telepac.pt
www.cvrdao.pt

Bairrada

Wine has been made here for centuries but only recently has the Bairrada, on the Portuguese 'Litoral' from Aveiro south to Coimbra, become a demarcated region. On a heavy clay soil the Baga grape produces the majority of *Bairrada* reds, and the white grapes, *Bical* and *Maria Gomes*, are used to produce sparkling wines, some of Portugal's best.

In the centre of the region, at Mealhada, 'Leitão' suckling pig is the speciality of all the restaurants: an oven-baked delicacy that goes very well indeed with the local red. The Buçaco forest is well worth a visit, and so is the Palace Hotel, which has been producing its own red and white wines since 1917. These great wines can be sampled only in the restaurants of the Palace Hotel and its sister hotels; prepare for a treat.
Wine route: 231 510180.
cv.bairrada@mail.telepac.pt

Fragile Earth series

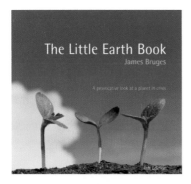

The Little Earth Book
Edition 4, £6.99
By James Bruges

A little book that has proved both hugely popular – and provocative. This new edition has chapters on Islam, Climate Change and The Tyranny of Corporations.

The Little Food Book
Edition 1, £6.99
By Craig Sams, Chairman of the Soil Association

An explosive account of the food we eat today. Never have we been at such risk - from our food. This book will help understand what's at stake.

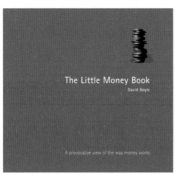

The Little Money Book
Edition 1, £6.99
By David Boyle, an associate of the New Economics Foundation

This pithy, wry little guide will tell you where money comes from, what it means, what it's doing to the planet and what we might be able to do about it.

www.fragile-earth.com

Six Days

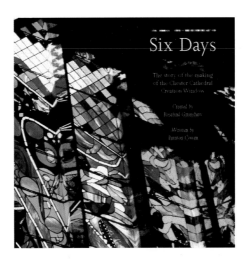

Celebrating the triumph of creativity over adversity.

An inspiring and heart-rending story of the making of the stained glass 'Creation' window at Chester Cathedral by a woman battling with debilitating Parkinson's disease.

"Within a few seconds, the tears were running down my cheeks. The window was one of the most beautiful things I had ever seen. It is a tour-de force, playing with light like no other window ..." Anthropologist Hugh Brody

In 1983, Ros Grimshaw, a distinguished designer, artist and creator of stained glass windows, was diagnosed with Parkinson's disease. Refusing to allow her illness to prevent her from working, Ros became even more adept at her craft, and in 2000 won the commission to design and make the 'Creation' Stained Glass Window for Chester Cathedral.

Six Days traces the evolution of the window from the first sketches to its final, glorious completion as a rare and wonderful tribute to Life itself: for each of the six 'days' of Creation recounted in Genesis, there is a scene below that is relevant to the world of today and tomorrow.

Heart-rending extracts from Ros's diary capture the personal struggle involved. Superb photography captures the luminescence of the stunning stained glass, while the story weaves together essays, poems, and moving contributions from Ros's partner, Patrick Costeloe.

Available from Alastair Sawday Publishing £12.99

Order Form

All these books are available in major bookshops or you may order them direct. Post and packaging are FREE within the UK.

British Hotels, Inns & Other Places	£13.99
Bed & Breakfast for Garden Lovers	£14.99
Pubs & Inns of England & Wales	£13.99
London	£9.99
British Bed & Breakfast	£14.99
French Bed & Breakfast	£15.99
French Hotels, Châteaux & Inns	£13.99
French Holiday Homes	£11.99
Paris Hotels	£9.99
Ireland	£12.99
Spain	£14.99
Portugal	£10.99
Italy	£12.99
Mountains of Europe	£9.99
Europe with courses & activities	£12.99
India	£10.99
Morocco	£10.99
The Little Earth Book	£6.99
The Little Food Book	£6.99
The Little Money Book	£6.99
Six Days	£12.99

Please make cheques payable to Alastair Sawday Publishing. Total £

Please send cheques to: Alastair Sawday Publishing, The Home Farm Stables, Barrow Gurney, Bristol BS48 3RW. For credit card orders call +44 (0)1275 464891 or order directly from our web site www.specialplacestostay.com

Title   First name   Surname

Address

Postcode   Tel

If you do not wish to receive mail from other like-minded companies, please tick here n
If you would prefer not to receive information about special offers on our books, please tick here n

REPORT FORM

If you have any comments on entries in this guide, please let us have them. If you have a favourite house, hotel, inn or other new discovery, please let us know about it. You can email info@sawdays.co.uk, too.

Existing entry:

Book title: _____

Entry no: _____ Edition no: _____

Report:

_____

_____

_____

_____

_____

_____

_____

Country: New recommendation:

Property name: _____

Address: _____

_____

_____

_____

Tel: _____

_____

Your name: _____

Address: _____

_____

_____

Tel: _____

Please send completed form to ASP, The Home Farm Stables, Barrow Gurney, Bristol BS48 3RW or go to www.specialplacestostay.com and click on 'contact'. Thank you.

Bilingual booking form

Á atencão de:
To:

Date:

Estimado Senhor/Estimada Senhora,

Agradeciamos que efectuassem uma reserva em nome de:
Please could you make us a reservation in the name of:

Para	noite(s)	Chegada a: dia	mês	ano
For	night(s)	Arriving: day	month	year
		Partida a: dia	mês	ano
		Leaving: day	month	year

Desejamos	quarto, :
We would like	rooms, arranged as follows:

Cama de casal	Camos seperadas
Double bed	Twin beds
Triplo	Individual
Triple	Single
Suite	Apartamento
Suite	Apartment

Também desejamos jantar: Sim Não Para pessoas
We will also be requiring dinner yes no   for person(s)

Agradeciamos que nos enviassem confirmação desta reserva para o endereço acima mencionado. (Pode utilizar este formulário où uma fotocópia do mesmo com a sua assinatura.)

Please could you send us confirmation of our reservation to the address below (this form or a photocopy of it with your signature could be used).

O nome: **Name:**

O endereço: **Address:**

Tel No: Email:

Fax No:

Formulário de Reserva - Special Places to Stay: Portugal

- New Maps
- Hotlists
- Extra pictures
- Extra links
- Extended searches
- Full write-ups
- Owner content

Discover your perfect self-catering escape in Britain...

We have launched a brand new self-catering web site covering England, Scotland and Wales. With the same punch and attitude as our printed guides www.special-escapes.co.uk celebrates only those places that we have visited and genuinely like – castles, cottages, bothies and more...

Special Escapes is a shining beacon among the mass of bleak holiday cottage sites cluttering the search engine pages. Each place is described in the style for which Alastair Sawday Publishing is so well known – and since it won't be published in book form, you'll be able to read the full description along with details about amenities and what to see and do locally.

Russell Wilkinson,
Web Site Manager
website@specialplacestostay.com

The Portuguese love *festas* (festivals), *romarias* (religious pilgrimages) and *ferias* (fairs) and there are lots during the summer. If there's one on nearby, don't miss it, and do check dates with the tourist office as they may change. Here are some of the major festivals:

February/March: Carnival in Portugal and Madeira: fairs, parades and fantastic costumes; notably in Viana do Castelo & Loulé.

May: *Queima das Fitas* celebrates the end of the academic year in Coimbra; Fátima Pilgrimage (10th); Flower Festival in Madeira.

June: *Feira Nacional* at Santarém lasts for 10 days, starting on the first Friday; *Festa de São Gonçalo* in Amarente, first weekend; *Santos Popularos* in Lisbon are celebrations in honour of St Anthony (13th), St John (24th) and St Peter (29th). There is also a festival in Porto for St John (24th).

July: *Festa do Colete Encarnado* (1st two weeks) in Vila Franca de Xira with Pamplona-style running of bulls through the streets.

August: *Romaria da Nossa Senhora da Agonia* in Viana do Castelo, third weekend. Feast of Our Lady of Monte (14-15) Madeira. Most important religious festival.

September: *Romaria da Nossa Senhora dos Remédios in Lamego*, Pilgrimage; 6th-8th New Fair in Ponte de Lima, second and third weekend.

October: *Feira de Outubro in Vila Franca de Xira*, more bull running; Fátima second great pilgrimage of the year (10th).

November: *Feira Nacional do Cavalo* (9th-14th): National Horse Fair in Golegã.

These entries have interesting festivals nearby - details sometimes given in brackets.
Numbers refer to entries in the book:
Minho • 2 (June, July & August) • 3 (Many local festivals - ask owner for details) • 4 (S. Sebastião - 1st Sunday in August) • 5 • 6 (Romaraia Sra. d'Agoia - Viano do Castelo - August) • 7 • 8 (July, August & September - Folklore festivals & Animation nights) • 9 (3rd weekend in September) • 13 (May) • 16 (S. José - 19 March) • Douro 25 (St John's Festival 23-24 June) • 29

Photo Laura Kinch

(Nossa Senhora de Aboadela - 15 August) • **35** (Gastronomic Festival 'Feira do Fumeiro') • **Trás os Montes 36** (S. António de S. Pedro - 24-29 June) • **37** • **40** (São João Festival 23-24 June) • **41** • **Beira 46** • **47** (Religious holidays: 24 & 29 June & 15 August) • **51** (20 January & 10-day festival in August) • **54** (September) • **56** • **60** • **62** • **66** (Every weekend during summer) • **67** • **Estremadura** • **71** (Several village feasts/fairs in summer.) • **79** (Festa S. Pedro - week of 29 June) • **81** (May-November) • **86** (2 festivals: Santo António in Lisbon 13 June & some days before and after & Nossa Senhora da Graça in village 5 October, also some days before & after) • **87** • **94** • **95** (Festival Popular - 12 June 'Marchas Populares de Santo António', Lisbon holiday & procession in typical dress down the Avenida da Liberdade.) • **97** (Festas de Santo António - 13 June) • **98** (June & February) • **Ribatejo 105** (Most weekends in summer) • **110** (Golegã Horse Fair November) • **Alentejo 118** (Large Easter Parade) • **122** (November) • **123** (Weekly market; local festivals in Summer; Carnival at Easter) • **126** • **141** • **142** (Many local, cultural and religious festivals.) • **144** (Festival São Pedro de Corval - 3rd week July. Many festivals in July, August & September; Pottery festival) • **145** (Monsaraz) • **148** (Medieval dinner with costumes and performances; traditional annual fair - November) • **153** • **154** (Annual fair 20-30 June) • **155** (Music, ballet) • **158** (Alvito annual Fair - 1

November) • **159** (March & October) • **163** (25 April - Independence Day) • **Algarve 173** (Sausage fair - 1st weekend March; Salted ham fair) • **176** (Festival 'Popular' end of June) • **178** • **183** (Festival dos Descobrimentos) • **195** (June - Boliqueime Festival) • **197** (Loulé Carnival - 40 days before Easter) • **207** (Feast of S. João - 23-24 June.) • **209** (June Festival 'Popular' in Tavira town) • **Madeira 210** (Carnival 5-9 February; Flower festival 9-10 April; Wine festival 2-4 September.) • **212** (Carnival - February; flower festival April; Madeira wine rally August) • **213** (15 August for 1 week) • **214** (1st Sunday in August)

Photo Laura Kinch

Quick reference indices

Wine production
Places of particular interest to wine buffs.

Minho 1 • 3 • 5 • 7 • 11 • 12 • 13 • 16 • 20 • 21 • 24 • Douro 28 • 29 • 33 • Trás-os-Montes 35 • 36 • 37 • 38 • 43 • Beira 46 • 49 • Ribatejo 113 Alentejo 115 • 122 • 123 • 130 • Algarve 176 • Madeira 213

Olive oil production
Places that produce their own olive oil.

Minho 11 • Douro 32 • 33 • Trás-os-Montes 35 • 36 • 37 • 38 • 39 • 40 • 43 • Beira 46 • 47 • 49 • 109 Alentejo 115 • 122 • 123 • 128 • 130 • 131 • 136 • 138 • 141 • 144 • 145 • 151 • 154 • Algarve 195 • 204

Wheelchair-accessible
These places have full and approved wheelchair facilties.

Minho 2 • 19 Douro 25 • 28 • 30 • Trás-os-Montes 35 • Beira 48 • 49 • 51 • 61 • 62 • 67 • Estremadura 69 • 72 • 81 • 85 • 90 • 91 • 96 • 100 • Ribatejo 106 • 107 • 109 • 111 • 113 • Alentejo 121 • 125 • 137 • 138 • 140 • 143 • 146 • 153 • 158 • 159 • 160 • 168 • 169 • 170 • Algarve 188 • 204 • Madeira 212 • 215

River / beach
Within 10km of a good river / beach.

Minho 2 • 3 • 4 • 5 • 7 • 8 • 9 • 11 • 12 • 15 • 17 • 18 • 22 • 23 • 24 • Douro 28 • 29 • 30 • 31 • 32 • 33 • 34 • Trás-os-Montes 35 • 36 • 37 • 39 • 40 • 43 • Beira 45 • 47 • 49 • 50 • 54 • 56 • 57 • 58 • 59 • 60 • 61 • 62 • 63 • 64 • 66 • Estremadura 70 • 73 • 74 • 78 • 81 • 93 • Ribatejo 105 • 106 • 111 • Alentejo 118 • 128 • 130 • 131 • 141 • 142 • 143 • 145 • 158 • 163 • 168 • 170 • 171 • Algarve 174 • 175 • 178 • 182 • 189 • 190 • 203 • 209

Courses and Activities
Either on site or nearby.

Minho 13 • Douro 33 • Trás-os-Montes 40 • 43 • Beira 46 • 47 • 49 • 51 • 53 • 57 • 60 • 66 • Estremadura 70 • 71 • 86 • 89 • Ribatejo 105 • Alentejo 115 • 119 • 123 • 126 • 131 • 141 • 142 • 145 • 148 • 155 • 157 • 158 • 159 • 163 • 164 • 169 • 170 • Algarve 172 • 173 • 176 • 178 • 182 • 183 • 199 • 204

Madeira 210 • 212

Accessible by Public transport
Owners will pick guests up from
bus or train station (possible extra
charge).

Minho 1 • 3 • 4 • 5 • 8 • 9 • 12 • 13
• 14 • 15 • 18 • 19 • 20 • 23 • 24 •
Douro 25 • 26 • 28 • 29 • 31 • 32 •
33 • 34 • Trás-os-Montes 40 • 42•
43 • Beira 45 • 46 • 47 • 49 • 50 •
51 • 53 • 54 • 55 • 58 • 59 • 60 • 61
• 66 • 68 • Estremadura 69 • 71 • 72
• 73 • 74 • 79 • 80 • 81 • 82 • 85 •
86 • 87 • 88 • 90 • 93 • 94 • 95 •
97 • 98 • 99 • 100 • 102 • Alentejo
123 • 140 • 141 • 145 • 151 • 154 •
155 • 158 • 159 • 163 • 165 • 166 •
170 • Algarve 176 • 178 • 183 • 185
• 190 • 191 • 195 • 196 • 197 • 203
• 207 • 208 • 209 • Madeira 210 •
211 • 212 • 214

Walking & cycling
Less than 5km from a walking or
cycling route.

Minho 1 • 2 • 3 • 8 • 9 • 12 • 13 •
20 • Douro 28 • Trás-os-Montes 36 •
43 • Beira 51 • 53 • 54 • 57 • 60 •
66 • Estremadura 70 • 71 • 72 • 78 •
79 • 81 • 87 • 89 • 90 • 91 •
Alentejo 118 • 116 • 122 • 126 • 127
• 128 • 138 • 140 • 141 • 142 • 144
• 145 • 150 • 154 • 155 • 158 • 163
• 164 • 168 • 169 • Algarve 171 •
173 • 174 • 176 • 178 • 182 • 188 •
189 • 196 • 197 • 205 • 207
Madeira 211

Casas Brancas
www.casasbrancas.pt

Alentejo 165 • 166 • 167 • 168 •
169 • 168

Montes Alentejenos
www.montesalentejanos.com.pt

Alentejo 126 • 127 • 128 • 129 •
130 • 131

Index by property name